five years

five years

thoughts during a useless time

by paul goodman

vintage books

a division of random house/new york

VINTAGE BOOKS EDITION, March 1969

Manufactured in the United States of America

Foreword

I wrote in these notebooks when I had no one else to write for or talk to. The notes have the kind of life, and lifelessness, to be expected in such a case.

When I finished the first draft of *The Empire City*, there was no chance to get it published and I did not even try. Whatever bright schemes I had to improve my city or the schools were also evidently not wanted by anybody. There were no signs of political revolt, certainly not among the young, to give me courage. The really desperate efforts for sexual happiness that I made got the reception that is given to desperate efforts in this line. But worst of all, I suffered from bleak hours of nothing to do or plan during lonely walks along the river or nursing a beer in a bar. It was in these circumstances that I started regularly writing down my thoughts in pocket notebooks. I was 45 years old.

By 1960, when the notes start to peter out, although I was not much happier, I was much too busy to write in notebooks. I was deeper and deeper involved in the disturbing love that I reconstructed in *Making Do*. I was embarked, at 50, in the odd but grateful episode of being a Student Leader. Several times a week I was on the aeroplanes bound for conferences on social planning. Magazines and publishers had begun to seek me out. Encouraged, I fell into the benign habit, when I was bemused or indignant, of straightway writing angry letters to public servants and the *Times*. These letters, published as *The Society I Live In Is Mine*, date from the administration of John Kennedy.

Thus these notebooks have the theme and tone of an interim of withdrawal. They complain privately about the world, and they pass judgment on myself. Nevertheless, as I copy out the thoughts, I see that it was no interim at all, but myself as I have always been and still am —only less distracted by other business and excitement. Or bluntly, the unlucky truth is that all my life I have existed in an interim, but only for those 5 years did I write in pocket notebooks. The truth is that I feel like an Exile —from paradise; and I mean, as will be clear in the following pages, a very bread-and-butter kind of paradise. *Um'-pnei hataenu galinu meartzenu,* "but because of our sins we are exiled from our land."

During the same 5 years I wrote most of the 8-line poems that I call "Sentences and Little Prayers." That is, on my walks or in bars, I either wrote little poems on scraps of paper or I wrote in these notebooks. I am not sure why I made the distinction between these kinds. I doubt that the prose is more detached or unemotional than the verses. Maybe I wrote poems when I had a "first line," according to the theory of Paul Valéry. More likely, I wrote a picture, thought, or incident in 8 lines when I felt that it could be so shaped and contained; but if it seemed to be an epigram or to want a discursive explanation, I wrote in my notebook.

When daily something in society had me by the throat, I reflected about it instead of telling somebody off. Obviously I had persuaded myself that nobody listened. Today I understand that they do listen—indeed the corporations are very touchy—though of course it still makes no difference.

These are not Diary notes. I did not write down events or appointments to keep a record, like Gide. Nor did I keep a sketchbook of ideas and plans for literary works, like Hawthorne. I wrote down only independent "thoughts," to concentrate my mind or distract my mind (it comes to the same thing). Unlike in Pascal, however, almost all my "thoughts" are physically autobiographical; it is usually clear where I am and what I have been doing when I think this, or what I have been reading and what is in the news. It is not hard to reconstruct the man in the city who had these thoughts. He is not interesting to me, nor especially likable or unlikable, because I am used to him; but he might be an interesting type to some readers.

To preserve the biography, when, where, and what doing, I give the notebooks in their chronological sequence and have added almost nothing, except to dot i's and cross t's. *Within* each notebook, however—it took me about 6 months to fill one—I have collected the scattered thoughts of that season under a few shaggy headings like "art," "psychology," etc. The purpose of these categories is to make it easier for the reader to read a few consecutive pages without continually having to change the entire realm of discourse. And since one does keep mulling about an idea for weeks and months, the arrangement frequently does result in a connected argument. But of course, as in all my other writing, the categories themselves are inexact: When I speak of "psychology" I am speaking about "society"; and I always speak of both of these in terms of a "method" of inquiry and, indeed, in terms of "myself" and what I am after; but to speak about myself is to speak about how I am in my only world, it is to speak of "art" and "God."

I am pleased to be able to edit at this time these thoughts of 1955 to 1960. If I were closer to them, I might still be too engaged in them, and perhaps embarrassed by them, not to argue them further or perhaps to camouflage them. A few years from now, on the other hand, if I am still alive, I may not be able to remember what I was batting about, and I hope I wont care. At present, however, I still think that it is worthwhile to publish them in a book.

P.G.

New York City
January 1966

five years

May to November 1955

i. people, places, things

:   There is a new fill of rock along the Hudson, south of Dyckman Street—ash, glass, broken cement, bricks. Where is bedrock, fertile soil, or noble ruin? But the earth bears also this junk patiently. She smiles at me and says she likes the messy animal man.

:   The dog shitting a hot turd is mildly interesting to me, but the cold turd on the street is disgusting to me. Yet on a rural road the turd is not offensive because it will decompose into living soil.

:   Worried brow, piercing eyes, determined jaw: the captain steering into the seas in a storm; the bartender when the tipsy rough begins to act up; the psychotherapist when the patient's syntax begins to break down.

:   One of the cyclists is in panoply, with a coonskin hat and totemic jacket, and on the handlebars foxtails and the flags of the United Nations, plus horn, mirror, speedometer, and other accessories. The other cyclist has the functional style; the wheels have no mudguards, the handlebars have no grips; he is barefoot and wearing a singlet and threadbare jeans; he would ride naked if it were allowed.

:   Of the 3 kid cyclists at the red light, one keeps his seat, foot on the ground; the second stands on a straight leg, resting the other leg on the crossbar; the smallest stands, holding the bike; and if I could draw, this is what I would draw.

:   Her hands seem to crawl or dance on the piano. It is not enough evident that they are touching the piano.

:   The gentlemen who sleep drunk on the sidewalks and in doorways are usually past middle-age, as though it took a lot of living to get rid of the conventions inhibiting normal lust for ease.

:   Portrait of a Young Gangster: seated in the subway like a tired droopy child, his gun held by the barrel in a tired hand, the handle drooping between his legs. "Nature Reasserting Herself After Violence."

:   Party decorations, streamers and balloons, can be stuck to the walls or even to the pictures on the walls as their solid foundation. But these pictures, and the painted and plastered wall they hang from, are only decorations of the steel and concrete structure. But the buildings of the city are only party booths in the natural scene. (We dwell as if in tents.) And that scene itself is Maya; I can think it away. Contrariwise: When I was a boy looking from the Palisades, I could see the hills of Inwood, Fort Tryon, and Fort Washington as the big masses. The railroad bridge across the Harlem was interesting but small. Now all these are dwarfed by the man-made structures, the Henry Hudson Bridge, the Paterno apartments. Unfortunately, I have been unable to achieve an intimate or trusting relationship with these new foreground masses; and the hills I loved, and love, have become tiny. My place in my city is small because I do not love the things that are now big. I cannot think them away.

:   Like the bull who picks out his home spot in the ring, when I have spread my gear on the beach and built a fire I am at home, and could indeed stay forever, improving and decorating. But if I must get a permit to camp, then it is all spoilt, for the center is elsewhere than in my simple election. I find it desperate that they will no longer let me pitch a tent on Fire Island. I am trapped in New York.

:   After the full moon rising opposite the sunset, we see on the next nights that the moon is an hour late, two hours late.

:   I was disoriented on the lake, for the east where the moon rose was not where I had expected. At once I felt like the mapless primitive: this water might never end; it might be the ocean; this ocean might never have another shore. Although I could *see* the shore.

ii. psychology

: He is continually organizing his own life, making a whole for himself with whatever is available, just as you are. The part of wisdom is not to want to be in that organization of his—you cannot work at it hard enough—but to hope that his outgoing moments will be of interest and profit to you.

: In fact he will continue to see X; you must make the best of it and accept that or have nothing. This rational compromise is perhaps not so worthwhile to you as a more perfect spiteful (self-spiting) triumph; but the question is whether you choose to have also an interpersonal world with its laws, for instance that a body cannot be in two places at the same time.

: When both of a married couple are writers, the problem is, How to cope with the excellence of the Other? You may respond with either envy (he has it and thereby proves I don't), or pride (we have it). When one of the couple dies first, pride is easy: the survivor has an object of devotion and the busy-work of furthering "our" fame, getting the manuscripts published, etc. To be content while the Other is alive, you would have to feel yourself always included, consulted, useful, and this is difficult indeed to believe. After the Other is dead, you have him (or her) your own way.

: The less vitality turns to the more vitality who gives promise and interest to her life by stimulating her repressed vitality. He accepts her; she gives him a field to exercise his powers, and these days it is not so easy to get a fuck, one cannot afford to turn something down. But she cannot really come across, is frigid. He is dissatisfied. And now appears his weakness, for he constrains himself in order to satisfy her, to bring her to orgasm, and this soon makes him feel inadequate, failing, a failure. His effort makes her the more tense, but it also attaches her closer. He is bored and would disattach, but he is afraid (or wishes) to hurt her. A harsh word from him makes her sullen, and by her sullenness he is paralyzed and fascinated. Perhaps a more violent attack would break her down—as no doubt she means to provoke—but he is not born to wield the whip; he won't give her the satisfaction. So far so bad, but there is worse: By paralyzing him, boring him, making him impotent, her inferiority wreaks a triumph. He understands this, how determined weakness is stronger than impatient strength; he is enraged, humiliated. He abstains from her in mere pride.

: Ways of making her man feel he is necessary to her: (1) She throws herself on the ground and clasps his knees, "Please do not leave me, my life is empty without you, what can I do to hold you?" (2) Matronly, she takes his head on her bosom and chides, "You silly boy, you make a fuss for nothing; when have I failed to be there when you need me?" (3) They are partners engaged in an experiment in reasonable living: "These jealousies are unworthy of you, of us. If we are to serve as a model for the others, etc." (4) They are both lost babes in the wood. Alone, the prospect is too bleak for either. They mix their tears and cling to one another.

: Dilemma of the Double Standard (Puerto Rican): The man has sexual freedom and is in so far fearless and aggressive; the woman, because she is inhibited, is afraid. She overestimates the disgrace of transgressing and is the more afraid. She is then easier to subdue and keep in her place. But on the other hand, since he thinks it is bad for her to be sexual, she becomes the forbidden mother and is not frankly approached; he is guilty in what approaches he does make, he does not let go with her sexually; he is more and more in the wrong. This combination of *machismo* and childishness is precisely calculated to make him a fool and to stunt his growth. He is *macho* but never grows up.

: When they are losing or have goofed a couple of points, adolescent Puerto Rican handball players tend to grope their penises before each serve. This phenomenon probably warrants a careful count and a questionnaire, but I don't intend to do the research, so it's up for grabs.

: Vindictive wishes his enemy to succeed where he is not deserving, so that the glory of it is soured by self-doubt, guilt, and resentment against the unsuccessful superior; and all the better if these feelings are unconscious and produce ulcers, bursitis, etc., etc. Meantime, the unsuccessful champion sleeps well, but in waking life he is bitter and frustrated.

: Impotence is positive, a cutting off of feeling, and you cannot explain a positive effect by a negative cause. It is not that the queer boy is not attracted to the girl, but that he begrudges giving her anything. His "homosexuality" is irrelevant except in so far as he regards it as a further grounds of resentment: "Mama won't let me enjoy myself as I wish."

: "If I bring up the sexual problems of the kids," says P., who is teaching shop in junior high, "the others will say, 'Stick to your woodwork.'" This is the time for Socrates' question: What is woodwork? The lad can't hammer a nail because he doesn't hammer on the outbreath, he holds back his anger. They want them to have skill and strength, but they will not speak of aggression. They want the work to be beautiful, but they will not speak of sex.

iii. myself

:   I distrust women clothed. Naked, they are attractive
to me like any other animals. Male dress passes—but I
have to reach for their penises, to make sure. This has
damaged my reputation.

:   He seems to me to be unbearably beautiful—I could
weep for it—and he also somewhat notices me, makes a
little nod, almost of complicity, whether because of my
adoring look or because this extreme of attraction really
springs from an affinity. But then he is shy. I think I know
what I want; he does not know what he wants or what I
want. It is the time for management and patience. Instead, I am abrupt and direct and I frighten him just in
proportion as I might be lovable to him, which he fears.
When this has occurred, I feel bitterly mournful for myself as I am. I could hate the sexuality that defeats me,
except that it is my energy of recognizing Paradise at all. I
say "I think I know, he does not know," but neither of us
knows what blindly we long for and would fearfully be
plunged into. It is to escape *that* anxiety that I make my
brusque approach. Anxious, I make him anxious. What
survives is remorse.

:   "Unbearably beautiful": You can (1) eat it up, (2)
fuck it to orgasm and lose the energy of desire, (3) be
heartsick because it will pass away, (4) weep for paradise
lost.

:   Beauty is the shapes of Paradise. Its attraction, my
being sexually attracted, is my motivating awareness of
Paradise. How else could I know about that? But because I
have starved and feared, it is this very attraction that I feel
ashamed of and doubt. Yet indeed, my experience has
been that just where I have come to have sex with some-

body we make up a simple ordinary world that requires no explanation.

: Venturing boldly, he builds his bridges behind him.

: He behaves in the world just as if it were his own home, with plenty of boring sex, etcetera.

: Instead of suffering my conflicting needs and tormenting myself for not coming to a decision and being esteemed as the kind of man who controls his wife, or casts her off, etc., let me take myself as the kind of man in whom just this conflict occurs. My hunch is that this would come to accepting that I am an artist, generous and greedy, instead of shrugging that off as rather trivial.

: I ought to listen seriously to simpler folk who surprisingly esteem the powers I indeed have, that "I write like an angel," "tie it up in a package so neatly." I take these things for granted and as of small account, for I do not feel their lack. And instead, I expect too much of other people, assuming that they have powers and are failing to use them, which indeed they do not have and cannot.

: There is dirt under my fingernails and G's father says I "do" it either in defiance or carelessness—and he concludes I must be equally careless in my profession. Certainly there must once have been defiance, brushing off a demand or expectation of people I didn't care about. But I don't think I am careless, rather that "I like dirt," an infantile coprophilia. But the whole issue is wrongly posed. Clean nails, brushed hair are a costume, a handsome shining that has its special quality and must not be taken either as the norm or as a mere mask. The laundered sailor looks beautiful for that: it is a cosmetic, it is appropriate, it belongs to the sea and to going ashore afresh. His problem is to dirty himself up gracefully, and then his usedness will be even more attractive. Thus, my unkemptness is not carelessness, but not bothering to dress up; my vice is that I am not happy and interested enough in the ordinary occasions of life to dress up for them. But in the system of social fears and hopes, of course, every no-costume has a destructive effect, no matter what my own motive is.

: That "my" truth is the same as some ancient wisdom —this I used to feel, and say, as a defiant complaint; but now it makes me cry for black loss. It is too much to have had only one life to live, in an unlikely society, and also, after all, to have been right. But feeling "right" is defensive and stops the warm grief. It is better just meaninglessly to bawl.

: I undo myself because of a theory that I, alas, believe: that happiness, satisfaction, is the necessary ground for the full exercise of power. It is not that I am miserable, I can really put up with that philosophically; but that, being miserable, I am wasted. Then all is lost. And because of this conviction, I fail to make an exertion of power that indeed I could make, putting in the "extra ounce of strength," like Beethoven. I guess there must be some positive purpose to my willful passivity. Whose will do I want to break? And what if she won't?

: Jealous of my mother, when I could not exclude the other lovers I cut her off—except for that kind of clinging that is performing dutiful obligations. So with my wife. But My Only World is attentive only to me.

: I guess I am the most widely unknown writer who is so highly esteemed by a few. The most interesting group are those who know me peripherally and dislike and condemn me. These are the ones I should seek out, for they put me to the test, they get me angry. But just by seeking them out, I would make them not peripheral and disarm them with my characteristic artifices, and perhaps real charms. Indeed, so-and-so's chief objection to me is that I don't happen to have paid attention to him. Surrounding any source of power we can find the Four Rings of Saturn: (1) positive transference, (2) negative transference, (3) those who blank it out so that it does not exist, and (4) after a while the pearly ring of accepting Fame.

iv. society

:   Why are we so well behaved? It seems to require so few in society to deter the rest. I can think of two factors. First, it is not the present threat or risk that deters, but childhood fear and guilt that were implanted when disproportionate strength was indeed brought to bear: the policeman is papa and mama writ large, so we are still disproportionately small. A psychopath is relatively free of these particular internalized fears, so he calculates only the present risk, which is often not great. But for most, a small deterrent keeps the old time spasm of fear from thawing out; we remain in a state of deep freeze; and so a few easily prevent the happiness of all. Second, this frigidity is pervasive in institutions which are inflexible and unfunctional, and most institutions are that way. This makes direct and spontaneous action extremely awkward; it cuts down the possibilities in the environment, so that it really is too difficult, or at least too much trouble, to act out. The world is not enough "for us," in the present. Or more accurately, the world that *is* for us is most easily encountered, in the present, precisely by resignation, frustration, complaint, rebelliousness, symbolic satisfactions, symptom-formation.

:   In the big city where all are strangers to all and the convention is not to talk to strangers, then if one forces an acquaintance and it is accepted, there is already the presumption of complicity, in some vice, with a lurking suspicion of robbery, entrapment, betrayal. When the big convention is broken, there are fewer conventional defenses in depth, though always insecurity. Similarly, as Cocteau said, "vice is vertical": if a child smokes he also masturbates, since he might as well be hanged for a sheep as for a lamb.

: In an essay on "The Psychoanalyst and Society," he asks: shall he be a therapist in ordinary company? shall he marry? and so forth—through the whole list of questions that would apply to the clergy. He states the problem as if psychoanalysis were a prophetic vocation, but it's not. I think, on the contrary, that precisely in psychotherapy the best is to confront the patient with the reality, oneself just as one is. The problem is not that other people expect the therapist to be different than his ordinary self, but what is his ordinary self.

: Grounds of distinction among our fellows: (1) A prophetic mission that sets one aside as touched with mana, (2) priestly profession, a part of the division of labor, entailing corresponding sacrifices of oneself, (3) being "chosen," as one who knows better and has to act out this unjolly power.

: 19th Century rationalism in France was an ideology of the establishment, peculiarly without revolutionary threat. The schoolteacher and the priest were rival figures of comedy. This co-opting and alliance was nauseating, so that French existentialism has been driven to the most Wild West extreme-situations in order to escape Reason and God. What elsewhere would be a bold practical use of the intellect, in France seems to be an extreme situation, simply because it makes sense, as if to say, "This could make a difference, therefore it must be an extreme situation." The French Revolution fell apart into two fragments, its rationality that "succeeded" and was taken over by the new establishment, and its fraternity that failed and now the world is inanimate. No life left but in a "subjective moment."

: The scientific-socialist critique of the bourgeois philosophy was that it was ideological, illusory, unworkable. But it has proved to be workable, and now what? To be sure, the system has changed by incorporating its adversaries, but by and large what we have is a fair extension of what was premissed. What was missing in the beginning is still missing, and belief and élan are now also missing. I am continually nagged by my original sin: to be Virgil and manufacture a meaning for this Empire. But instead I come on like a Cicero who has never had his day.

: My one literary theme has been the Community, as in *Parents Day* or *Break-Up*; in *The Empire City* it is the band that acts as if it were the community and as if the others, who don't make sense, didn't exist. Logically, I could have the correlative subject: the workings and disasters of the non-community that indeed exists, e.g. the young man cannot get a job that uses even a small fraction of his powers, yet it would be better for him to have that job than none at all; and in the job he finally gets he must concentrate all his soul on some triviality, e.g. defending his status with passion. So in sex, education, politics. The enormous passion of electoral campaigns for mediocre candidates concerned with non-issues, for offices in which they will be largely powerless anyway! This could be my vast subject—but please, it is so sad, so gray. To have to write the endless pages of this impasse! relieved only by admiration for our human courage and patience. . . . Murrey suggests a more plausible alternative: to make my subject the man faced with just this problem: in no community and aware of it as his problem. My Angel Roeh-El, who comes down among the daughters of men and soon leaves in dismay, and of course he can't make it in heaven either.

(1966: Murrey's suggestion—now that he is dead— turned out to be the theme of *Making Do*.)

: Longinus says, "Write it for Demonthenes, Homer," the ideal audience. But I am ashamed to come before my future audience with situations based on our present-day repressions, inhibitions, prejudices. The fellow in the subway panicky protecting his virginity: what would Demosthenes make of *that*? And my own "interpersonal" conflicts rise from these same mores—how could it be otherwise?—and I myself cannot take them seriously, though I suffer them in the flesh and soul. . . . Good. Then be the practical scientist and alter the intolerable to the possible, e.g. as Marx said, tragedy will be possible again in a classless society. This is the scientific truth. The artistic truth is still larger—the imitation of Paradise. Truth is to make beauty possible. I am impatient, just writing these words.

:   Artemis the huntress comes to Aesculapius to ask him to revive Hippolytus, the hunter. The physician is nauseated by these destructive virgins, both the dead youth and the goddess, but he goes, *noblesse oblige*.

v. language

:   The articles "a" and "the" in natural languages are not adequately translated by the logician's "x" and "a,b,c . . ." and "Ǝ". The articles in the natural languages say that there is something to *notice*, particular, and definite or indefinite, quite apart from the question of existence or implication. They involve attentiveness of various kinds and so bridge the gap between psychology and semantic. The problem is how something is given for judgment to begin with. This is, of course, the theme of Kant's *Critique of Judgment*. It is neglected by the logicians.

:   The primitive plural "skies" is better language than our analytic singular "sky." It says what is the case.

:   Jespersen points out that in Elizabethan writing, "hath" and "doth," the more correct and ancient forms, were used in serious conservative prose, whereas poetry began to use the colloquial and newly spreading forms in "s."

In more recent times it is poetry that employs "hath" and "doth," because they are archaic and strange. Both functions are validly poetic: poetry should use the newest and colloquial as its base, and may then play with the strange and archaic.

: Writing the sonnet "God damn and blast," I made a correct use of literature, for I was pent up and there was no person there to talk to. Worse, indeed, Sally and Nilo *were* there but could not understand what I meant to say. But I could say it comprehensibly to empty paper.

: There is little communication in the shared content of speech, what is usually called "communication," although it produces a sentiment of "understanding" and approval. In fact, each one rearranges his own filing cabinet and masturbates at peace. Contact, dialogue that makes a difference, occurs in the "meaningless" passage from one structure of meaning to another; it touches the background, of which the proposition is the foreground figure; it disturbs the structure. (Similarly, the authentic democrat does not persuade people to his proposition but helps them to formulate and realize their own proposition.) This notion of speech is frighteningly lonely—or it envisages a soul of quicksilver that is not lonely at all.

: So-called "complex words," poems and orations, that develop into feeling and action—akin to the songful polysyllabic concretions of primitive speech, as Jespersen reconstructs it—are the premisses in ethics. The positivists are in error; ethics does not consist of prescriptive commands and the sentences deduced from them; rather, it states the relations in the soul between how I am in the world and what I command myself to do. Poems and rhetoric give us these premisses in a synthetic form; the implications must be drawn out by criticism. This justifies the vague and seemingly pompous carryings-on in the literary reviews. As Arnold said, Literature is the criticism of life, but it is not easy to know what it is saying. Similarly, belief is expressed in puzzling scriptures that require rabbinical exegesis. But there is no help for it. Simplicity or precision is not to be hoped for. It if is achieved, something is wrong, since ethics and faith are in present motion.

Except on some such view as this, it is impossible to understand how ethical propositions can be motivating. Why would I obey the command unless it engaged me as I am? Conversely, it is not the "proposition" that God created War-Horse and Leviathan that is convincing to Job— at best this could lead him to servile identification with his powerful conqueror. Rather, the ethical proposition is the moving poetry, which engages us, and so we move of our own initiative. The speech of Adam in the garden is Jespersen's non-analytic syntax and song; it is neither abstract or value-neutral, nor does it state "values."

: "United States" no longer connotes a federated political structure, and it only routinely refers to a nation, as in "President of the United States." But it comes alive as a brand-name on a commodity, "made in the United States," or painted on the side of a bomber.

: After the quarrel, I say to her, "The fact that I could say it meant that it was no longer so." This is true when the inhibition of the *saying* has created a tension in the field—especially inhibition of anger, in order not to hurt or risk retaliation. Then the saying itself changes the situation of which it says. In other cases, however, the saying rather confirms the situation by "witnessing" it, by giving it an interpersonal environment and a formula of operation, a bridgehead to go further. If such a self-confirming statement meets opposition, it becomes an important rallying center and a flag. If it proves itself when said, it is accepted, assimilated, forgotten. One good kind of philosophy is truism. Another good kind is battle-cry. The best use of philosophy has been to get rid of silence and superstition; that is, to simplify the situation just by its being said. The chief abuse of philosophy is ideology, the fetishism of mere speech, preventing confronting facts.

vi. method

:   I learn from Sherrington how our sense-organs, nerve-endings, etc. are of the same order of magnitude—billions, trillions—as the minute energies. This gives us a closer woven warp and woof of the organism and the environment than I had thought. What, then, are the problems of unifying a physical (mass-gravity-electricity) and psychosomatic theory? Start with quantifying. If we take the "least perception" or threshold as the unit, my guess is that we will find *phases*, analogous to the passage of water to steam or ice to water; it takes an accumulation of energy to break suddenly into the *presented* surface, to be something for attention. The surface, therefore, *always* tells a forceful secret. A "fact" *has* more energy in it than a possibility; and that is why it occupies a privileged place in our calculations.

:   Phases: (1) Threshold of perception or fantasy, (2) passage into muscular action. Both these require a prior accumulation of latent energy. The passage into muscular action is known as "will." There is an interval during which the "idea" does not change, but much energy must be added to it till the result of overt behavior. In this context, however, we must also contrast deliberateness and spontaneity. In deliberateness much energy is extrinsically employed in inhibiting other activity, in *paying* attention rather than being "distracted" (attracted elsewhere). In spontaneity, it is as if we were already well toward the phasic change of state, so to speak "over the hump"—and so in spontaneous action there is little "idea"; the idea does not continue to be energized, and the energy of the idea itself merges into the overt act. E.g. orgasm is murky.

:   Let us make an arbitrary assumption that the constancy of the speed of light means that the scene is immediately given: the light is simultaneous with its vision. I

think this was what Aristotle meant to say. Then, if the
sun is 8 light-minutes away, it means that the sun is *not*
immediately given; *we* have withdrawn from, or cut off,
the vision of it. Put otherwise, this is its apparent magnitude, a small disk, rather than the fire filling all the sky.
But can we catch ourselves at this withdrawing and relax
it? or is to withdraw, or cut off, the condition of the sense-
organ itself? I fancy that for Adam the sun fills much more
of the sky; he receives its light more immediately.

:   Continuous or field theories and discrete or particle
theories seem to be contrasting attitudes of observation,
one relying on the flow of spontaneous energy, the other on
deliberate interventions and impositions. It is the same
distinction as between ancient natural law and Hobbes'
positive law; biological naturalist vs. biological experimen-
talist.

:   In nuclear fission, when the parts are less bound,
there is new energy: is this energy "released"? or is it a
property *of* the freer condition? So with combustion. In
evaporation, and in the expansion of a gas, heat is absorbed; can we not interpret this as that the less confined is
able to contain its energy, but when compressed or bound,
energy is given up? This seems to be the opposite of the
theory of cohesive forces, the so-called mesons.

:   Primarily, I see this gray and the other gray, whereas
some people seem to see the piece of driftwood on the
sand. Of course at need, for use, to manipulate or speak or
"have a world," I too can organize the scene into things,
see the "driftwood" when I need a piece of firewood.
Perhaps this use-function was what Kant meant by his categories; however, once one is close in the immediate scene,
there seems to be little use in organizing in the categorical
way; in progressively getting into contact with the scene
there occurs a sufficient organization for one's changing
uses.

: When I was in school, I was a good mathematician in working through theorems and problems in my own way; but my mind was, and still is, balky and stupid about following other people's chains of proof (so I find it hard to read mathematics in a book). Yet I have no such trouble with empirical studies like biology and history, where I am docile to the facts and make up my own schemes of them as I listen along. It is out of this experience, I guess, that I have always leaned to Kant's conception of mathematics as a synthetic production of the imagination, a producing by the imagination. The formalist conception of mathematics does not fit me; I have to give up my own spontaneity in order to "think abstractly." [1965] It seems to me, therefore, that programmed learning and teaching machines are desperately inefficient. They do not take into account that different people mathematize in different styles.

: We are born in a physiological time, after a certain number of mitoses and at the closure of a genetic figure; but we are born, after 270 days, *into* an astronomical time of days and years. Thus begin our astronomical birthdays; but these again are not the time in which we mature and die. They would seem to be irrelevant, "a man is as old as he feels." "But how old do *you* feel then?" "Ach! 43 years!" The conditions of society go by astronomical time and they have done me in.

: Awareness is simple presentness, both perceptual and motor. Experience, in Aristotle's sense of the grounds of inductive truth, is present memory and habits. Consciousness is limitation of presentness to the subvocal and the safe perceptions, and the confining of motor response to the deliberate and the delaying, excluding the stronger passions which are motoric. Fantasy and dream are largely pure consciousness. Hope is largely fantasy and merely conscious, but the unlimited present component in hope is faith, in the fixed attitudes of ambition, determination, confidence, risking. In its most precise form, rather than in its fixed attitudes, faith is always "groundless," although *a posteriori* its grounds are generally apparent.

: Knowing is an existential condition, a way of being in the world, with its specific heroism and passion. You can see the style best in Aristotle, e.g. the irritated tone of *Metaphysics* 4: "If only he will *say* something (sc. significant), otherwise he's no better than a vegetable!" All of philosophy is made to depend on the fact that somebody means something and speaks up. So *Oedipus Rex* is Aristotle's only poem, the hero of knowing who tragically doesn't know after all, but whose grandeur is his will to find out. And Aristotle's prejudice here traps him, for he does not perceive Oedipus's hybris, his will *not* to know. He speaks of Oedipus's unconscious ignorances as "outside the play"; but Sophocles has put them in the play. And to Aristotle, theory is, to one's astonishment, identical with happiness, but Aristotle *means* this odd proposition.

: Science vs. Humanities: The principle of the sciences is to accumulate more and more elegant and accurate knowledge, making a sounder foundation; but the principle of the humane studies is, in the end, to reach presentness, *not* knowing, not thinking of knowing. Socratic ignorance is empty faith—in the fertile void. As science, sociology aims to know more and control; as humanity, to know less and less, proving everything to be mere superstititon, in order, suddenly, to live happily. But alas! my own experience has been that, although often active enough in my faithful void, I am growing old through incompetence and/or frustration, and now I often find that I have not a Socratic ignorance that liberates, but just forgetfulness and stupidity. I must get used to the idea of being a fool and (worse!) of being known as a fool.

: Marie Coleman speaks of some incidents of telepathy, etc. as "hair-raising, spooky," but such things never seem to me to be eerie or uncanny, but interesting and somewhat reassuring. I wish that these powers exist and could be practical, as if they were primitive instinctual manifestations; to me the primitive is not destructive as such, but it puts it up to us to cope with it and make the required cultural changes, which I am only too ready to see come about, if only out of spite. I do not remember feeling anything of this kind as evil or hostile-uncanny, as, for instance, I feel that psychotics are uncanny (though I sign them off by becoming bored rather than creepy). The tone of catastrophe that seems statistically to accompany telepathy might be simply that we do not much notice and note down what fits in with the regular order of nature; and what is extraordinary, what goes counter to the regular order, is usually disastrous, as the "picturesque" is disastrous. Anyway, I hope it is the case that our ordinary contact with one another is grounded in non-sensory communication. But the idea makes me sad, for I feel excluded—not because I do not have such powers, but because, if I have them, I am not letting them breathe; I have woven them too closely into my unfortunate methodical views and habits. An example: it seems to me quite impossible that the fellows who get on so well with one another at the bars are doing so by what they are saying; there is at least some animal bond working subliminally, and why not a telepathic bond? But I *notice* all this, I cannot avoid being explicit and self-aware. To sum up: when telepathic or hypnotic phenomena are discussed, I no longer know whether they are talking about what I have never experienced and cannot understand, or about what I experience as an ordinary thing and perhaps at the very moment of the discussion.

vii. art

:   Most of the photographs in *The Family of Man* tell us nothing. The photo of a child tells us little about children; it must be a photo of how the child sees. You don't show "man's labor" by a picture of a man hammering; you must somehow convey the difficulty and necessity of the task itself, perhaps by bringing out the resistance of the matter worked on.

: *Ars Celare Artem.* This might mean (1) artisan is an inferior class, so the work must seem "effortless"—"a gentleman doesn't practice the flute"; (2) proof of the creative grace of heaven—spirit "without works"; (3) the work is "like a living animal" without the attachment or intervention of the ego—"there is no Homer in the Iliad"; (4) total respect for the medium, as if *it* generated the work—"the sculptor finds the figure buried in the stone and releases it." But on the other hand, effort is itself expressive, e.g. Beethoven's marking *prestissimo* means to play faster than you can, to be impatient with the mere medium. So tour de force and virtuosity, camping, exhibition of the artist as a child showing off. An aristocrat of the métier, he plays with the medium.

: The "forgery" of *Ossian* must be taken as an integral part of its formal structure, as an example of letters in 1750. It expresses the up-coming Romantic impulse, as if to say, "What I'm feeling doesn't make sense, but it belongs to a deeper—more archaic—part of myself."

: In Rimsky's *The Sea and Sinbad's Ship,* the mighty element is dramatically opposed to our sailors; it is a monster of dream, the projection of a childhood totem, and the whole a fairy tale. (Contrast *La Mer,* which is more "like" the ocean, but less like us.) As the conflict approaches its climax, there is a moment when the sailors seem to be wounded and their music becomes modal and passionate, suffering—they have already given up hope. The climax is the fortissimo of this passion, the sailors' part; it is not the crashing waves—the sea, rather, is freely flowing and the wind whistling through all the registers. The structure of the whole is: first the majesty of the element, up to the moment when the men suffer; the element becomes softer and threatening, and finally free and effortlessly pervasive at the climax, the death of the men. The structure is pretty much like the sexual orgasm.

: The more expert and able to release his power an artist becomes, the worse—because of the awful irrelevance—the let-down after a work is finished. He has had his excitement; he is unfit for life.

: Soon, having heard through a perfect art-work a few times, we say, "Good! now it is just beginning—more!" But there is no more. (We know under what tension, walking a tight-rope, the artist was able to get that much down complete.) Hearing, we're in a fine world, that makes us forget this world. We want to go further in that world. We begin to breathe, we are thirsty. . . . On the first hearing, on the contrary, we were anxious: Can it prove itself, make itself through? . . . So the only satisfactory hearing is the single one when we first know the piece and recognize it working itself to its tonic.

: There are two kinds of dramatic sequence. (1) The sequence of happenings and actions in which and by which the person moves. This sequence is dramatic if it involves him more and more closely, and the moment of character change, or change of fate, is climactic. (2) But there is also a sequence in the ways of taking the events, of being in the world. For instance, anger will flush after resentment is unlocked; tears may occur after anger has flared. This inner motion is not a relation of the person to the events, it is more like a sequence in generation and corruption. . . . The distinction between these kinds of sequence is important for direction. Usually we direct the successive scenes toward the mounting climax, the beginning toward the end. But in *The Young Disciple*, each scene should be played absolutely toward its own climax. The following scene is not led up to, but hopefully it emerges after the previous corruption.

:   *Coup de Théâtre* is the cubism of the stage: it is the identification of plot and the medium, acted spectacle. Pirandello is all *coup de théâtre* but the plot is schematic, not strong enough. Racine is the master of *coup de théâtre:* the plot expectation, involvement, forward impetus are great; all that is necessary is for the personage to appear on the scene: *"Dieux!"*

:   I want to say what is indisputably true and presently important and that you do not want to hear, with such clarity and direct application to yourself that you are held there betrayed by your need. Everything in the play makes you restive and wanting to get away, giggle, scoff, but you hear another surprising home-thrust that unbalances you and keeps you from getting out of your chair. My purpose is not to teach, nor move, certainly not to please, but to shake your assurance. This is the High Boring Style. As if you are confronted by a lover (whom you don't much like) who pays attention to you and recalls your buried hope of glory as if it were present and possible. Naturally you panic.

:   The problem of drama comes down to this: how to get the audience to make the responses and sing the chorales. I could invent words that you could honorably say, but I don't know how to get you to say them. If only the audience will act something, we can act. Now what they do act is to come and look and listen. Then my test of success is the edge of the chair, where they are about to get up and leave and no longer look and listen, and yet they stay. "My play was a great success, very few walked out— though, to be sure, afterwards they advised their friends not to go *there*."

:   Defiant, panicky, desperate, I lay the stress on my difference from the audience and say, See it my way and we'll be friends. I do not first rely on our likenesses, and hope to grow into an agreement on the disputed points.

:   When I turned the story into a play, I made the narrating "I" into the Young Disciple. This freed me from too closely imitating myself and gave me a new live scene, the Boy's tantrum at the end. The difficulty in this trick of composition is to care enough about the alienated "I" to write his history down. The bottled-up justified complaint that I *need* to air at least gave me a motive. (Another kind of motive would be the superabundance of joy that needs sharing—how long ago that rings!) Simply to write the history of misery is not, for me, a sufficient motive to write at all.

:   The problem is not how to be an artist in the world that does not come across as I wish, but how to have an expressive relation to that stingy world, any relation but withdrawing—it is enough to kick at it, to be spitefully Utopian, to bawl. Indeed, art is precisely the cheapest and least perilous expressive relation, and we are lucky who can manage it. But the next problem is how to be happy being an artist, where happiness is in the glancing acceptance, in the fact, in good Grace. Frank O'Hara says that Whitman and Mayakovsky identify with the world and its faults and so are not ground under the wheel, they are at the hub of the wheel. But this seems to me to be a cheap victory, masochistic. A *part* of God's plan is my wish, and it is at peril of losing everything that I would fail to keep both contestants in the field, I and the world. (To be sure, my stubbornness also stands in the way.)

viii. God

:   I want something. Quite different is what works out historically, including the history of me. This objective history is God and God has a relation to me.

:   Deciding that I am loyal to the *Workman* of the Six

Days—and giving up my thoughts of Paradise—I have gotten into livelier touch with the real world. The first day of this has given me cause for shame, anger, and fear—far better than stewing in my juice.

: Like the ruined boxer clinging to the time of his fame and fortune, when he bought $40 hats and was good-time Charlie—our advice is, take the situation as it is and go on from there.

: In *Paradise Lost*, X the devils become serpents and the expected applause turns to a hiss, yet Satan is still "greatest in the midst," a Dragon. Milton cannot conceive how to humble pride, for instance to make Satan just a modest kind of snake among the rest. (Perhaps he, vindictively, does not want to give him that kind of comforting satisfaction.) It's like the fellow who says, "I'm the worst fuck-off there ever was. *Nobody* is such as schmuck as me."

: No holy day is so high that the Jews eat their forbidden animals on it, the "prescribed excess" that Freud talks about. It is their negative theology: "Not this occasion, not even this occasion." The prescribed sacrificial animals, the sheep, goats, and chickens, seem not to be totems but a shared meal with the creator. The Christians go all the way by frankly eating up the man himself, frequently. What *is* the Jewish totem? A pig? some species of shell-fish (Dagon? or another idol of the surrounding indigenes?) Oh! the terrific and glorious occasion when Moses will be on the mountain as a wild Boar or a horned Snail shone round by light.

: The Buddha commences with accepting Misery, that the world punishes and thwarts. Giving up the fantasy of getting loving-care, he dissociates it as his own ego-ideal, Compassion. This reaction-formation he can always control, by patience and concentration; he can make it stick and become the reality, by retreating to the attitude where he himself calls the shots. In this limited area he can enjoy complete love by spitefully annihilating the rest: Total absorption in a limited attitude annihilates the sense of limits, and this is Nirvana. Nevertheless, Gotama's spite is the spite of the high-born and happy; he is specifically introduced to us as rich and sexually successful. Thus we must believe, or at least seriously entertain the possibility, that he is dealing with reality as it is, such as it is; make the best of it. Do not ask metaphysical questions, for they might offer grounds for hope or more likely resentment, and reopen old wounds. . . . In general, if peace of mind or even "pleasure" is the goal, one must find a retreat, ποῦ στῶ, where one is safe and can be effectual; then it is possible to let go and be flowing. From this place one can return, like Ecclesiastes, "Then I returned and saw . . ."

: There is no happiness without virtue, and no happiness without luck that gives the glancing present, opportunity. Now some characters make their breaks, by skill and hustle, or at least their virtues are compatible with luck. But in my case there is almost an incompatibility between my virtues and my readiness for luck. My virtues are to be enduring, prudent, effortful, to see beneath the surface, not to be bought out. But luck requires to be quick, present, colloquial, prone to illusions that become reality by believing in them, and to be somewhat venal. As an artist, however,—and art consists very much of strokes of luck,—I am fairly open, and I husband and use my luck.

: If we see Abraham as moment by moment continuing his job of being-a-father, there is no dilemma in his navigating the trial of faith, moment by moment. But Kierkegaard does not understand natural relations like fatherhood, so he comes to hard crises and Wild West solutions. But it is wicked to toy with extreme situations. The problem is to find the extreme in the ordinary. The man of faith does not know he has faith until you press him, or tempt his despair. He is a happy-go-lucky atheist.

:   "If only I knew the truth!"—concerning, it was, whether I really wanted my wife to leave me—or me to leave my wife, whether or not my intuition of her not coming across was justified or a projection of my own, whether my "deep impulse" was really my deep impulse or just another illusion as I have had many. And indeed, if I knew this truth, this complex of truths, I should act on it. Oddly, this is the first time in my life that I remember wanting to know the *truth* as a basis for action. (Not, that is, to know the "truth" in a jealous fit, where I would do better to consult what I myself wanted and not try resentfully to deprive somebody else.) Consider the series: (1) to know an objective truth—this is fairly idle for the likes of me; it is either a divine play that I sometimes enjoy, or it is a withdrawal from involvement that I happen not to be subject to; (2) Horatio's maxim, to "know" the "truth" that indeed makes him happy to believe; this is at least a truth that works, it is "his" truth; (3) but now, to *need* an objective truth, in such a way that knowing it I shall indeed act on it. That I come to this third possibility is the idea of God that I thought of the other day, the history—including history of me—that in fact comes to pass. Finally, (4) there is the truth that one can in fact make to be, that wreaks itself, and the world is now *this* way.

:   I have become philosophical skipping a step. I am not worth the truth because I have not dared to succeed with "my" truth. So I lordly understand what my opponent is arguing, I give him place and swallow him up; or lordly also, I brush him aside or spitefully destroy him. But "my" truth is not put into the competition. For I have already given up on its efficacy. I preserve it safe as an imperishable complaint.

Winter 1955-6

i. in a hospital

: I choose to have an operation for long chronic hemorrhoids; not with the hope or even purpose that they will be cured—for how should I remember vividly what it would be like not to have that chronic ailment?—but simply to clear myself of an obligation, "I did my best, now let me live with it." In this frame of mind, I choose not to be given an anesthetic and the pain proves to be so astounding that afterwards I can remember it only esthetically as "exquisite." I recall—too late—that studies have shown that surgeons are a little sadistic, and why not Dr. Z.?

: I say to a nurse, "I tried to shit and I spattered blood all over your bathroom. I suppose it ought to be cleaned up, no?" To my surprise I am soon given a public dressing-down by the head nurse for my vulgar language. "They say nursing is low, but it's patients like you that make it cruddy." I was concerned about myself and the other patients; the nurses are concerned about the word "shit." They imagine I am expressing contempt for them. My brother proceeds otherwise. The "lower" in status the one he talks to, the more he puts on a pseudo-Oxford accent, and they say, "Oh, he's a fine fellow, a real gent," since in fact he does treat them as equal human beings. But I address everybody with the same familiarity, disregarding their assumptions and presumptions, and then some regard me with contempt and others think that I hold them in contempt. In the sequel, of course, I get closer to them than he does—as I want to and he doesn't want to.

: Under sedation, I have a moment psychotic to the point that I think, "I am losing my grip and they'll put me away." The conditions seem to be these: (1) Sleeping pills that don't work, (2) pain and fear, (3) inability to get attention to ask for help, (3) being deprived of my usual security measures of smoking and masturbating. I cannot smoke because there is an oxygen tent in the ward;

I cannot masturbate because I have no genital feeling. My floor signal is broken. It is a busy day on that floor of the hospital. My mind strays and I realize that there is a cosmic plot against me, swiftly taking away my resources and neatly trapping me by the simplest means. "Whom God wishes to destroy, he first makes mad." So swiftly to this point! Obviously I live with little reserve of strength—yet I do feel the moment with a certain bleak humor for its simple technique.

: "Don't let me die today. I have just learned to sight-read and I am going to read through the piano literature."

: I am incapacitated by a post-operative condition and I complain to the surgeon. He shrugs it off, "It's of no clinical significance." "But I don't function!" This he doesn't understand. Instead, he tries to impress me by airing his opinions on Tolstoy. Drive nature out with a pitchfork, she comes in at the window.

: Once it becomes clear that the doctor is my friend and sits on my bed and chats, I am treated much better by the staff. *This* I find contemptible, and I understand a little what it must be like to be the Puerto Rican orderly at the low end of the totem pole.

ii. south

: Children of Georgia are pouring out of, presumably, a white school. Most of them look like little English farmers crossed with Negro and a dash of Creek Indian: muddy blond hair, sallow skin, flashing black eyes, big square teeth. If the purpose of segregation is to prevent miscegenation, it is a little late. But obviously there is a desperate need to manufacture a distinction, to exteriorize some internal split in the soul. I get the impression of two periods of history, with different economies. There was a secondary invasion of Negroes, perhaps from a different region and certainly differently exploited in the field, into a white-Negro society well on its way to integration. None of the whites is white, but many of the Negroes are very black.

: The Fortress of San Marcos, in St. Augustine. The Spanish used it to keep the British enemy out. The Americans use it to keep the American prisoners in.

: At the road-stand I said, "Give me a black cow." "We don't serve ice-cream sodas," said the big washed-out blonde, "just cream in a dish or cone." "O.K., give me a dish of vanilla and a bottle of root beer. Can you give me a glass?" "Gee, you Yankees are funny; why cancha drink outta a bottle like everybody else?" I began to put the ice-cream in the glass. "No!" she said, "I know what you're up to!" and she snatched away the glass.

: These fellows in Jacksonville, sailors and barflies, have the right of it; their way gives them courage, ease, friends, a good time, a task, whereas I am anxious, lonely, dissatisfied, and unused. I try to merge with them, but they say only foolish things, prejudiced assertions from preposterous assumptions. Of course their opinions are not a big deal with them; they serve merely as a background orchestration, or as a kind of blazon for mutual recognition. But unfortunately my opinions are integral to me; so in the circumstances I am reduced to my convictions as my only action, and I keep a notebook like Hamlet. I try to belong, but soon I am looking on contemplatively. I am not timid to turn against them, occasionally, and say how their say seems to me, but I feel irrelevant and ask myself, "Why are you banging them a tea-kettle?"

: But the beach-settlements in pretty colors are so immodest as to be hideous. People's impulse to get out to the ocean is unexceptionable, but they do not humble them-

selves and hide in the dunes. Yet the brazenness, like the
boastful advertising, is not conceited, or it is only childishly conceited. It's a craving to be recognized, to communicate, not to be shut off. I feel it keenly, traveling alone.
They do not understand what a tremendous claim it is to
establish oneself in the natural scene. Not that a man may
not assert himself—man too is part of nature—but it is
safest to begin by humbling oneself to the site and
shrewdly asserting oneself from there on up, adding another wing. In old settlements, enough human energy has
accumulated over the years to make the men belong.
However ugly the old town is, there it is. What a relief
when we at last draw clear of the last settlement and there
is again the sea, the sand, the dune grass, the scattered
palmettos, long inured to one another.

:   Crossing Alabama, the conductor orders me out of
the Negro car where I am just getting friendly with the
pleasant sailor I am sitting with. "You don't know your
place (white)." Because of my illicit sexual intentions toward the sailor, I protest only feebly and go into the other
car, and then feel like a dog for having let him down on
the issue that must be important to him. (If we had gotten along further, I guess, I should have put up more of a
fight and gotten thrown off the train.) At least in New
York I am humiliated and ordered out of the bar for what
is important to *me*. But it's all of a piece.

:   Downtown New Orleans seems to bustle more even
than New York. Since the folk are more approachable,
each unit has more individuality and therefore the busy
motion of the crowd has more sentimental momentum.
And the buildings and traffic are less out of human scale,
so the sense of the crowd is not overwhelmed. It's an
urban place, the people are sophisticated, but one is embarrassed by their lack of urban pride. To entice the tourists, every doughnut is "since 1840" and the gumbo is always "famous." The city is really not that provincial, but it
makes itself so by accepting the national norms. Possibly

television does seem glamorous when watched at a distance from the source; in New York we see it bigger and worse by looking out the window. The provincial believes that it would be interesting in the capital; the New Yorker understands that it's not so interesting after all, and his humility—"we don't have much of a culture, nobody has"—allows a margin for freedom in the void. But what they do have in New Orleans, and that rouses in me envy and a repugnance for my native city, is a city shape, a more human scale, an easier community.

: If we meant to compare our high culture with, say, the medieval, we must carefully locate where our culture is, otherwise we seem more culturally unproductive than is possible. Our Piazza San Marco is probably the enormous fleet of cars on the freeway and the throughway, billions of dollars of investment. Not mainly utilitarian—the drivers are active and giving themselves, and for many, certainly, driving is one of the few solitary hours still available. It is remarkable, too, how such a multitude goes through such complicated maneuvers with so few accidents. I have seen a thousand drivers on the highway carefully, without direction, grasp the whole situation, thread and untangle a traffic jam around a wreck, day hot, motors boiling over. And given the vast geography of the country, these drives and excursions and migrations do make some use of the whole that would otherwise go fruitless. To be sure, all the towns and stations have become standardized; one gets quicker to where there is no point in going. And though both the individuality and the community of the drivers are amazing, they don't add up to a very rich culture, do they?

: I like my kitchen and my person; I lavish care on them, keeping the dishes clean, heating my rolls, making oyster stew, getting the laundry out, and remembering to buy soap. These are real satisfactions, good enough meals and being able to appear in society that occasionally pays off. But my bedroom is dark and crummy; I do not help by neglecting to make the bed or sweep—I would if I had a bedfellow. The cruelty of the neighbors to each other and to the children and the dog disheartens me. But I like to sit outside on my little porch in the sunset, while the roast is on.

: I am comically betrayed by a difference of convention. Meeting a lady for the second time, I am surprised and delighted when she exclaims, "I'm so glad to see you again!" and I proceed on the assumption that she is glad to see me again. But it is merely the conventional southern expression for second meetings, and in fact she considered me a bore at the first meeting. She, and the others, go on to disregard me utterly, talking among themselves, and I am offended; but then I learn that this too is usual and not aimed at me, whereas up North we conventionally make an effort to include the stranger, to put him temporarily in the center. I am myself so childishly literal-minded that I prefer conventions as low-pitched as possible, say, a solemn acceptance of the introduction, perhaps repeating the name, as is practical. Then if some one expresses more lively interest, it may or may not mean anything personal about me, but at least it will mean he is a sociable creature and I can act accordingly. Myself, I find I must answer the conventional questions. At "How are you?" I can rarely refrain from explaining how I am, a very difficult feat; and the rougher and ruder, "How you doin'?" I cannot resist at all, but am drawn to a buddy or repelled by the too forward alcoholic. On the other hand, "Charmed!" or "Enchanté!" freeze me to such a degree that I find it hard to proceed from there—I grit my teeth, "If that's the way they use words!" All I really want is the guarantee that no knives will be drawn nor punches thrown.

: "God you're dull!' said the Assistant District Attorney, "you don't write that bad." So I am and so I don't. My dull presence and conversation is of the species, "Are you saved?"—a very dull kind indeed. And my explanation would be even duller: "When I write I choose my company and my subject—I meet a better class of people in my dreams. Frankly, you people don't enliven me, and I try to remedy that by remedying you." Ow!

:   When I overhear the brutality of the neighbors, I am almost convinced to Proust and the Buddha, anything to put a stop to it. My bother with the life of compassion seems to be only that it would be easy for me, and I could be happy and guiltless in it.

:   At the hustlers' bar, they are constrained under the Saxon rules for the settlement of private quarrels, and under the Norman law against felonious disturbance of the King's peace. But at least they are exempt from the Puritan code.

:   The quick lights in the mirror and the light in their animal eyes. The knife of speech and the murmuring fantasies. So time stops for four weeks. But there are tiny biological motions, fingers twitching, heads bobbing.

:   The saxophone slung around his neck, he wears like a badge of servitude, but he plays the horn carefully and amorously as if trying to woo the song from her, not as if it were part of his own body and *he* were singing. A moral boy: my side of the river.

:   Here is a lad from Dallas with elaborate silk shirts asserting, at age 17, that success is preferable to excellence. I point out to him that his behavior at the hustlers' bar belies him, for he suffers frustration and humiliation from an impossible fellow who happens to be his idea of excellence, such as it is. In his flesh and feelings he craves for a real good, obscurely glimpsed. I point out consolingly that the unjust have to live with their injustice; they may buy the body with their wealth and beauty, but they likely get only the hard on and the pleasure that they are capable of. So what? What good does this Socratic wisdom do for me? For I too don't get what I want, and my enjoyment is corresponding. Yet there is a difference. When, by exception, I get even a crumb of actuality, my orgasm brightens up fine, to my surprise.

:   My act of rescue seems to be to give the cast-off boy a father. I am moved to nullify his orphanage. I can put up with his surliness, his testing me by raising the ante, his sponging—all this I bear with cheerful patience if only he indeed accepts help and uses it; and I come back again and again with extra kindness that he did not demand and that undermines his dead set. I really perform quite powerfully in this line, and indeed I would adopt him and guide him and put him on the high road, if I had the resources; I do so to the extent that I have the resources. I will not pay for sex, but I hang around—almost like a scavenger—to give a meal and a bed. These physical gifts I can guiltlessly give and they do go beneath his vindictiveness and need to triumph, so I am loved. So far very beautiful, a reasonable reactive denial of my own fatherless state. But two things are amiss: (1) I do not enjoy fathering my *own* son. This is because he has a father—it happens to be myself—so he is one of the sleek lads whom I envy and hate from of old. Lucky for him that I am such a good father that I do not take it out on him worse! (2) The cast-off lad is rescued, but *I* am not rescued; nobody undertakes to father me. And my behavior inevitably casts me in the role of being depended on, never of being cared for. I set up with skill and determination the situation in which I get security, honor, gratitude, activity, but precisely not the satisfaction I want and need. Soon, he invariably turns over to be fucked. I am trade's trade, as Edouard used to say.

:   I look at the old man and think, "Oh! if I can reach that age without disaster, jail, disgrace, violence done to me, 3rd stage of syphilis, *then* what can my critics say?"— as if I had to prove that "after all, it can be done." To whom must I prove that what can be done? But attaining to a decrepit old age seems to me to be Victory. I will have foiled them. No lion, but an excellent fox.

: As if in despite of myself, and contradicting my usual self-consciousness, I sometimes find myself in a noble attitude, perched on my bicycle and peering at the route ahead; impartially critical of what they are saying, my right arm on the back of the chair; frowning at the difficult situation that the unfortunate fellow presents, but not doubting that we can live it through and that *I* will think of something. I realize that I am one of the law-barons.

: It is true that my kind heart has made me loved here, used, respected, exempt from the usual bitchery—they spread remarkable little malicious gossip about me. But in a place like this you have to have a heart as big as a watermelon, and mine soon bursts.

: A sexy young man, his sturdy erection is bent to the right from left-handed masturbation.

: "I get passionate, I'll do anything!" (sc. "eat pussy"). He means he's not responsible, and nothing "really" happened. Thus, the young sailor acted with surprising directness and charm when he was hot. Afterwards, on the occasion for repeating, he saw everything as a danger, a telltale sign; and next morning it was, "I never met you." It is, therefore, always the *second* encounter that could make a difference, what Kierkegaard meant by "repetition," for in the repeat the ego-defenses are involved, a friendship could be formed, a feeling could become a poem. The first passion, surprised, works in a looser organization of the instincts, vulnerable to surprise; but the second has to dissolve obsessional precautions and undoing, it alters how one takes oneself. Similarly, the first creative impulse, the idea, does little for a work of art; it is the courage to compose it, rather than mention it, that makes an artist. Let me give an example: Outside the railroad station, where I went to buy a ticket, I was surprised to see the blue-eyed daisies (like Susie's eyes), but I at once thought, "How surprising to see blue-eyed daisies!" and so copped out.

:   After a while, when my superficial timidity has relaxed and I can reach for what I want, and still I do not find what satisfies, suddenly my animal nature withdraws altogether. I am estranged from the human beings, their tiny faces on their bodies like planaria the flatworm; or I see them as bundles of tubes. Reading in Hume's history, I am disgusted at their petty violence, idiotic, ruinous, repeating. So I have come out here to Tulane's orderly campus, where the rule and reason of these grounds seems to be the immortal counter-protest: the people are made small, yet *something* human is aggrandized. But it is not interesting—it is an empty field with a few buildings, like a carefully planned suburb. There is no enclosure or community. What do I want? The natural human disgusts me, the artificial human is pointless. . . . Yet sitting in the coffee shop and watching the young veterans cheerfully and courteously playing cards, somewhat brings me back and reconciles me to living.

:   Off and away cycling when I was twenty, I used, either curiously speeding to the next place or just idly pedalling along, to find myself much further than I had planned. It was hard and long to get back in the evening, into the western sun. But now here in New Orleans, I find it hard going on the outward trip. I lose my way in dead-end streets. There is a punishing Gulf wind. Soon I prudently give up and turn back without having gone as far as I planned, not even to Lafitte not to speak of Grand Isle. I return rapidly and am home too early.

:   And so, after feverish desire and trembling anxiety, fearful of dangers that proved to be non-existent, but immediately succeeded by other fears equally fantastic; and day-dreamy hopes and plans for the future that did not take the other persons into account at all—suddenly I am made free of all that by an outcome that had nothing whatever to do with any of my thoughts or wishes, but that indeed occurred in the order of real events in which, to be sure, I participated by holding back from them, and committing myself to nothing (which is what I reap.) I am relieved, so that I laugh; and plunged back into my empty world, so tears are in my eyes.

: When I consider the breadth and height of my pretensions, and how unsuccessful and ineffectual I am, I become unsure. But when I place against these pretensions the fact of my cowering timidity, my illusory hopes and fears, inane projections, the pettiness of my wishes—as measured against this heads-up outgoing look at the Mississippi (from Baton Rouge over to Port Adam)—then I am at a loss. I can think of no reasons except those of faith or superstition. I am left not unsure but just baffled. A little braver.

: Waiting in the railroad station is again like checking in at the hospital for an operation. We give our lives into their impersonal hands. Cut off from the past. It will be "done to us."

: To some of us, trains, planes, stations, terminals, and even subways and local busses are the lively places. We do not find traveling a bore, whether we cruise the passengers or watch the scenery—it comes to the same thing. There is an anonymity and democracy in travel because the concerns of career and identity and the insignia of status are in abeyance in the passage in-between. We who have not found happiness in our settled lives, but only discouraging entanglements and disappointment, here start afresh where all start afresh. Possibility revives and with it courage. All are captive in the vehicle together, and occasion for beginning is given by the way. And "whatever happens doesn't count, for soon we'll scatter on our own ways." But you must not cheat by cruising the station when you are not going the journey, for then you don't belong to the not-belonging. I've made some nice acquaintances on the way, but I never pursued one after I arrived.

iii. psychology

:   She is in fact stabbed by jealousy. Her knees go weak and she has frightened headaches—probably rage turned against herself. He in fact is lusting after another woman and to give her up would be to give up his liberty and manhood. The facts conflict head-on. Nevertheless, there is a free space for motion: if, instead of being frozen with guilt and resentful of her demands, he notices that she is indeed suffering and acts out his concern, "I must continue to make you suffer but, dear, let me hold you around."

:   The three roots of love are lust, taking care of somebody, and feeling secure from anxiety during excitement. Normally, these should enhance one another, pleasure leading to affection and protection, gratitude and confidence unblocking feeling, and so forth. Instead, they usually seem to embarrass one another. Secure lust threatens to make us lose ourselves and we panic. It is hard to wish those we love to be free and strong. Those we feel easy with are not exciting.

:   Christmas season, parties, Saturday night dances are like musical chairs; there is reshuffling; somebody gets left out. Such parties operate advantageously among the unattached who are looking around, and among the happily attached who can find refreshment in the "prescribed excesses." For the rest of us, they cause more pain than they are worth, unless to touch the wounds to the quick is an advantage. The unattached come home either with a partner or with a bright fantasy to masturbate to. The well attached come home not on speaking terms, but they quarrel and make up in bed. The poorly attached do not quarrel, at most they bicker, and there is still another pretext of guilt and resentment. As for me, I lose out in the musical chairs, yet I get a certain peace from observing the game; and the fact that I observe it rather than playing it hard is probably the reason why I lose out. I come home exhausted.

: When I consider the long lineage: Paris manned Oxford, and Oxford Cambridge, and Cambridge Harvard, and Harvard Yale, and Yale Chicago, etc., I realize that I am not a scholastic nor a university man—though I ceremonially defend them. I am a humanist, that kind of Renaissance free-lance. At present I seem to be seeking a different lineage: Charcot to Freud, Freud to Reich, and so forth; but I am significantly unable to belong to it. In fact, I was born fatherless.

: You call an author to task for his dangerous opinion and threaten him with sanctions unless he recants. This creates a life-problem for him; he is anxious and in pain. He concedes on the specific issue, because he is afraid. But he is an author, and indeed you have inspired him to write another and much more dangerous work, for now his inner problem has deepened and the old sanctions have become trivial. In the end you have to burn him.

: Alfred and Wallace are examples of the rebirth of the Hero by going back to primeval society. The hero is outcast and flees to the swamps and solitary forests. He gradually collects his forces one by one among the people. Guerrilla warfare is grounded in social nature itself. The hero is not now inwardly betrayed by guilt of arrogating authority; he has no longer come into the kingship by mere convention, using unknown soldiers as mere things. That is, the Hero loses all, withdraws, is reborn in the natural matrix of society in the wilderness.

: "You love me for my body—you love my money,

etc." Of course we do; they are excellent goods, and hopefully one thing will lead to another. Why do they alienate
their gifts as not themselves and even regard them as a
curse? They usually mean that we are not up to coping
with our craving and greed, to come to the human feeling
that they, like others, need. We will take the generous
beauty for a whore. (By the way, this particular vocation
of saintliness has not been much studied.) More likely,
however, they are afraid of their own shallowness. It is
they who are trapped in their goods. For instance, the
beautiful and rich are not much put in the way of learning
anything. I remember how Mme. S. used to 'phone me
enthusiastically, "Oh, grab a taxi and come right down!"
when in fact I didn't have ten cents for the subway.

:   At first, the teacher has a hard-on and makes love out
of lust, but the student, who likes and encourages the advances, thinks he is still being teacher, making love to test
him, to give him a useful problem, and so forth. This
makes it impossible for the student to be simply himself,
to accept or reject; he feels tested, is concerned for his future development. "How am I doing?" He trusts the
teacher as a lustful man, but not moment by moment.
And indeed, the teacher is a teacher and cannot fail to
notice this or that detail, and since he notices it to point it
out, "Why don't you take a breath? why don't you move
your pelvis?" It is just when he is most blind, inconsider-
ate, and selfish that he is most lovable and safe—for he is
trustworthy when he acts blindly; but when he is teacherly
and considerate, he makes the poor youth impotent. Noticing this too, he holds back. He creates a climate of desire and waits for the student to make an advance and take
equal responsibility; but the student doesn't, because he is
a student. They become angry with each other.

iv. method

: To concentrate on an ever simpler and more defined
object leads to more profound results. For it fills the attention, without distraction. Nevertheless, as soon as there is
a "pure" abstraction from the background altogether, all
life vanishes, the process becomes sterile. The too con-
trolled experiment ceases to tell us anything, except about
the experimenter. The too abstract painting has not explored anything new, so it achieves no reality. The profound moment is quiet but is in high tension in the environment. This is just this and nothing else, yet this is *with*
everything else, maintaining its difference.

: A theory of Communication requires at least 3 factors: (1) the symbols and the structure in which they are
interchanged, (2) the solipsistic interpretations by which
each accepts the structure of symbols according to his own
interests and character, but (3) a moment of contact in
which the communication makes a difference, the solipsistic characters being altered, the structure being altered, the
symbols being altered. Communication is a species of
growth. The first 2 factors give content and security, but in
the end it is only novelty that is really communicated. The
better the communication, the *less* the interchange of a
structure of symbols and the *more* the direct action of the
communicants on one another. This is what Artaud means
by Theater of Violence.

: Our big society is a society of sub-societies, groups
with varying mores but employing an identical technology.
This has many advantages. One can be idiosyncratic as
part of the big society, yet approved in the appropriate sub-
society that he gravitates to. The difficulty, however, is
communication. The sub-groups seem to communicate because of their use of common instruments, but they do not
really understand one another or profitably agree and dis-

agree. The language of poetry is supposed to communicate the common sentiment. Popular culture seems to do this but in fact does just the opposite: it is so devised that differing groups "share" in it by projecting onto it each one its own fantasy, and what they are really sharing is the common technology. At present, culture is really shared mainly when there are heated quarrels about censorship, comprehensibility, and so forth. The only possible art is advance-guard art, which unfortunately is not the best art since it is so busy being advance-guard.

: In music, consider the bass as the background, a background of harmony, figuration, and beat, that gives a way of being for the tune, its assumptions. The glory of music is that it creates so much of its own world, both assumptions and assertion. The scale itself is a chaos already formed. (Naturally, my own left-hand at the piano is insecure, I do not keep the beat, not otherwise than I find it hard either to share the common assumptions or firmly to impose my own, when I happen to know them.) If we had a common culture, common to all mankind, common to man and the universe, we could *rest* in the background assumptions, take them for granted. The bass would be inaudible. This is the Monophonic style. The background undelineated but present in the texture of the Raw Silk.

: Amiel says of the 100,000 sheep, "The result is wonderful but wearisome, wonderful in material strength, wearisome psychologically." No. If it is wonderful, it is not wearisome psychologically. It fills and interests the mind as a whole. But the bother is that there is then nothing to do *besides*. Taking in the block of 100,000 sheep has used up all my available resources. It occupies the world, and I find myself without a world. So in the city, we find that only the demolished wall is interesting. But we see a wild child and life revives.

v. God

: In an essay for *Commentary* I mention 3 articles of Jewish faith, which I universalize and up-date: that there is a Creation, that God is not a body, that the Messiah will come. But I do not mention the usual 4th article, that God has a covenant with His Chosen People. In fact, I am ambivalent to the idea. I sometimes say—and they tell me I often act!—"we chosen," meaning the creative, the dutiful, the practical, all those to whom I apply the expression *noblesse oblige*. But as an article of faith it sticks in my craw and I usually compulsively act out the contrary, egalitarian democracy. All *are* my peers, not "could have been" or can be. This can be quite destructive, when I attribute to people powers that they don't happen to have. For instance, I resent that my wife doesn't come across, rather than learning that she won't or can't; if I relieved her of the pressure of my expectation, perhaps she would come across. I look for friends in impossible bars and don't find what I look for; and I don't seek out my obvious peers, though we're at ease together when we meet. Why do I insist on the article that "all men are equal," not merely equal in law but equally noble; that there is a community, and it is a democratic community? Perhaps because I am afraid of the Unchosen. My behavior, a kind of incognito, looks very like protective coloration. Yet there is something more. There is no use in salvation if these others are excluded; if any are excluded, I am the one who is excluded. In Paradise these distinctions of status or belonging cannot exist, though in glory every other particolored distinction, and I will not give up on Paradise.

: Buddha is awareness. By awareness we come to non-attachment, and by non-attachment we can temper and escape our wretchedness, and reactively create the compassionate world. But indeed there is that of which we are unaware, and towards this our attitude is Faith. We hope in it as providential. Such are the Jewish and Christian religions. Now the choice between a therapy of awareness and a religion of faith is an empirical question; it depends, for instance, on the quantity of one's misery, the amount of opportunity that there seems to be, the degree to which one's childhood has preserved or destroyed one's animal faith. The psychology works both ways: The high born and happy—Gotama—can settle for awareness without seeming to be shamefully avoiding experience; but the wretched must hope for a total miraculous transformation, miraculous because it is so out of touch with what they experience, namely Jesus on the Cross; it is the substance of things unseen. Or on the contrary, those who have lost confidence in the possibility of an aggressive and creative change must content themselves with ordering their errors and desires, and they pray for peace; but those who have been more lucky can still believe in a New Heaven and New Earth. Luck is the grace of the holy spirit, that gives sense to the glancing present as it comes to be; it is God's favoring countenance.

Or we can ask, what is the metaphysical status of pain? If pain is, objectively, chaos—causing the confusion of form and the sensory excesses that we experience as ugliness and pain—then *either* creative love transforms it into New Heavens and New Earth, *or* it remains lurking there as pain, to which we ineluctably return when we cease being distracted by our illusions. This is an empirical question.

: The Kingdom of God is within me surely, but I don't live there.

Spring and Summer 1956

i.   persons, places, things

:   Meantime meantime patience. General Deep Freeze, the king penguin, stands in the show-window of the pet-shop on the corner, a position of little dignity as he climbs a ramp onto his box of ice or sinks to the ground and lies down clumsily, usually keeping closed his square-pupiled eyes, often hiding his head under his wing, but sometimes pecking savagely at the plate-glass. And he is let out for display-advertising to a department store in Brooklyn. Nevertheless, when the new Aquarium will open at Coney Island, General Deep Freeze, they say, will be the chief penguin, a position of high dignity, gaped-at instructor of my native Empire City just by being himself. To be sure, none of this is the freedom of Antarctica, the glacier, his own people. Last week the petshop failed to provide the ice and General Deep Freeze was visibly drooping and dying in the sun that beat through the glass; but an old gentlemen, learned in the needs of penguins, saw it and indignantly notified the A.S.P.C.A. It is impossible to die of maltreatment in our city. O penguin! I can hardly bear to look at you there, you fat and beautiful bird. And I think of Bodhidharma, the wall-gazing Brahmin, who stood for nine years at the wall of Shao-lin, quiet and happy and becoming aware. But I do not have the courage myself to renounce longing for what I do not attain. Often General Deep Freeze stands there so still that passersby think it is only a stuffed penguin, and that also is very well.

:   The black fellow I fuck is like a wild Fijian, with his long nigger hair starting out in all directions, his black mahogany thighs, his monumental erection. I suggest that he paint white spirals around his breasts and get a shield and a spear and appear and frighten the Coral Bar. "I'd frighten myself," says he. He seems to regard me as a kind of diabolical White Shadow.

:   The chameleon is beautifully the color of the broad

leaf he lies on. He is safe. But in the beating down sun, if you look from the underside of the leaf, there is the chameleon sharply drawn in silhouette.

: The big rocks terribly break off from the Palisades and tumble down at us. We line them up to make a wall along the river path to keep people from falling in the water. We make them into rustic tables and benches for picnic lunches. "Leopards break into the sanctuary," said Kafka, "—after a while it becomes part of the ritual."

: To the end of the old pier reaching into the river, where you have to pick your way in order not to fall between the broken planks, come (1) adventurous boys, (2) queers following the boys, (3) hung-over winos to sleep it off undisturbed, (4) persons in distress or elation, often weeping women, seeking calm from the sight of the water or meditating jumping in, (5) old men to sun-bathe, (6) philosophic gentlemen puffing on pipes, (7) fishers of the deep. Such is the State of Nature.

: Sweet and striking in their gaudy silk shirts, two Puerto Rican youths are petting on the corner of 23rd Street, in love, and love it is makes them brave, callous, careless.

: We say, "The mist lifted and the sun appeared." But it is the sun that lifts the veil of the mist to make his own brilliant entrance.

: When the lowering northeaster abated and the sun broke through, Sally began to hum "Good King Wenceslas," likely by association with the words "looked out."

: In the wake of the flooding rain, the road has deep puddles, the ponds are brimming over, but the sea is no fuller than ever. It is low tide.

: A hundred gulls loll on the currents of air and veer

and circle, not unmelodiously squealing, till first one bold one turns off and heads into the wind across the Bay, then two or three who follow, and then the tribe. I can hardly see the leader in the distance.

: The small child, age 7 months, has in her eyes a look of perfected intelligence. It is only that she cannot yet manipulate the environment, for example the path from her hand to her mouth. The Gestalt-forming Attentiveness seems to be fully developed. As Plato says, the soul is like a man in a ship. Or better, as Averroes says, there is one active intellect for all mankind—and there it is.

: In a religious rite, style of the 6th Century, the slave takes the Sacrament, his chains fall off, and he stands forth free, while his brothers sing the anthem.

ii. psychology

: If a man becomes quickly and unreasonably angry when he is frustrated, you may suspect that his desire for the thing is shallow; he is forcing himself to seek it against his nature. He's touchy because he has to keep down his own rebellion.

: The structure of passivity is that in the developing feeling there is an unchanging "objective" element. The structure of activity is that an objective element is destroyed.

: Pleasantly masturbating, I have two fantasies of how things should be: (1) I am sure that my beloved loves me, she clings to me with trust. I am confronting the enemies who would prevent us, but I am confident and laughing because I have the rights, the strength, the weapons—for example, they can't stop us from just going off to Tuscaloosa. The essential premise seems to be that I am chosen; I do not have sole responsibility for the sex. (2) My enemy is gunning for me. We draw and fire. But the bullets collide in mid-air! This occurrence is so unique and interesting that it becomes the subject of lively discussion between us; and we two, who were hostile, are soon firm buddies as we engage together in this objective activity.—The meaning of homosexual love is that we both have penises and engage in sex.

:   Living to serve and so finding identity. But if they are not let to serve, they bite at you with spite, to hurt you, to get attention, not to be nothing.

:   With simple assurance, and giving reassurance, I tell old X. to go off to Europe without that wife of his. I am all on his side—anyway she has a grown daughter to keep her company. Then suddenly I recall "Uncle Charley" who became the step-father of my friend Y. During our adolescence. (There is partly an association by resemblance, for both X. and Uncle Charley are retired portly red-faced real-estate men, cheerful and tending toward apoplexy.) At *that* time I empathized with my friend's hostility. I was against the interloping man. Obviously the way to my changed attitude is to have a wife who gives you a hard time and doesn't make you feel loved. That makes you resign at least this much of the Oedipus Complex, and good riddance to bad rubbish. (Written down this Fourth of July.)

:   The patient is sitting in a noble pose, legs crossed, small of the back straight and supporting, head up, freely breathing from the midriff—and then she begins to laugh. At first her laughter is anxious, the relief of tension. But then the laughter deepens and becomes spontaneous. It is the Homeric laughter. "What fools these mortals be!"

:   Laughter is infectious, yawning is even more infectious.

: There are two states that balk me as a therapist: (1) Jealousy. I empathize completely. I can predict the next sentence and the course of resentment, anger, fear, and grief. I even know how to alleviate suffering by holding oneself more erect and lessening depression (the mind goes blank). But I have no perspective. I do not know how to drain energy from the insanity. It is with the patient as with myself, we are forced to rely on time and chance and flattering rationalizations and resolutions. (2) Blocked blank inability to speak or have a next thought of feeling. Here my bother is just the contrary. I often have to deal with this state and recognize it, but I have no empathy with it, I do not believe it. It leaves me out, and I don't know how to woo him forth. I myself can always think of something—except just when I am balked. I can write something even when I am balked.

iii. language

: "Now don't be crushed if after all Bob can't take you fishing?" Matty said, "Who, me? I won't be crushed, I'll crush *him*."

: Between the river and the tracks they have long been making a wide fill, and now suddenly about 30 yards of the area is fenced off as a car pound of the Department of Sanitation, with a sign No Trespassing. I stroll through the gate, hoping to get past and continue my walk along the rocks. The cop whistles and stops me. I explain I am going through. He says you can't do that any more. "What? am I supposed to climb the fence onto the track and go around that way?" Seeing that this is my disposition, he shows me a hole in the fence to crawl through. "I've been making this walk 40 years," say I. "You and a thousand more! I know it! That's why I made the hole in the fence." Now how to explain his strangely literary expression, "you and a thousand more"? We must take into account that his action is out of the line of duty and is suspect; it is daring and boylike and on the side of nature. In these circumstances (1) his embarrassment makes him pompous; (2) he falls back on a literary language that for him embodies the unusual and adventurous; and (3) perhaps for him this language still has a vestige of the original exclamation. We who are used to sophisticated language would consider the heightened expression hackneyed; we cannot express live feeling in this worn jargon. But common people, moved, suddenly talk soap-opera. Trying to imitate their being moved, we search for the "common" speech, manner of Wordsworth, and we imprecisely avoid the literary. His sentence "I know it" had a simple consecutiveness and logic that he uttered precisely with awkwardness and a little self-mockery, as if it were out of the way for him to be direct.

: I write pretty much as I speak, from the same impulse and with the same syntax and almost the same vocabulary. The difference is in how I feel toward the listener. When there is somebody to respond, I talk; when there is no one and yet I have something I need to say, I write, as if for the blank paper. Thus, the opposite of the usual, my writing tends to be more disconnected than my speaking. I lose the thread, I indulge myself, for there is no audience. I lose the literary audience—and they accordingly neglect me. Also, I write longer paragraphs than I speak, because when I speak I soon see that there's no point to it, no continuing response, and I swallow the ending. (Except when I give my two-bit lectures regardless.)

: I used to write with the liveliness of my speech, and now that my speech has taken on the dullness of my propositions, I write these notes with the dullness of my speech. I used to undermine statements that had content with an irony that nullified them, and now I am left with pointing out the remarkable lack of difference between six and half a dozen.

:   Gone are the days when the editors didn't edit or cut
my prose—which they didn't publish either. Now they not
only edit and cut but they insist on my agreeing and revis-
ing their revisions. The problem is to reduce 304 lines to
300, and whether "shit" or "crap." Let me hasten to explain to the next happier generation that I wrote "shit"
and the editor emended it to "crap." Of course the reason
for most of the editing is that the editor, like anybody else,
must prove to himself that he is working for his salary.
The 4 lines must be pruned for "format." But often the
editing of obscenities is not by the editor at all, but by the
linotyper who, like anybody else, has his craft ethics.

iv.   art

:   At Willy Poster's last night, we generally agreed that
there was no more comedy, whether from Hollywood or
The New Yorker. And that this was because Eisenhower is
the supreme object of fun, and since they can't make *this*
comedy they can't make any. We used to wait for *Punch*,
now we wait for the weekly press-conference. It's Ike's
rhythm—one cadence of it and you're rolling in the aisles.
It never fails.

:   In *Hermann and Dorothea* Goethe uses an elegant
structural device to show that the possible is possible: to
ordinary happy-making wishes he opposes feeble obstacles
that at once dissolve. There is enough obstacle to keep the
narrative going, but never enough to arouse conflict or
fear, so the whole is delicious and glorious in effect. To
meet the girl, fantasize about her, and get what you want
all in the same uninterrupted day! The weak conflict is the
big effect. But if you look at the poem closely, everything
is problematical. The boy is bashful, prone to hurt feelings, cagy. The woman is both forward and sanguinary and
safely domesticated. All says success and courage, and all is

timidity. As he says in the *Divan*, "How to ascend to fame? By defending yourself."

: When you develop the incidents in the story, introduce sentence by sentence whatever works for any merely "literary" reason: rhythm, contrast, irony, surprise. Don't worry about the action. From the details you have literarily introduced you will find ways to advance the action, and the action will then seem "natural," that is, it will be imbedded in the written world which is all that the work is anyway. (This was what Cezanne meant.) Commit yourself rapidly to plausible invented details, regardless of their necessity for the plot or theme; but then be consistent and parsimonious, and you will be forced to remain in the constructed world.

: I'm fairly well into Musil's book. It's good, pity it's not great. He has a kind of structural observation that reminds me of myself, but his points do not then surprisingly cohere and drive him far. He does not let them breathe and generate dramatic moments that he did not expect—what Rilke does so astoundingly. Another way of saying the same thing: he plays favorites for his hero against the other people. He interprets their behavior from above, with a certain contempt; they are not absolutely justified just because they are people; therefore they cannot at any moment take over, to his surprise. His hero is always fully justified, especially in the crises, by the concept that he is a Modern Man. But once that's been explained, why bother to explain it again? Anyway, there *is* no "modern" plight, because we *could* change the premises if we cared and dared. Like Max Weber, Musil believes that technology is fate. The disproof is that its working out becomes just as boring in the book as in the world. Can Fate be boring?

: My wife has said once too often, "Soon you'll carp at this book too." My judgments are *not* bitter and overnice, they are my judgments. I cannot be sent when I am not sent, and I often find myself disappointed after a promising beginning. The author presents a new point of view, but then he is not consistent to it or he does not let it wreak itself come what may. I am tired of making allowances. I am coming to feel in me a certain iron.

: A work of art is not in any way crippled or dismembered, but covered from head to foot with scars of battle and healed disease, ruddy of face but lined with experience.

: I compose some tunes on a recalcitrant wooden flute. It has no tones below middle-C. It won't play that if it's wet. I don't finger it carefully so I'm always doubtful about the sharps and flats. Then I get home to a piano and oh what ease and range, all the tones prefabricated, and they stay there put. Only—there is no difference between E-flat and D-sharp, and no way to find the pure melody. Soon I forget what I wanted and am satisfied with what I hear. I grasp at anything that makes sense at all and wallow deeper into banality.

: Lothar's Scale: a system of leading-tones. "But you can't have a leading-tone without a tonic." No! it was this dilemma that Lothar solved, solved it by keeping it doubtful that the dilemma was hopeless, and we watched in an agony of fascination his heroic effort to make home—until we shortly die.

: The patter-song goes faster and faster, till absolutely fast it becomes a trill and turns into the distant tonic of a slow, short, quiet aria floating on the speed.

: A tragedy "ends in death specified by the circumstances of the death." So when J. finally wrecked his automobile, as indeed we had all predicted and refused to ride with him, now very clear was the proportion between this and his manner of painting, total immersion, drip, and accident. It was all of a piece, no one is surprised, but one is unprepared even so. And naturally the painting itself now becomes better—not seems better, but proves itself better. It is more fixed in its style and means its style more. When any of us dies, however he dies, his art comes into its own, for it meant all along that each of us was a dead man. Rank calls this abstraction the "imitation of immortality." The work of art is like that Emperor of China who never died because he never lived.

: "No matter how you twist it and turn it, the fact remains that So-and-So has enormous talent." And can't you see the poor fact of a fellow very twisted and very turned by his critics?

: The poet knows untaught and he shines, to the disgust and perhaps wonder of laborious and obsessional scholars. But then, losing his flair, he is worthless and has nothing solid to support him. He may have intuited what is next, but he is not up to it, he is not there where he is. Ceasing to think of something on the spur of the moment he finds himself speechless, stupid (*stupeo*). "We poets in our youth begin in gladness, but thereof come in the end despondency and madness." I dream that I am about to go on-stage, but I don't know the lines, I haven't rehearsed them. I don't know the plot, so I can't even improvise. I am not in a panic but in a cold despair. My shame and stage-fright are repressed even in the dream, if I indeed feel them at all.

: Here I am filling a third little notebook of thoughts, always grudgingly and disparagingly—"Are you writing anything?" "No."—as if I would rather be writing something else. Even guiltily, as if because I write this I do not write something else. Yet I know that later, when I am writing something else, these notes will seem very fine to me; even now I sometimes put something down in my notebook eagerly. I know, I know that what comes to me to write is given me in its time. I really do have this confidence and therefore am able to write—it is just this that is lacking to the lads who can't write. So rather than saying that I am only writing down little thoughts, let me say that just this year the creator spirit wills me to write down little thoughts. And there, I smile at it instead of frowning. If this is an illusion, at least it is a comforting illusion.

: The little prayer "I do not much collaborate" was a masturbation fantasy. Now who else has such a masturbation fantasy? And who else, having this poem, remembers and calls it a masturbation fantasy? The same person, and it is I. And this is my poetic mission, "Among the Americans, to say how a thing is."

v. method

: What is needed is a gentler curiosity.

: It would be useful to develop a theory of architecture from its strictly active elements: screening, sheltering, entrances and exits, zoning, lighting, locating, and a few others. Develop each of these and their combinations as a formal calculus. Elements are architectural in that they imply other elements as parts of a dynamic configuration; they are "expressive." Thus they are distinguished from the atomic elements of engineering. We distinguish shelter from shed, doorway from hole in the wall, seat-in-and-toward from support-for-the-body. These active elements give the formal cause; materials and construction give the other causes.

: The Hollywood movies are essentially imitations of vast, ambiguous, quasi-conscious consensual psychosexual types and life-attitudes. Parker Tyler sees this clearly, and that it is the role of the critic to name them. It is pointless to look at these films as works of art, and it seems idle to treat them sociologically rather than finding the sociology

on the streets. They are psychological actions. Producers
subsequently doctor the films into inconsistent and threadbare works of art; for such "secondary elaboration," as
Freud called it, is necessary to make them tolerable. But
what if we did not dilute them, but rather intensified and
expanded the symbols in their purity? The audience would
scream and panic.

:   A difference between dream and waking is that the
waking world is "real," it has a feeling of possible public
validation. It is not that we feel dream as fantasy, we do
not. Rather, it is peculiarly conscious, phenomenally complete, not theorized or theorizable. Waking is real just in
that it presents the possibility of being doubted, of its reality being questioned. Dream is not questioned, though
often, dreaming, I feel that the whole thing can be turned
off. But this is *not* done by pinching myself, by questioning this part or that part, but precisely by waking.

:   It is an annoying style in argument to listen intently
until you catch the crux and then cut him off, saying,
"Yah! I see your point, but it's beside the point. The point
is this—" Most often you have grasped the point correctly
—sometimes not—but your opponent is annoyed at being
interrupted, and it doesn't help if you have caught his
point correctly on the fly. Nevertheless, though annoying,
this style is necessary, for if you hold your water you cannot keep paying attention: you can't pay attention to what
is beside the point, or to a point once you have grasped the
point. You become bored and surly. This is therefore a
bad dilemma. Here is a possible solution: Attend to the
speaker even after you have got the point; watch the fact
that, whatever the merits of the point, he does hold and
advance and expand (!) this point. Listen to the tone of
his voice, his syntax, the wrinkles on his brow and mouth.
Intuit, while you are waiting, his psychosexual nature and
the incidents of his childhood. And when it comes again
your turn to speak, you will have become concerned with
this complex object; and it is to this, rather than to the

original point of argument, that you will now address yourself. Thus you have acquired a style of argument that is still more annoying.

:   I get a vague signal to shit; I have the theory that it's good to perform animal functions without delaying; I go and shit; and *then* I get a belly-ache. It's the same with everything I do: I cruise for sex because of a vague dissatisfaction and a strong ideal ("sex is grand"); if I find anybody, I get a hard on; then, when the bout is all over and gone, I lust. Now no doubt this is neurotic, a defense against dangerous excitement, operating by safe controllable thoughts, which are also domesticated as "justified." Yet instead of just brushing my character off in this way, let me regard it as a viable psychological type, in the manner of Jung. Different characters have different styles of first contact, whether thought, conation, or feeling. What matters is that the experience is total in the end. Next, let me try to notice in which situations I begin one way and in which another. What are the structures of the various sequences?

:   Freddie, the substitute bartender, is reading the story about the Parris Island marine base, and I am watching Freddie reading it, the saccadic motions of his eyes, etc., also keeping in mind his responses to the story. I am closer to the reality, the man taking in the words. I do not suffer from literary identification, a kind of fetishism. Yet still closer to the reality is the actual interpersonal situation, my lust for Freddie, Freddie's vague and avoiding behavior toward me. But *this* reality one must not observe, though one may notice it; but accept, act, risk identifying with its unknown future.

vi.   society

:   "What military historian," asks Marc Bloch, "would dream of ranking among the causes of a victory that gravitation which accounts for the trajectory of the shells?" Ah, the great one! the great one! the Zen master. If we took the fundamentals into account, there would also be different events to narrate.

: I am merrily fanning a wet fire at D's, smoking up the house. She pushes me aside, unmakes my fire, starts afresh, and makes a blaze. I am offended and angry, especially since my fire was getting along fine according to my standards. She imagines I have the opinion that women shouldn't make fires, the "romantic" work, but should stick to patient drudgery—as if women didn't always do the cooking and make the fires. Obviously this is *her* problem. But what I despair of making clear to her is that we sport with the fire, we piss on the fire, it is not man's work but child's ritual. Her home is blest with many things but it has the wrong kind of fire.

: "Natives" "Denizens" "Aborigines." Aborigines are savage and have wild matted hair, whereas Natives tend to be Barbaric with elaborate hair-do's that belong to the adolescent culture of decorating one's own body. But Denizens live in remote bogs and secret forests; they infest areas where something higher has established itself, either like rats who were always wild, or they are Degenerates who have retreated from a higher civilization, e.g. the Irish. One can be also, in a picture in the *Herald-Tribune*, a Denizen of the Bowery. On the positive side, Aborigines have mysterious Chthonic Powers; and Natives have Rights to be Respected, they must no longer be exterminated but kept in museums or reservations so that no aspect of Culture is Vandalized. But nothing is done for Denizens, who are part of the flora and fauna. Denizens are just tolerated.

: Reading C. D. Burns' *The First Europe*, I feel I have nothing to do with this European tradition, its concern for the individual soul rather than the outgoing act; in place of immediacy, a sense of guilt, symbolic proof, vocation, etc. It's quite indifferent to me; I guess I'm a psychopathic personality. By contrast, I feel like a classical Mediterranean, but of course I'm not that either. What frustrates me is the social problem that the *others* do not come across, initiate, pay human attention to one another; what delights me is our sharing in achievement. Slavery and compulsion are abhorrent to me, but no Greek would have caviled about them. Yet I take lightly the individual sense of privacy, obligation, sexual guilt, so that the Europeans abhor me. ??

: Distressing, that these handsome fellows become policemen and probably out of circulation. But *quis custodiet custodes?* So much by way of a joke—what else is there to do? But the case seems to be as follows: (a) The police do not much directly impede my behavior; I have a measure of success under their noses—so they are not intolerable. (b) I shall surely be arrested one of these days, simply by probability, given the number of occasions—I am fairly prudent, fairly careless. The prospect alarms me but does not throw me. (c) But my spirit is spoiled by their power, and consequent right, to molest me. This is largely an ideal consideration and therefore suspect—think of Negroes and Puerto Ricans who catch police brutality—but there it is and I ought to fight back. I am guilty that I did not indignantly intervene when I heard that C. was arrested.

: In the afternoon I was with the beautiful wild boy who plays by the river, sexy, amiable, and on the loose so that he will come to nothing. But I could happily spend all my days with him if I dared. I would not be bored in his company—I have plenty of resources of my own; and I'm not oppressed by not getting anywhere myself or by my lack of prestige, except when I see how others suceed and I am envious. But in the evening I was in the great new aeroplane flying West, and I was abashed and made small by that machine, society with a big S. The corporation handled us psychologically to allay our discomfort, to calm our fears, to preserve each one's self-respect. In that big operation there is no place for animal or spontaneous disturbance. Why cannot I identify with this wonderful thing? that takes me back to the campus at Tulane which is our immortality, and whose book-store features comic books of trivial private caprice. By the river I am myself, but I am afraid, vulnerable to the police and weak against the hostile hoodlums who patrol there. Finally, at night I was at the conference, leading a company of my peers who seem to accord me attention and respect, and even (as it turned out) interesting sex. I spoke well, absorbed and spontaneous; a good deal panned out; I downed my misgivings and asked for what I wanted, and somewhat got it. But that was yesterday: what is their reaction now that I am gone? I am again faced with an empty day, yet I have less impulse to throw myself back into the wild and its fears.

:   My social existence is absurd. In God's creation I'm a kind of juvenile delinquent, a little Manfred. But I move in a society so devoid of ordinary reality that I am continually stopping to teach good sense, to give support, to help out, as a young gangster might help an old lady across the street on his way to the stick-up. So I cut quite a respectable figure, though on the pious and boring side. All this does nothing for me except to confuse me and use up my time. When the Devil quotes Scriptures, it's not, really, to deceive, but simply that the masses are so ignorant of theology that somebody has to teach them the elementary texts before he can seduce them. When long ago I threw in my lot with Cain and Ishmael because they were able to get to talk to God, I little realized that I was dooming myself to become a pillar of humane culture.

vii.   God

:   Men don't act until the case is desperate, until there are no other alternatives and we feel desperate and those who have set their minds on inadequate alternatives are running around like chickens without their heads. Our action is compelled and this is a pity, for then it does not have the grace of free choice and divine superfluity, calm, clear, unhurried, and decorative. Nevertheless, action out of desperation has its own style, simple and close to brute nature. The gaunt and fumbling style of acting out of desperation saves man from his baroque pretensions, from missing the point altogether.

: Some intelligent Jews nowadays, e.g. the Zionists up at *Midstream*, lay all their stress on survival, having survived. The Jews are those who have survived, and modern Zionism is not a return to sacramental glory but the engine of survival. *Is* this the way to survive? It seems to me that one in fact survives by having an idea which—surprisingly, but one was not thinking about survival—outlasts the roundabout forces of destruction; it proves to be a stronger way of organizing energy. To work at survival as such is like trying to be happy as such. Not that the "idea" is to be taken at face value, nor that survival isn't more important evidence. But to use survival pragmatically is bound to make it boring and we'll destroy ourselves just for spite. To boast of surviving tempts Nemesis, our deeper impulse.

: It was 35 years, not one lifetime, between the death of Bach and Mozart. All that style was almost a fad! It was not two long lives between the settlment of Boston and the Revolution! I am 45 years old and I recall most of my life, such as it has been; it takes 120 such remembered spans and we have all of human culture from the Egyptians and the Chinese. 120 pretty good biographies and there is History. By "immemorial" we simply mean infantile forgetting; the infantile amnesia of 2 generations is eternity. When we see that the whole of history is so brief, it becomes again possible to be an agent of history. The change we can make in history might be small, but it *is* commensurable. Indeed, these days when I read the *Times*, I find that the doings of my acquaintances make up a large part of the news. Every day more so. When I was an adolescent, up to about last week, I certainly did not consider the great world as the stage of me and my friends, but now, alas! it is precisely we who have become the actors of that great world. This makes me think poorly of the great world, if I and my friends are its actors; but perhaps I shall come to think bigger of me and my friends, since we act out that great world. (I doubt it.) Surely there must be some other value, some quite different kind of experience, "outside" this History.

: The above history-conscious lucubrations I wrote down on the eve of the day that I hoped, but did not expect, that G. P. Putnam's would agree to publish *The Empire City*. But they rejected the book, as I expected, and today I feel less like an actor in history; I don't know how to go about it. Not that I am crushed nor terribly cast down, though saddened and empty, and I do have an important new perception to carry with me. This has been my career in general: I do not achieve a success that I can act, but from time to time I have an opportunity, or the fancy of an opportunity, that keeps me going and stimulates thought. If this is my basic relation with God, frankly, it's thin gruel.

: Here's a poem I hope to write, before I am robbed of it by disappointment: "Thee God we praise! I have had a stroke of luck, with all the earmarks of surprise, unlikelihood, and utility for my further activity. And not undeserved. The result has been to animate me and make me resolve to do a job, within my powers, classic in proportion and rich with baroque decoration." P.S., the premise did not pan out.

: Philoctetes is frantically worried for the decay, or fancied decay, of his unerring bow, while he himself mildews in exile. The wood, he thinks he sees, is drying out, or it is rotting with the damp. Naturally there are no proper oils among the savage rocks. And the empty days of solitude and their dry tears and bitter taste. When the torment of his wound occurs, however, he wants only to die, to destroy, spitefully to destroy his best thing, his unerring bow; and he breaks his hateful bow. At this moment, of course, come the Greeks to make amends and make human use of him again. But the God—before our startled eyes—makes the cracked shaft cohere, supple and strong. Such is the play of Philoctetes. But I am unable to create it.

: Somehow I must do two things apparently incompatible. First, simply disregard evil, folly, prejudice, timidity, lethargy, and cheerfully assume that you aim at the sensible and happy-making. When I do this, I rouse your disbelief and contempt of me, then your irritation, but finally I get you to laugh at yourself. I *know* that this is right behavior. I have always done it when at my best. The defect of it, however, is that it is too thin in content. I must take more seriously your world as it is for you (and richly for me). I must *not* glibly bypass it, as I tend to. Yet I must meet it with neither frontal assault nor with acquiescence. God is in the world, including you, not in my intuitions, even the soundest.

: The days get longer, and on St. John's day you go crazy, it's too much. You become self-destructive, as in *Meistersinger* and *A Midsummer Night's Dream*. Having gone so far into joy and light, more! more! But there is no more. At the Winter Solstice we grow mad another way; in fear we retreat to imperishable hope and dream up a Savior. I am crazy for the Midnight Sun, my emblem. But how far North one must go!

: Giving up my planless and fruitless search for company, I go far off on the empty beach. And what if I were Robinson Crusoe? I would collect kinds of insects and shellfish, whatever has a will of its own. Everything—the waves, the sun—has a rudimentary will of its own. Soon the nature of things becomes a Thou for me. There is a return of the forgotten and the landscape is peopled with its gods. This company of the chosen solitude, or resigned solitude—it comes to the same thing—is what I really want, but I am so impatient.

:   I go up to the lonely moor behind the dune, where no one ever goes but me, and no one can see me. By short stages of association—"moor" "lonely moor"—I think of the verses, "God be my help and stay secure, I'll think of the leech-gatherer!" I ask myself if I can resign from this Purgatory, and I at once think of Rabbi Tarfon's sentence, "It is not incumbent on you to finish, neither are you free to leave it off." All my deep advisers say the same thing, but I only shake my head, dumbly disssatisfied, while the sobs rise in my breast.

:   June 30, 1956: I swear, by this wild-rose bush in the bank of honeysuckle, and the visiting bee, to maintain the peace with my only world.

viii.   myself

:   If I breathe softly and let my underlying face reappear, it is the child crying himself to sleep. There is no complaint or demand, that's all over. Then I yawn, and at the yawn I spontaneously smile, because it's interesting how the reflex carries itself out: yawning after relaxation. So I guess I'm cut out for a philosopher. I have the two philosophic faces of final woe (Heraclitus) and merry curiosity (Democritus). I pass lightly enough from one to the other, without desire or effort. Indeed, I am *not* much in touch with the desires and disappointments that I gripe about so bitterly. And I must get *some* satisfaction from my philosophic faces, or I wouldn't have camped there so long ago. I write from these faces: my writing is sad and it is alert. It is authentic writing, though it changes nothing for me. My griping is not authentic, and it also changes nothing.

:   When I lay about me in my rages off the top of my head, then beware first those who by neglect have done me a small wrong that I can cunningly latch onto and make a symbol of the world's neglect. But treated still worse are those who like me and do me small services, for they must bear the brunt of my accusation that their efforts are worthless. I render them speechless by my implacable reasons. Yet I really don't mean to make them feel bad. I am waspish. I mean, "Don't bother me, for instance by existing." Wasps don't attack, they just sting you if you bother them—I like wasps—but it's hard to know what bothers a wasp.

:   Since I do not remember (in the fiction that I accept as my biography) a moment of confidence, of feeling that the world had great possibilities, of ambition toward an unquestioned goal, I never suffer from feeling bogged down, having lost impetus. And since I never experienced a love that was "pure, clean, gave me a good feeling," the way some people speak, I do not feel that I am no longer innocent. Paradise is lost, but I didn't lose it. Similarly, if I had ever wanted "to be a writer," as the kids say, I should probably suffer at how I miss the mark, at how little I do the right work that suits my genius. But since I just got half-ass involved in writing one piece after another, and so became a writer, I have often enjoyed a complacent satisfaction at how bully my writing is.

:   I see an attractive fellow far off, but as I approach along the beach I see he's with his wife, to my no small frustration. She smiles at me, and I, pursuing my New Policy of immediate impulse, of saying it out and having it out—a policy to which I was driven after I finally caught my death of boredom—I say, "Stop grinning at me. I don't lose any love on *you*. Why don't you fly a kite and lose yourself, so him and me can be men together and end up sucking off?" But he, the booby, feels that he has to protect her, and I—my immediate impulse now having changed into self-defense—hardly get off unscathed. What could I have seen in such a stupid, hen-pecked type—as it turned out?

: I have hunted the wharves from 23rd St. to 38th St. so often that they take me as belonging there, on the job, either going about my business or having a break for lunch. This is an advantage. It makes me less strange. (But the truth is that I come from about 2 blocks further away and work at a different job!) Now curiously, even when I am elsewhere I am taken as if I came from the wharves: "Are you a seaman? Do you have a truck? work on the railroad?" Do I? am I? I have succeeded in making myself more Catholic than the Pope.

: "You look younger than when I saw you 6 years ago." Ach, that looking younger began about 4 years ago, so now I'm growing older in that being younger, and it shows.

: As his hair became gray his chest broadened, he drove a longer ball and learned to dive, the things that would have been of great advantage to him as a boy. Meantime he neglected his studies and his need to speak and write became less, the things that would be of profit to him at the age he was.

: I have gradually been refining from my behavior the bluff, the false dignity, the evasive maneuvers, the actions performed to make good the bluff. But this is a dangerous course, for soon I come to see that the whole is false *en bloc*, it is "not myself," I am "not really interested." And I am baffled as to what altogether different thing I do want, under the cotton-wool that muffles my soul. My only world! She will finally lie there naked like Maja Desnuda and I have no recourse. "Put up or shut up." *What* shall I put up? If only I had a hard on! I cast my eyes wildly about, looking for a commission. And I am taken by an overwhelming sloth.

: It's admirable and touching how Sally and I always carry out the mission, often a hard journey over hundreds of miles, and we drive old cars. But we suffer no mishap, we are on schedule, nothing has been left behind, we deliver safe and sound. Meantime each journey has less satisfaction and less importance for us, and we are increasingly distant from each other. Then one time it is likely that we shall *not* accomplish the mission—not arrive on schedule —something left behind—delivered *not* safe and sound. And this without any change or crisis, but just as might be expected.

: My eyes are glazed over—something must surely crack. My daughter is very ill and it drags on. I don't know what to fear or even hope for. I go to the hospital afraid to ask. Being with her, I feel a warm affection, even simplicity, and it's not boring to spend the whole day there. But it wears me out. I know nothing about it medically and I cannot intervene, but I know that what they are doing is not good enough, is not the best that could be done. On the train there is a sexy and inviting fellow, and again my feelings are eagerly warm and simple, but I am on the way to the hospital. I remember my old guilty theory that my pleasure will bring on disaster to somebody else, yet I *know* that animal vitality creates health. Everywhere I feel disapproved—by the nurses; tonight by Dr. Northup, for my quick remarks about the ineptitude of these hospitals. My bluff manner annoys people, but I can't help it. Here, here we see the result of my good head and full heart long disused and out of touch. I no longer know anything with confidence, and I know very little; and what I do know and perceive better than anybody often contains a proposition that may be disastrously wrong. This throws me utterly. The few things I know surely and simply I cannot effectually present and execute, because of all the garbage in my head and all the garbage in other people's heads. I am anxious that the car will wreck. I am superstitiously anxious about finishing this notebook on this note, for it is the last page.

September 1956

i. growing up

:   My daughter is stricken with polio and her legs are seriously involved, but I want her to get out of bed and walking in a few days. I am set on this one thought and nothing else will allay my hope and fear.

At the hospital, however, the doctor speaks of transfer, after the acute stage, to another hospital for rehabilitation. He mentions months of time and wearing braces, or even sitting in a wheel chair. I reject these ideas violently and hate the man who utters them. I will not discuss the hospitals he names and their various advantages.

A few days later, when she is not making progress satisfactory to me, I am sure she is not getting the right treatment at the hospital where in fact she is. I now fear that she may not ultimately—in several months—fully recover. So I try frantically to have her at once removed to another hospital. But there are obstacles; she does not yet meet the criteria for discharge and re-admission. I refuse to accept the obstacles. I am now set with great determination on this new thought, the other hospital, the very idea I had so recently violently rejected.

I work hard at this, and succeed; whereas with my previous hope and fear I could do nothing.

:   This is an important sequence of feelings. By cumulative repetitions of it we grow up, for better or worse. Let me spell it out.

1. Our primary wish cannot be worked at and is intolerably anxious. Therefore it slips away and we push it away.

2. We accept the defeat of our wish by making the very content of its defeat the central goal of our second striving.

3. The new goal is pettier. It is not desirable in itself, but good in the circumstances, a lesser evil.

4. We do not forgive the person in authority who

thwarted our dear first wish. We try to escape from him.

5. But his painful idea persists and becomes central.

6. We ourselves betray our first wish, no longer willing it single-mindedly. But we frantically combine elements of it with the idea that defeated it.

7. The new combination has now become our "own" wish; we work hard at it, and boast of any success we achieve.

8. The primary wish survives in isolation, as a distant hope, exempt from the test of present reality.

9. We learn a new adjustment to reality and go on.

: Betraying one's wish and embracing the content that defeated it occurs inevitably in the conditions that are prevalent in early life. In the present case, these conditions have re-occurred:

I am ignorant in the situation and cannot take practical steps of my own, so I am awed by an authority. He does not win my trust, respect, or affection, and I want to defy him, rebel against him, and take over on my own. But I am afraid of disapproval and punishment, and I cannot cope with the consequences without him. I cannot assume responsibility.

He is almost like a successful rival who has unworthily won authority in the hospital. I doubt his ultimate skill and daring, and have more secret confidence in my own. It seems to me that he disposes of my daughter (and me) without the earnest attention that I would give. He really does not care.

But my antagonist is strong, and my own wish is ambivalent and weak. Reconsider it: I want my daughter to get up and walk quickly. If this were a simple desire, the alternative—of a slow and perhaps imperfect recovery—would *not* seem like an antagonist, but like a hard possible reality, in which to be patient, prudent, determined, and hopeful of the best. Instead, the wish was panicky as if I myself were attacked. The idea of my daughter crippled endangers my image of myself: nothing practical can follow from such a fantasy.

Certainly the first wish does not *center* in the girl and her welfare. My compulsive denying of her threatening fact is not far from denying her existence: "*You* have no right to be in danger. Be as I need or don't bother me."

Children are inevitably caught in this kind of situation. Powerless and ignorant, they are subject to demands by big and knowing authorities who do not win their trust and assent, but whom they cannot quit and against whom they cannot rebel. Matters become worse when the satisfaction of many of the child's desires, whether narcissistic, erotic, or ambitious, is further made impossible by fear, guilt, shame, and deprivation. The child is soon out of touch with what he needs, and he is shaky even about what he thinks he wants. Therefore in a crisis, he easily gives up the content of his own wish and identifies with the wishes of his authorities. He is then safe, blameless, and even boastful.

: As an adult I am not quite so powerless. I rally and draw on new real resources and so do not altogether repress my original wish. Since I distrust the authority in the hospital, I consult a physician from among my friends. He suggests various hospitals and, although perforce I give up my literal wish, I judge in terms of the same criteria of speedy and complete recovery, and I make a choice. On inquiry, I find that the care that she has been getting is indeed all that can be done at this stage (according to present knowledge), so I am more reconciled to the physician-in-charge and I apologize to him.

Within the limits of prudence, I venture to exert my own two bits of therapeutic wisdom. I see that my daughter is in a panic of fear, and this I can alleviate. I give myself to all-day visits, I somewhat calm her fears and lighten the long hours. And since action leads to feeling and feeling to understanding, I now have her as a real object of affection, and I see the whole matter in perspective and more practically.

Tangentially, I engage in a good deal of bitter griping

to my friends about big hospitals, etc. This energizes political and social ideas of mine.

By these means I cannot at all resolve the problem, but I can diminish my anxiety and, unlike a child, I can keep the matter out of repression. A child can adjust to "reality" only by repression and identification. But a creative adjustment can find new truth and excitement in the problem itself. New life springs from the collapse of the *status quo*. One draws on new resources, of compassion to remedy, of study and invention to make prosper, of patience to endure.

My own behavior falls midway between the childish adjustment and the creative adjustment. I have a kind of patience, but it is nagging and worrying. I can act, but erratically and with unnecessary friction. My anxiety is not allayed because I am attached to myself in the past and I do not embrace the faith that destiny is providence. Yet I am able to diminish my guilt and resentment by coming, in many small ways, closer into contact with the situation, so my anxiety is manageable.

Winter and Spring 1956-1957

i. persons, places, things

: One boxer crossed himself before each round and the other did a little jitter-bug, but I don't remember which one won the fight.

: Outskirts of the city. The car pound of the Department of Sanitation. Weeds have sprung up on the fill along the river. The set is like the beginning of a crime story, and it is here that I hopefully look for adventure and the beginning of a new life.

: Hungry. Nothing during a long walk but top-shoots of milkweed, a few dandelion flowers, and a pipe of burley. Very nutty, sweet-and-bitter, and fragrant, but thin thin.

: Pissing, he spattered on the hot gray slate a circle of beautiful diminishing polka dots. Swiftly each one evaporated from the edges to the center. There was a whiff of ammonia.

: On wet pavement on a rainy day, the blob of spittle smoothly slides for a couple of yards, pretty as a picture.

: Some Negroes are so sweet with the upper lip childishly retracted from their creamy teeth.

: Our School (of Hard Knocks) antedates Paris by several thousand years.

: "Auld Deer is the worst of the year": February 16. It is the last reach of winter before the illusory promise of spring—as 3 A.M. is the hour when people die more frequently than at other hours.

: It the tobacconist doesn't know the brand and has to fumble around for it, don't buy, it will be dry.

: Usually Matty avoids the doctor and won't take the

medicine. But when he had an attack of asthmatic bronchitis and couldn't breathe and cried out, he insisted that we send for the doctor and he was obsessional about taking the pills on the minute. "Other children just gasp and don't notice it; he reacts to this disease like an adult," said the doctor.

: The big Negro, basking in the sun in the back of the truck by the river, says he keeps his hard on down " 'cause I can't afford to get a hard on"—he does—but he is pleased to jerk me off and watch me come 'cause I can just change my pants and get these dirty ones washed.

: The April days are warm and delightful and every clock on 23rd Street tells a different story. This one says 2 o'clock, that one 4 o'clock, this one 20 after 3, and that one stopped at noon. I have to return and consult the old pendulum of my wife's dead uncle to find out the right time.

: A problem of ratio: to embrace your wife just enough to feel secure and get to sleep before the contact gives you a hard on and lands you in a fight.

: The hundreds of big trucks and trailers around you, loaded and *looking* heavy, make up your space and the massive world. Then if suddenly one truck begins to quiver and a trailer backs up toward you, your environment breaks up as in an earthquake. You came into this dangerous landscape looking for love, but you have gotten an excitement you didn't bargain for.

: Above the clouds in the sun; in the blue! If you look down, impenetrable mist, but no doubt you have lots of gasoline.

: Flushed with lust and praise. Gee!

: "If I could lift up my head to look at my face in the mirror, I'd finish the self-portrait."

ii. method

: It is not important whether we take as primary the phenomenology, the nomenclature, the classification, or the etiology, but that these be related in some coherent structure.

: I am waiting anxiously for the doctor in the lobby at St. Luke's hospital. The door of the elevator opens, but it is a Negress in a green dress. The outer door opens and a red-haired mother comes in with her little boy. Suddenly the inner door opens, a Puetro Rican orderly limps by. One would think that it is just this arbitrary factuality that would convince us that the world is material, is not our idea. But indeed, it is just in these cases of anxiety that the world seems most like paranoia, rife with "reference." Certainly the world is not our idea; but the contrary *proposition*, that "there is an objective world," feels very much like either obsessional disowning or paranoia.

: There are three theories of pain, (1) as a feeling the "opposite" of pleasure, (2) as the excess in any sensation, (3) as a specific perception with its own sensory nerves. Physiologically, the last is the case. But we must then ask, "What is the specific object of the perception of pain?" as color, solidity, pitch, heat are specific objects of specific organs. Is the painful an objective property of the environment? It is the chaos or unorganizability-for-the-organism of the environment; that is, it is the contrary of the esthetic. Or it is the brute factuality of the environment, contrary to purposiveness or ideality. Such an answer is at once compatible with the other two theories of pain. Chaos is the material cause, excess is the efficient cause, and unpleasantness (inactivation) the formal and final cause. But if this answer is valid, the occurrences and varieties of pain must be used as evidence of the nature of things, a painful idea. To be sure, most common pains are proprioceptive, intra-organic, but this does not sweeten the picture.

: Wittgenstein says that the meter at Paris neither is nor is not one meter long, for it is the Meter. Does not his operational theory here lead him into an "odd" way of speaking, as he would call it? For instance, the meter at Paris has length and so must be quantifiable. It is 39-plus inches long and so is equal to a meter long, and so *is* a meter long. The operational theory of meaning is a good way to make sense, but like other theories it mustn't be pushed.

: Measurement is a cause of length but it is not length, which occurs as part of the object's total configuration. As Aristotle says, the cause is not in nature but is the way we explain nature.

: Hobbes argues that the law is essentially positive rather than natural. But if this view is pushed too far we have the paradox that the lawgiver is a psychopathic personality, for the law is not legal, being the standard of legality. To be sure—though this is not Hobbes' intention— History has been that the lawgiver *is* a psychopathic personality. He arbitrarily assigns a rule, often by some fantastic impulse that dominates him. Indeed, in some cases he makes a law to still an inner conflict of conscience and stay in control.

: Three or four miles high in an aeroplane, I lose scale. The mountain ridges and the rivers look to my unpracticed eye exactly like the runnels in a small field. And worse and more disturbing—since the material is quite different—I see the "sea" of clouds and "islands" of other colored clouds. When there is space-travel and no gravity to fall by, experience will be even more illusory. We fall into stereotypes of perception, with a fearful loss of materiality. Ha! but the need to get down to earth out of the fire and the gorgeous blue empyrean, *this* sharpens one's material perception: "the featureless sea" of cloud becomes very like smoky cloud, that you can't see through.

iii. language

:   I sometimes hear a good quick past-infinitive: "I would like to had it." "I aim to been there before I die."

:   I use: "Whom Joab was the first—" for "of whom." "Whom Joab came and offered him the water," for "to whom."

:   The school grammars take Here Now Then There as pro-adverbs for "in Chicago" "last Wednesday" etc. But this is not how they work in contactful speech and dialogue, only in disowned or discursive speech. And the words usually called "pronouns" are not pronouns. Especially You I Now and Here are more proper names than John or Tuesday. They name something immediate and present in the dialogue. He Then There express the immediate excluded. Proper nouns and common nouns with the definite article are less concrete. "I" is sometimes an immediate noun, sometimes (in autobiography) a proper noun, and sometimes a pronoun. "You" seems to be the most usually immediate noun; it is hard to think of it as a proper noun, for "you went" is direct address and not merely biography, whereas "I went," especially in neurotic speech, sometimes has no present reference and hardly names the speaker, but merely fills out the sentence-form like a pronoun. "You" does not seem to be ever a pronoun except in How-to-Do-It books, or when used as a substitute for "one." I You This Here Now can be uniquely singular and perceptually concrete. "John" is singular but not concrete. "Apple" is one of a collection and abstract.

:   In "I am dizzy," I is a proper name and Dizzy is an

adjective. In "(I am aware) I am dizzy," I has become an immediate name and Am-Dizzy is a verb.

: In a stream of narrative, to modulate from one tense to another is stronger in effect than musical modulation from key to key or even mode to mode. The narrative tense conveys not only meaning and feeling but attitude. In *Parents' Day* there is a good modulation from the past to the present in the narrative of the Fire, in the paragraph "The fire was no longer an exciting spectacle, etc." By the change to the present, I mean to achieve an endlessness, a static presentness, of licking flames, small changes, nothing going on. I accomplish the modulation by a generalization, expressed naturally in the present tense: "The thought of it, when there is not yet a fire, rouses suffocating anxiety etc." The next sentence, "The firemen have put down their hose," can still refer to the general proposition; and its present-perfect tense is not too far from the previous narrative past. But the next sentence, "They stand and watch," makes it likely that I mean *these* firemen, not firemen in general; and then at once, "Here across the brook, I can see—" in the full historical present. But I come to the present not for historical vividness—the passage does not much have this effect—but for lyrical immediacy, a little poem on the word "fire," which word I repeat as often as possible. In *The Galley to Mytilene*, I try the difficult, odd, and unusual modulation to the narrative future. I set it up by abruptly commencing a new section in the present—"The city of Mytilene is at rest"—whereas the previous narrative was in the past; but it is really in the *next* section that I mean the modulation to occur. This section again takes off in the present, a participial present, "At sea the existing is gently arriving . . . is blazing." The first verb in the future is then sneaked in: "Will tack as close as she dares." Without a subject for the verb, as offhand as possible; and I return at once to the present, "The sail drops." I then repeat the same sneaky approach: "The moon rises at a bound and we'll see how it is. We jump etc." Then full future: "The other galley will have sunken," in the future perfect! Oh what a tense is the future perfect! that leaves the decks clear and ready for a new beginning, which is what I am here trying to say. Again, in Chapter One of *The Dead of Spring* I come to the future by a simple repetition: "There is an instant in which we do not notice anything. Section 5. Will be an instant in which we do not notice anything." And at once, "Even before Horatio comes flying" (tense ambiguous) "some of us will have been—" Again, a sharp future perfect, and from then on the narrative is in full future. But in this novel, it is the *next* tense, *the historical present in the future*, that I am really after, for that is the utopian theme. First, I continue my future for a good page; then, to blur the transition, there is a sentence with only a participle, no tense, "Horatio's left hand resting familiarly etc."; then boldly, "Dave will glide . . . for the vibration *has ceased.*" This present perfect in the future is like a leading tone from beyond. "Will it have ceased? 'I can't!' *cries* Lothair." We have returned to the present, but it is the present of a utopian future. And the narrative persists in this utopian tense for the rest of the chapter and the next.

: "Water washes me clean." This is the whole poem. To the poet it means, pregnantly, that he hasn't bathed in a long time, his habits have been dirty, he is regenerated as if by baptism, and so forth. But the natural magic of the fact he is describing cannot be conveyed in such sparse words. The trouble is that as a pure modern artist he takes the speech *in abstracto*, scrupulously unconscious of the audience; he does not use speech as an interpersonal action, to evoke, move, make clear, bring home, and so forth. How enviable the rhetoricians of the 19th Century! so willing to be long-winded, and to what patient readers!

: In the line "They also serve who only stand and wait," the "and wait" is tonally isolated; and I choose in *The Structure of Literature*, chapter V, to read "wait" on a higher pitch, by no means as a period, and ever so faintly louder. But oh! if we read it not higher, but normally dropping down at the period, and not louder, with forced hope, but neutrally, then—it is simply true. I cannot read it this way without shock and beads of sweat on my brow.

iv. art

:   It is May 9th and my wife does not fail to congratulate me on "my" holiday. (It is the day on which the story *The Ceremonial* occurs.) I walk self-consciously down the street as if in a parade or an academic procession, in front of the city and human history, and under the sun we have earned, whether or not people know it. They don't. There rises in me my sorrow for all of us artists, as innocents-by-experience, for it has never proved itself to us—indeed, we create it otherwise—that the world is corrupted and paradise is lost. On May 9th I am proud of us and sad. God grant that once before I die I shall be proud and glad.

:   The beauty of it—as I write my little pieces of music and explore further, and hit on something new to me— the beauty of it to find that our illustrious forebears have invented an ingenious notation for what I want.

:   Composing, pruning another tone out of the chord, I have the impression of carving the song, like wood-carving. It is as if I were starting with noise, the solid rough noise of my existence, and liberating, as Leibniz said, the song. Nobody asks you to do it, but since you undertake to make a work of art you must start with the ugliest, the truth.

:   "Determination" is the will to have terminated. It is not merely persistence in staying with the undertaking, but the will to *have* finished with it. We are determined toward what we will to be rid of. This is the primary characteristic of the artist, he finishes whole works; it is what distinguishes him from the amateur who does not need to finish. And so from the beginning we keep choosing and rejecting so as to allow the work to be finitely completed with the knowledge and the energy that we have available. It is so these days that my art consists in making little 8-line Sentences that I begin in hopeless cafés and finish as I trudge home.

: Grief, so that in a blink it is dark from the horizon to the pole; and then jokes and bizarre actions; and somewhere, as if in the background but growing stronger, the high and clear music of Paradise. To start from a gloom as uncompromising as melancholia, till there is a delicate psychosis. . . . Related to this, no doubt, is that I laugh, and even heartily laugh, at only what is scrupulously real and accurate, without exaggeration. But when I write what is funny to me, most readers take it as serious; and when I'm most serious, they think I'm joking, for "he can't mean that." Sometimes I can almost portray the impregnable frustration of my gloom, and I break down by becoming still more accurate till it's a joke. But the clear high music comes from I know not where. I guess it's the same as the voice of the Dog in Kafka's story, "torn from his chest."

v. myself

: I have a bothersome conviction that anything I do easily is common practice, belongs to everybody. This works out badly. If I think of a catchy tune, I am convinced I am remembering it and hesitate to use it; or worse, I trick it out to justify using it "again." When I visit pleasant and secluded spots along the waterfront, I hopefully expect that somebody else will be there to strike up with; but nobody is there—and indeed, if many others did have the same bright idea, the spots would not be secluded.

: Granting that I am an idiot and a coward, yet in

many big ways, my work, my art, hunting, handling of
money do make more sense than what I see about. I try
too hard, like an addict, for immediate satisfactions; I do
not patiently lay a good foundation. But other people seem
to be in a maze or trap. They never do *anything* simple.

: I am lonely outside the barrier watching the fellows
tossing a basketball at a hoop. I am attracted to several,
especially one youth who keeps clutching at his prick.
Sometimes the ball bounces over the barrier toward me
and I punch it back onto the court, and my lust is increased by this much contact with the game. But now a
ball bounces a good distance away. I retrieve it and throw
it back hard. After which my lust is somewhat abated—I
write this observation down—I am more detached—
enough to go away.

: For *Philoctetes:* "That wound one must not allow to
heal over, the wound inflicted by contact with frightful
reality."—Gide, 1934

: For *Philoctetes:* Just now I do not love anybody,
there is no one I look forward to, or whose perpetual absence would very much disturb me. Negatively it's not so:
there are several people, son, daughter, wife, sister, several
patients, whose distress makes me anxious and to whose
aid I at once rally; and I do not myself feel abandoned. I
feel the same resignation with regard to my works. I no
longer try to get them published. The publishers will have
to come to me—it is not in the offing. Will I then write a
new work if this is how I feel, and what kind of work?
Freud says the work "solves an inner conflict," but the
conflict is solved! the problem is solved! Let me pray, "Do
God exist in order that I may adore Thee." It is a form of
the ontological argument.

: And here are some further reflections about myself
that occur to me soberly but with little affect. (1) Either I

was crazy then, or I am now. Then when I felt I was excellent and was angry and bitter that others did not accept the love and art that I was eager to give them; or now when I suspect my abilities are mediocre, and also that the others are what they are, not interested and not interesting, and I am not excluded but isolated *in* the know. (2) I, like everybody else, am in physical jeopardy in the city, from a crushing blow with the butt end of a revolver, the tortures of the cops, the gang of queer-killers, etc.; but I do not accept the Social Compact that Hobbes thought up for this; it is not my Way. (3) When occasion rises—but it arises rarely—I can become alert, friendly, self-reliant, scarred by healed suffering. Certainly I have done some good things to be proud of and have little to be remorseful for. I can hold my head up and I do hold it up. What does it mean that I think of these 3 things? That I am freeing myself from clinging. Good! But "just now I do not love anybody" and it seems that without the illusion that I am right, great, misunderstood, etc. I do not know how to take the world at all; I have never learned how. Oh God! *can anything be salvaged from all that effort?*

: My awareness of failing does, by diminishing my conceit, give me more scope for other people to exist. Yet this has not resulted in my having more world, if anything less. I wistfully think that success would have given me more world and also diminished my conceit.

: It is even simpler. Part of my misfortune comes from people's misunderstanding of me and occasional envy, but the most part is due to the fact that they *really* don't like me, find me offensive, and find what I stand for offensive. I don't get the rewards of being wanted simply because I am not wanted. I come to see this remarkable causal connection between my behavior and my deserts, but I have no impulse to alter my behavior. In prospect, the rewards of being different from me are not interesting to *me*. Yet I wish I weren't so damned ugly—I would try harder. I wish I weren't so ugly, period.

: He praises me for a good teacher, that I pay attention to the questioner rather than the poorly phrased question, and I try to answer what the questioner is after. I don't know what to do with his praise, but embark on a pedantic explanation that there are several types of good teaching, etc.

: He presses me with a friendly question—I stop and become aware of the one same feeling: the hot flush and swollen eyes of having bawled myself out. My ear hurts. I have cried myself to sleep. I am afraid to wake up. So for 40 years.

: I am sick. I am a sick man being in the world as I am. I do not feel that the disease is mortal, that I am going to die of it. Nevertheless, it is mortal, and so forth.

: I point out new possibilities to him, express high hopes. This has first the effect of flattery, but then it exerts an intolerable pressure. He sits bolt upright and says, "I'd be happy with a second rate destiny." And of course this is what I do to myself, except that I am tied to the strait-laced taskmaster; I can't walk out the door.

: I say, when I have to say anything, that my patients are artists. But in fact two of them turn out to have been Eagle Scouts. There it is.

: A gentleman from *Life* magazine writes a letter attacking me, and I write a lofty and insulting rejoinder in my manner. The result will be that those people will say, "See? there's no dealing with that type"; while the lads in college will say of me, "What a very lofty-minded fellow that lofty-minded fellow must be!" In brief, everything will be just as it is. Yet I suppose I am lofty-minded—in this company. It is the obverse, and reward, of my abject sexuality, quite beyond humiliation.

: And suppose that what I have called my abjectness is

really humility, that this is what humility is? Here's a disturbing thought.

: It's hard to know how it is with other people; when they vanish down into the subway, you do not know where they come out. But I think I get involved with a wider *range* of persons than is usual. This afternoon I was pretty intimate, in successive hours, with a distinguished academic, a merchant mariner on the waterfront, a famous painter, and the delivery boy; and I meet the solid bourgeoisie on fairly equal terms. With all these, I am quite myself, hold the same views, have the same emotions, and hardly temper my language. Far from being all things to all men, I am pretty equally unacceptable to all. The advantages of this indefinite ranging, to which I tenaciously adhere, are obvious—simplicity, humility, humanity. The great disadvantage is that I cannot share the divisive prejudices of each status, and so I belong nowhere. Most often I do not insist, when I'm with the academic, on my experiences that are too plebeian; nor being on the waterfront, on my ideas that are too academic; but sometimes I slip up and estrange myself. Probably I am "refreshing" or "interesting" to them—so both the professor and the sailor have told me—but I don't get much out of it.

vi. God

: God, like any other author, knows the world because he makes it up as it will be. But oh, if he is like me, he makes it up as he goes along, with only a rough plan or none. Sometimes there is a block, he is unable to continue for a while. He rereads what he has done and mulls it over. He makes abortive efforts to go on, and scraps them. Here, meanwhile, are we. . . . The whole is certainly rich in texture.

: As Kafka said, the disorder of things is finally mathematical. X. likes Y, but is not attractive; Z. likes X. but is not attractive. There are psychological reasons that foster these hang-ups, but dammit! her nose could have been a little shorter, longer, etc. What *is* ridiculous, however, is to do what I do, to look for the juncture of incompatible traits: sexy yet sober, forward yet modest, playing hookey yet scholarly.

:   Inevitably we regard every successful advance that we make against our own bastion, and system of bastions, as a great progress of our thought, for indeed it throws us into turmoil; but our great advance is likely some quite ordinary point that others, who did not have our particular blinders, have been seeing and saying all along. So Wittgenstein, in his late book, gives up the positivism of the *Tractatus* and painfully fights his way back to common speech, but he still sticks to the notion that language is a "game"; though after a while he must realize that it is not a game with conventional rules, for it is an engaged behavior, a way of being in the world, as everybody knows who speaks. And so I keep asking myself, *Can anything be salvaged from all my effort?* If not, what am I to do? left with no orientation, no lust, no self-confidence. My dull clarity is giving way to a dull confusion.

:   Be patient, do nothing, cease striving. We find this advice disheartening and therefore unfeasible because we forget it is our own inflexible activity that is structuring the reality. We think that if we do not hustle, nothing will happen and we will pine away. But the reality is probably in motion and after a while we *might* take part in that motion. But one can't know.

:   I tried hard, risky, and in vain. If my friend came to me and said as much, I'd tell him to desist, that it was he who structured the bad luck into the world. But what shall I do with this good advice that I do not proffer to myself as a friend, when what I want is a rabbit's foot and a fountain to refresh my faded face?

: The bother with the young is not that they think they can do what they want, which is an enlivening thought, but that what they wish is a way by which they prevent themselves from doing what they can, which is often more daring and never feeds conceit. A sage, on the other hand, is a man who has come to want what he can do, and so he causes life to spring around him. Confucius said, "When I was 70 I did what I wanted." I used to take this to mean, manner of Coleridge, "I became the kind of man whose spontaneous impulse was acceptable." But it means also, "At 70 I could want what I could do."

: Suddenly, the last few days, everything is more practical to me. The world is both more spacious and more intimate. I am at home at home and at home on the waterfront. Glenn bursts out laughing and says that I am the only person he knows who would at once be happier if we lived in a reasonable society.

vii. psychology

: She arrives animated and babbling about things she has seen. If he is pleased to see her, he shares her animation. If he is resentful of her, he is annoyed also at her animation, which is a further proof that he is left out. My own response depends mainly on the content of the babbling. If it is interesting and well-observed, I warm up to it. If it is boring and false—then, if I am pleased to see her, I put on my tolerant face, as for a child; if I am resentful, I become bitter at this further proof of the stupidity of what I cling to.

: After Nietzsche and Jekels, I usually trace compassion to a refusal of injury to oneself. But the thought of Melanie Klein is also very valuable when she speaks of "reparation" for one's own destructive action, especially an

infantile wish taken as real. The child sees that in fact
Mama is not destroyed; his wish has not been a reality;
there she is good as new. This humbling but salving experience gives him joy and security. The compassionate man
works toward this experience of Repair.

: Reparation-compassion is a means of buying off retaliation. I am compassionate so that "some one" will not
take revenge on me.

: A strong personality makes an impression in a place.
He is invited for a few return visits. But then the vague
hope that he has aroused dies, and he is no longer invited.
Not only that he has failed and let them down—though I
know well how I fail and let them down—but also that, to
the extent that he has succeeded, the excitement was too
wild, it frightened them; as soon as they have learned to
repress it, they freeze against him. But afterwards it all
reappears in dreams: they dream of a forbidden joy, and
he dreams of a reasonable community to work in.

: My wife is uncooperative, forgetful, in helping me
publish a little book of poems. I am thwarted and miffed
by her neglect, and I mention the matter. She says I am
trying to make her feel guilty; but I'm not, I'm making a
desperate appeal. Indeed, it is I who feel guilty, by impos-
ing my project, on her and the subscribers, who are certainly not eager for these little poems. Thus, she retreats
into her problem of feeling reproached, and I into my
problem of feeling unwanted. And this further development, that each neurotic acts like a neurotic makes me
gloomier still. . . . She yawns and becomes droopy. I take
a breath, calming down. She: "Why don't you do it yourself? Isn't that what other people do?" I, bitterly: "*You*
write 20 books and get the reception that I've gotten. Do
you think it's like putting on your hat?" What hat? Neither of us wears a hat. Unable to bear the pressure of her
self-reproach, she puts on her coat and walks out. I write
in this book.

: Usually virginity and innocence are incompatible. It is very unlikely that a lively child will remain virginal, but he may remain innocent if he is lucky. It is almost impossible that an adolescent or adult virgin could be innocent; they remain virginal because of their dirty guilty minds. I dislike virginity because it is so filthy and squeamish. To others, however, there seems to be a kind of excitement and temptation in this squeamishness.

: Young persons who can't make up their minds whether or not to have sex with you because afterwards the "truth" will be revealed, that they are not "really" interesting. Yet (to me at least) it is just coming across and taking a chance that is truly interesting. It is precisely what they do, stalling, that is boring. (But it's my own fault. I pay such flattering attention that they think I expect Lord knows what.)

: Two episodes of the Oedipus Complex: (1) A.B. Jr. dreams that he goes to the Municipal Lodging House looking for his father "Joe O'Neill." He and the caretaker go from bunk to bunk flashing a light in the faces of the sleeping bums who flinch, snore, curse, or open their eyes wide in fright. (Meantime A.B. Sr. is at home in Westport, on $50,000 a year from Madison Avenue.) (2) The woman at the bar, trying for a little of the missed gayety of youth, is pretty tipsy, pretty dirty in her speech, pretty amenable to being felt up by the gentlemen, and carrying on pretty much like an amateur whore. But her behavior is not outrageous to the onlookers, except to her 10-year-old son whose nose is pressed to the window, his eyes wide with horror and hard with hate. (Yet the puritanical idealism of the 10-year-old is a vital relic of original paradise, though made narrow and fanatical by our anti-sexual mores. These kids are a pain in the ass; they make a demand we cannot meet—and it is a stupid demand; yet it makes us ashamed because they are better than we.)

: A feeling that is not deeply repressed—if you tempt it

too overtly or in a way that he cannot deny noticing, he reacts with angry defense, projection, counter-attack. But if the stimulus is covert or is felt as a "suggestion" and partly induced by himself, he responds by yawning and perhaps lightly napping. As Freud would put it, the repressed draws the cathected object down toward itself. Ordinarily his jaw is squared against the threat, and his teeth are grinding; now his jaw relaxes and he yawns. Since for various reasons I touch on the not-deep-repressed, I am surrounded by yawners. But I am also boring—perhaps for the same reason. "Is he yawning because he is interested or because he is uninterested?"

:   Continuing functional needs, like breathing and sensing, that require no initiative, are accompanied by only mild feeling. Recurring appetites, like hunger and excreting, build up tension that must be attended to and give pleasure in the satisfaction and strong unease in deprivation. Sexual lust and learning, which are more sporadic and require complicated initiative in the environment, are strongly motivated by longing and strong pleasure, boredom and interest.

:   "Desire" is different in kind from need, appetite, lust, and interest. It is immediately stimulated not by felt scarcity which appropriates or seeks out satisfaction in the environment, but by an external or internal image or an ideal to be fulfilled. It is sometimes initiated by the initiating self prior to felt need. In the neurotic behavior of greed, there may be no need at all, but the desire acts as if to answer a conceit of starvation.

:   Thus the counsel of ethical perfection has usually been to diminish desire, to make life simpler and happier. This in no way involves asceticism or renouncing appetite. (By rule and discipline, ascetics mistakenly try to disattach themselves from satisfying needs; they try not to initiate or be pleased at all.) Happiness enjoys, but it does not seek out enjoyment.

: Nevertheless, desire does have a positive life-furthering function. It attaches needy feelings and behavior to activity that has otherwise become meaningless through frustration, discouragement, and resignation. Desiring, one has to walk abroad and seek for stimulation when stimulation has become dulled. Because of frustrations and punishments, curiosity is inhibited, adventure is feared, there is no surplus of animal spirits. But desire urges us on; it is a kind of memory of a past that was less resigned.

: In the nature of the case, desire is usually deceitful and ineffecetual—hope is almost always so. Being ideal, it is out of touch with the present and what is possible. It is a poor guide, a bad provider, an augmenter of disappointment and misery. Everything that the Buddha says is certainly the case. But desire is nature's way of our making the most of a bad deal in a difficult field.

viii. society

: If the birds go in flocks, their chances of meeting and mating are enormously increased. Then, by in-breeding and selection, birds of a feather flock together. They flock and become of a feather.

: There is a point in colonizing at which natives begin to be taken as aborigines. They may then get more human treatment, for we pay attention to the exceptional—the retarded, the deliquent, the victim of muscular dystrophy.

: Going on the Parkway, you will never know what Rockland County is like. But the Parkway on the East Coast is like the Parkway on the West Coast. The Parkway has a culture, and colors, of its own—not the worst in America. It has an extraterritorial law: Keep Moving. If you break down, they will take care of you as far as Off. It

is another world! but you and your car have to be in shape
to survive there.

: "Nothing so confirmed Valéry's opinion [that history is useless] as the comparative study he was led to
make of the contrasting strategy of Foch and Pétain, the
former relying on the teaching of history, the latter judg-
ing, with superior wisdom, that history can be of no value
in the face of necessarily new conditions."—Gide, *Journal*
1933. Isn't this a lesson of history? I am reminded of the
young editors of *i.e.* in their issue blasting Harvard: by
careful sociological observation of students in the Harvard
Library, they prove that sociology has no human value.

: "I cannot esteem the courage that comes merely
from the feeling of one's physical superiority. It is easy to
strut when you have muscles of steel."—Gide, 1937. He
seems to think that it is by a moral and social accident that
one has muscles. But to have them is the effect of a way of
being, both aggressive and fearless, that allows the lad to
move, risk, make an effort, develop his muscles. The muscles are a moral fact, a habit, just as courage is a habit; and
no small part of the habit is the confidence that one can
make it good. It is always dismaying to find how little
Gide, the apostle of material joy, is in touch with material
nature. This is why he is so often stupid. He quotes with
relish the expression, "*Tu te fais des idées,*" and he himself was fairly exempt from moral "ideas," except the usual
humane principles; but he was a bundle of intellectual
prejudices and gimmicks.

: When a village ceases to be a community, it becomes
oppressive in its narrow conformity. So one becomes an
individual and migrates to the city. There, finding others
likeminded, one re-establishes a village community. Nowadays only New Yorkers are yokels.

: "New York is unfriendly." So it is. Living in the big
metropolis is like the pre-6-year-old condition of "commu-

nal soliloquy," as Piaget calls it. To accost a stranger is to invite polymorphous perversity or other childish naughtiness. Simple practical friendships, in which one is respectable and respected, are here not easy to make. Friendship must be worked at and grown up to, with luck; and few have the luck. But such second-growth friendship, if it can be achieved, is a powerful engine of change, of cultural invention, international art. It is growth in a mastered reality rather than a practical adjustment to reality.

I find living much easier in the small cities in the Middle West—perhaps because I always go there on a well-paying mission, with established status. Yet oh! to be back in New York where the boys have a sensual and knowing look, however hostile. They are not fed on corn, and damned if they don't look healthier for it.

: I am esteemed in the small cities of the Middle West where I mind my manners. I am described there as warm, friendly, informal, and "impersonal" or "objective." There are no hurt feelings. Needless to say, I am not esteemed as a poet in the small cities of the Middle West.

: At the Columbus Day assembly at the public school, they miss the chance, as always. The school, the neighborhood, is teeming with Puerto Ricans. One of the classes speaks only Spanish. And how nicely, in the play, they sing off Pinta and Niña, the i's tinkling sweet, and Santa Maria rolls off the tongue. But nothing is made of it—no poem from the Spanish, no stress on the Hispanic and Latin background of the story, no pride in the Pan-American holiday. Yet it's glaringly beautiful as you sit there: "Little Spaniard, little Indian, how do you come to be here?" "Because on October 12, 1492—"

: (Inevitably this Columbus Day grief throws me back on myself. (1) I am left out—they didn't ask *me* to write the masque. (2) I am isolated *in*—I alone am close to the nature of the situation, yet I am powerless to change it because I don't live in the same world as the powers-that-be. Now this looks suspiciously like a psychotic response on my part. What is the more likely case, at a quick frank glance? That I am a seedy unsuccessful writer who has some talent but doesn't make the effort to communicate. I blow a good deal and impress a few unimportant persons whose ego I support, as they support mine. I am a sexual failure and a medical quack with a flair. And all this I hedge around with reservations and interpretations to make it colorable and painless. All right, if this *is* the case, I won't be able to keep it up. I'll be more and more isolated. We'll see.) [1966: Ouch! *Now* I don't have a Goddamned moment to myself.]

:   William James, and we Americans in general, lay stress on the combat for "Rights" rather than the status of *having* the Rights. "Eternal vigilance is the price of Liberty," but at our best we regard it not only as a price but as the gratification of a need. The moment that is alive is not the moment of speaking freely, but rejoicing in the decision of the Court that affirms the moment against those who would dastardly encroach on it. Sovereignty is the source of Rights, and the meaning of our kind of democracy is to keep maintaining and indeed artificing our sovereignty. This provides a remarkable synthesis between the Natural Rights theory of law and the Hobbesian positive law. It is a program of orderly revolution. Unfortunately the Americans have not been up to it—but it was a great new idea.

:   Freedom is a juridical relation. Certainly man is not born free; he has this right if he can wrest it. Yet spirit is free by nature, for it is the matrix of inventions that go beyond existing juridical relations. The free spirit informs a person and transforms him into a son of freedom, inalienably extending the Rights of freedom. I suppose this is what Croce and other Hegelian idealists meant to be saying. As for me, I look at the Statue of Liberty with dismay because in my city I am not free in many ways that are essential for myself. I am in dismay and in rebellion because I have been corrupted by the freedom of the spirit, by too much study of works of truth and beauty, by not paying any mind to the popular culture, by not taking seriously the spurious politics.

Summer 1957, in Europe

i. the ship

:   The booms are lowering the cargo into the hold, and the gentleman from the company stands to his table at the brink checking off the thousands of items being stored in that voluminous belly where things are measured only by the cube. It is the most antique scene of the sea. The mate stands straight on the foredeck looking aloft, and gives rapid orders for departure.

:   "The more rubber stamps there are on a document, the easier it is to counterfeit it. But embossed seals, like the final papers in the U.S.A., are hard to counterfeit." Such is the wisdom of the Doctor trained in the Dutch underground.

:   The young Dutch sailors are rotten poker players. They still think there's a full house in the deck. So I have won eleven bottles of beer. But what shall I do with eleven bottles of beer? Give it back to the kids—heads they win, tails I lose.

:   It is unimaginable how Columbus and his sailors tempted this waste of the sea, especially in the drizzling dim night. I am afraid that I will jump into the water and vanish without even a cry.

:   Clad warm, I start my round around our ship into the foggy dawn, deep in my reflections, tireless. Finally the ritual works. I grow warm also from within. I raise my eyes to the horizon where, influenced, the fog thins, the sun begins to shine, the sea is blue.

:   When the sun breaks through, at once everybody's tone of voice is ringing and animated, like birds after the rain.

:   When the sun is visible through a thin cloud, a rid-

ing silver disk, it is a lonely star—and then what and where
are we, outcast in the abyss? But when he comes blinding
in the blue, then it is our Day and light of the enveloping
world.

: If I were to remain on this little ship "forever," that
is for a year, I would no doubt brusque my thwarted situation and try to make it more satisfactory; and very likely
find myself "in trouble." But as it is my stay is too brief. I
cannot learn the ropes enough to be daring, and my departure is imminent enough so that I do not concentrate on
despair. It is different in my little world as a whole, where
I shall indeed remain "Forever," that is for a year. There I
am more desperate and daring and I often brusque the
situation—circumspectly, circumspectly. But it comes to
much the same: I am dark as to any other way of living
than the way I live. But suppose I were indeed to remain
somewhere "forever," that is for so long a time that I do
not continually feel that my time is slipping away. Then
perhaps I would *not* brusque the situation but let it calmly
become as it will; or maybe I would brusque the situation
with a good conscience, instead of feeling that I am impos-
ing myself where I am not wanted. Let me summarize:
(1) Is there time enough to learn the ropes for an act of
daring? (2) Is the duration of happiness worth the risk of
disaster? (Frankly, this is a kind of calculation I rarely
make.) Rather, (3) Is the duration of suffering short
enough to be bearable, because escape is imminent enough
to be real? (4) Is there an *alternative* to making a go of it
here? (5) How long can I continue in my cowardly and
stupid course and not have finally failed in my duty to
glorify my only world?

: For a couple of hours I stood and watched, followed
and watched, stood near and watched Willem working,
climbing, painting—he is about 19, manly, strong, effemi-
nate. During that time all I felt was my frustration. But
now as I walk alone and begin to sing to myself, I have
found a lovely melody, in 6/8 time, syncopated, with tones

long drawn but that do not languish on the beat. A melody that could be endless, as I like. I have already forgotten it but it will recur to me at a later time when perhaps I can "make use" of it. At that time, however, I will not remember that this melody is Willem.

:   Some of the crew resent that they cannot play table-tennis on the upper deck, though the table is usually empty. (There are only 12 passengers.) In the evening, during the bridge game with the Captain, I abruptly bring the matter up and speak for the sailors' cause. He is annoyed, says it is out of the question for them to hobnob on the upper deck; but he paternally offers to get them a table for their own deck—which he perhaps will. The effect on me is that I am made to feel guilty about going down among the crew.

:   The others at the bridge game set great store on the latest scientific systems and agreed conventions, talk about them a lot, and regard me with a certain disgust for my ignorance. But I consistently win. The case is that we are all sandlot players and their formal knowledge stands in their way and misleads them. Their technique is too refined for their abilities, it is masters' play. I employ cruder old-fashioned ideas, but I do try to win and make occasional shrewd estimates of what the others are thinking. I am less trapped in form without content. Alas, there is another side to it. I think back to how, as an adolescent, the others learned to play tennis with correct form, often losing to me, but I could never improve my game, and they did improve. And I am still restive, stubborn, indocile. I am a fatherless boy who cannot go through the regular channels; I am touchy about the regular channels. But I do greedily absorb scraps of information that are dropped, and I use them my own way. Sometimes I end up well-trained; yes, and I even act with the confidence of being trained!

:   "I try to win" or "I want to win" is not the same as

"I like to win" or "I need to win." It does not imply that one is a poor loser, or even dislikes to lose. For it refers to the competition itself and is a finishable situation. But the man who needs to win is fighting not this game but an older fight that he will never win, not this time either. Sometimes he comes to the formula, "I don't care whether I win or lose," and then he is uninteresting to play with.

:   Young Dutchmen sound like euphonious moose.

:   This cargo Ship S. is not an image of the world, it is an adequate sample of the world. And as usual it is I who cause the evil sameness. Nevertheless! also as usual, here is the sailor Bloom who is not working on this trip and is therefore approachable, wants something to occupy his time, and even speaks English; but just he is not my type at all. We are back to Kafka, the disorder of the world is mathematical.

:   But behold the cliffs of Dover, and it is at these that I am staring with authentic lust. Like on the train in New Mexico, I forgot my friend when we came to the mesas. Those were red, these are white, and each in its kind there is nothing on earth so fair.

ii. three days in Paris

:   They're making a film in the ballroom of the Grand Hotel. When you look directly at the scene, the 1890 generals, the gypsy orchestra, the vedette, the dancing, it is simply idiotic. But sideways in the mirrors you see the chaos of wires on the floor and the battery of absorbed technicians behind the cameras. The scene is artificial but the mirror, because it selects at random, selects the truth.

:   My friends formally warn me not to mess with Alge-.

rians. Inevitably I am taken in by the fellow's poetic cour-
tesy and he robs me—but having been taught prudence-
when-traveling by my mother, I have little on me to be
robbed of. He is terrified of the police; he thinks I might
be a policeman. Yet I can neither protect myself nor,
being an anarchist, am I willing to call the police. Luckily he doesn't know my scruples. I understand also that he
and his people are burning with resentment. Probably he
was not even lying, according to their peculiar way of using
words; and not stealing, but violently appropriating self-
selected gifts.

: I must believe, if only hopefully believe, in order to
get a hard on.

: Seurat's method triumphs when he paints a few
blades of dune grass in the foreground. You cannot tell if
they are accidental scratches or the living grass, just as it
really is.

: I'll fare further—indeed I'm leaving tomorrow—and
not meet anybody so fair and simple as the Breton I spent
the afternoon with on the embankment. No use to ask,
Why go? That's an old story and I'm too late in it to alter
the plot. So I ask in wonder, Why was Jacques interested
in me, leaving his friends? No doubt the lively affection in
my eyes is attractive, he being shy and lonely; and at least
this proves I am capable of affection and showing it. Oh,
which is worse, to come home exhausted, having tried hard
and found nothing interesting in the world; or to go away
with a heart sick-full of impossible excellence with which I
cannot abide?

: The necessary lesson for me is Rembrandt's *Venus
and Cupid*. She is a bosomy capable mother; the child is
hurt—hurt feelings, sulky, frustrated. He is rudely pressing
his small hand against her breast, not caressing it but as if
sulkily demanding attention. He is beyond the age when
there will be any milk there. But she is holding him firmly

in her arm and drawing him to her firmly. I must learn
this, for I do not know it, although I do sometimes act it
out: past the time for unchewed milk, beauty holds me
and supports me and will not let me down in spite of myself, when I am bitter and sulky because I have been
Cupid of the impossible. I grudgingly grab at the beauty I
need. Yet meantime my eyes are full of tears because of
the Breton on the embankment, who was for me unavailable. His dark eyes were wide apart; his mother is Irish. He
reminds me—I suddenly recall—of D.M. whom I described in *The Ceremonial*, whose grand-uncle laid the At-
lantic Cable! I smile at my particular kind of snobbery.

: There's always a Right Bank and a Left Bank, but of
course in three days I have hit on the tip of the Ile de la
Cité to while away in the sun where the river divides. I
cannot learn the ABC's of civilization; I seek out the Neolithic era. My own way, or not at all. I am a stubborn little
autodidact.

iii. Switzerland

: I have come no further than a fortified town on the
Marne and I am already betrayed by the Tower of Babel. I
lodge near a half-naked fellow at the grimy little café. He
seems speechless, almost cretinous, but in fact he is Italian
and speaks little French. I retreat, or advance, to the language that is not verbal, offer the match, match the smile,
buy the drink, show my pictures, and timely grope him
discreetly. We are well in agreement and I go out on the
fortifications under the stars—the word "tout à l'heure"
has rung in common between us—the Corona Borealis
midnight end of June. Nevertheless we have got our signals crossed. I hear his motorcycle going through the alleys
looking for me—now near, now far—and I wander to meet

him through the black town. Finally his engine dies; he
has given up.

:   For mankind, speech with a capital S is especially
meaningful and committing, more than the content communicated. The outcry of the newborn and the sound of
the bells are fraught with mystery more than the baby's
woeful face or the venerable tower.

:   Pope's verse, "Alp rises upon Alp" had seemed to me
ugly, exaggerated, and not descriptive. But I see with my
own eyes that it is precise and even too compactly accurate
to be beautiful. The Alps do pile after one another without let, and each one is precisely an Alp, not readily partic-
ularized like the mountains I am used to, that have valley
and environment. These are more like a herd of sheep.
And like the Rockies, the Alps give—terribly strongly at
first approach—the sense of a disheartening formidable
obstacle. It is amazing how, and why, the farmers live up
there on the high slope where it is so improbable.

:   "Dein Land ist sehr schön," I say to the young
farmer on the boat (Vierwaldstättersee); in fact I am
awestruck at the poor chum. He spasmodically keeps pressing my hand. He works for his father and is late returning.
He had hurt his knee skiing and had been to the hospital
in Luzern, dressed in his Sunday suit. But suddenly his
voice rings out proudly, "Canton Uri! *Da* ist Canton Uri!"
He is from Altdorf. Would to God that I could say in such
a voice, "New York! Here is New York!"

:   I am moved to feeling something, I am interested,
and I end the day choked up. In my hypnagogic thoughts
occur the most frightful ancient quarrels, and a clutch in
my upper chest as though I were dying.

:   A lovely scenario that, as I go further into the lands
where I speak the language less, (1) I keep my fool mouth

shut more, (2) the simple sentences I can form are not
oppressive to the other, (3) he can feel secure in himself
and even amiably superior, (4) comes to my aid and likes
me because I am bright and willing, and (5) the thoughts
we exchange are after all the important facts of orientation: "Where are you from?" "what work do you do
here?" "where shall we go?" I can make out—so long as I
do not learn the language.

:   The important thing about travel in foreign lands is
that it breaks the speech habits and makes you blab less,
and breaks the habitual space-feeling because of different
village plans and different landscape. It is less important
that there are different mores, for you counteract these
with your own reaction-formations.

:   The Speech Reform Movement, of accurate reference to things that can be interpersonally shared, is a necessary consequence of the collapse of the Tower of Babel.
When people cannot spontaneously know one another
through mother-speech, they must at least get the security
of sharing implements for use.

:   Every primer of a foreign language is aimed at a specific purpose—e.g. to read Caesar in the 2nd year—and
also according to a specific conception of what communication is and what people want to say. And here I am on
the border of Italy with a primer of Italian made by the
school of I. A. Richards, designed for accurate reporting of
the objective situation and excellent in exploring the theory of relations of Bertrand Russell. "Formerly the book
was between the two books that were bigger." But my pur-
poses are, let us say, interpersonal, and in this little book I
cannot find sentences in "You" and "We," not to speak of
cazzo and *spicciare*. My memory is that Berlitz was more
practical.

:   In Luzern, in keeping with the mountains, the asper-
ity of the climate, the foliage, the manners of the folk, the

benches along the lake are painted beautifully, newly, a dark pine green, and every slat is of course in perfect repair. In Lugano, in keeping with the air, the flowers, the manners of the folk, the benches are painted newly, beautifully, a flaming red orange, and some of the slats are not in good repair but just painted over. The effect in Lugano is quite natural but it's too lush for me; I would rather thin it down, make the benches a French gray, counter the vitality.

: At the Casino in the Italian enclave, the old man wins several hundred in the first few spins. The croupier makes a gesture and says something in his foreign tongue. The old man is embarrassed and thinks they are ridiculing him. He plays differently and loses his winnings. In disgust he steps back from the table and cries, "I'm fed up with it. I'll never come here again." Then he claims he is bored.

: "Nous Bernois, nous avons toujours dominé la Suisse!" says the rigid prudish fellow burning with jealousy because his sister has a Ticinese lover. He is savage with self-righteousness. With grief I think of the farmer of Altdorf and his loving patriotism. Canton Uri can only liberate the land; it is Berne that governs it. Danton and Robespierre.

: They will ask me what I saw, and I shall say that I heard the ring in the voice of a hardworking man in Canton Uri. Only George will understand what I mean, for he perceives that I am an American writer, who wrote "Northward on Route Nine-West."

: I fumble with the language here in Lugano, and the customs are almost as foreign to me as those in the United States. But when the whirlpools of the wake turn after my dripping oars, and I lie down in the belly of my rowboat in the sun, I am as much at home as on Lake Seneca, a citizen of nowhere but an animal of the world. I am lucky to be able to come so far and end up in the same place.

:   I order a sandwich and lemonade. The water brings the lemonade. When he brings the dish, I have vanished, for I have gone to change a bill in order to tip him. By the time he brings the sandwich, I have returned, and I give him his tip. "Oh, merci beaucoup. Tu (!) es allé changer, n'est-ce pas?" This is at the best hotel in Lugano; but he is like a child, to whom the puzzle and the answer are more important than correct behavior. Also, I get the impression at these de luxe hotels that the help regard me in some sense as a pal, more hep than the other patrons.

:   My bother with the luxurious hotel is not the extravagance of it, while other people work so hard etc. This doesn't touch me. I feel neither the envy nor resentment of it, since I am persuaded, rightly or wrongly, that if I had cared for such things as a lot of money can buy, I should have made the money. (It's a long time since I couldn't go to see the one I loved because I didn't have the fare.) But I am offended by the fact that this lovely hotel, not quite in the season, has empty rooms while poor transients are walking the street. The universe that would please me is one in which this kind of waste did not occur, in which our material and human resources were put to use.

:   "What! shall I wear my yellow shirt, my pretty? and then have it to wash in Venice—just because it is my last night in Lugano?" But my generous impulse prevailed and I put the pretty shirt on. Walking in the soft, too warm night, I met Peter, a Swedish youth as beautiful and friendly as cool water. I told him my best truth, making my lame German run the course, as he deserved. Acting with a little more spirit, I was rewarded with a little more beauty.

iv. Venice

:   It's convenient, sociable and permissible, to offer a cigarette. But I am a pipe smoker sucking on my, as we are, unsharable pipe. The smoke that was precisely the smoke of fellowship, passing around the bowl, has become the refuge of solitude. And it is packaged identical cigarettes that form society, such as it is.

: Ciro is a good kid; what a pity that from time to time, unaccountably, he smells bad and I draw back. But it's not Ciro who smells, but the whiff of Venice, the marsh, the Adriatic.

: The city of St. Mark—Mark was the evangelist of fear and trembling—affirmed its collective immortality, shuddering each man at death. The Lion of Venice has in his paw a book and the book says, "Pax tibi, Marce."

: That improbable blue field of the gold stars and the gold lion. Yet on a summer night, the sky *is* this very blue. Does it therefore work? A splash of the naïve in the sophisticated: perverse child genius.

: The vast crowd, especially of tourists, fits the Piazza San Marco; it was made to show off to travelers. Unfortunately our crowd has no *business* in Venice, and so the crowd is too big and Venice too small, for now she is looked *at* and not up to or around at. The Venetians are living on this accumulated capital of their ancients the way a good-for-nothing inherits a million dollars. But as Wordsworth said, "Men are we, etc."

: You give 500 lire to a couple of unemployed Neapolitan lads, to eat, *not* for the movies. They enthusiastically make you trail along to the restaurant and insist on buying you a bottle of beer with what used to be your money. When you demur they are indignant, as if to say, "When I don't have money, I can't treat. Now that I have money, you won't let me treat. When then shall I treat?" Of course the bill comes to 600 lire and you reach resignedly in your pocket, but the waitress shoos us all out with a laugh.

: I have gotten an immense respect for the fellow who, by exception, earns an honest living at a job that *might* be useful, e.g. apprentice mason; and I feel pity (not unmixed, of course, with contempt) for all these decent fellows working at phony jobs. How hard the world is; what nice lines one comes to draw! Why do I have to? why can't I take people as they are, as they have been compelled? Yes, I do have to. For it rubs off on their humanity. A merchant sailor is decent, he is something or might come to something. A navy sailor begins to stink and stinks worse.

: The childishness of St. Mark's comes from how they picked up pretty pebbles on all those beaches they plundered. The prettiest are here; the left-overs are scattered in the other churches. Nothing fits together exactly, yet the conception is strong and cunning and the whole glitters harmoniously.

: In the Piazza a noisy symphonic band has been playing rhetorical Italian music, so that one squirms for mankind in this setting. But now suddenly he has chosen to play the first act of *Otello*, and the scene has sprung into a vivid and terrible night. At the storm, I inadvertently look up at the sky to see if the lightning will flash and strike. I hear the mocking chatter in the back alleys, where last night I was led on a frightening adventure. And lastly there is the faery grandeur of the love music: as Coleridge pointed out, Othello made a perfect world of his love, like a crystal globe; but if it had a crack, he was cast into hell.

: What is most noble in Venice is the *absence* of the centerpiece between the horses of San Marco. I don't know if there ever stood anything on the middle columns, but what could be there now? When the world again has a center, then we shall put something there. As it is, the absence of the driver of the team of four—the absence of the charioteer and the warrior, and one of them divine—

this absence is, alas, the only honest thing in Venice. Let me pray: God grant that we—one of our young—will find and place this missing centerpiece between the horses of San Marco, over the middle door. [1966: Let me pray, Thank God that I, at least, thought of this utopian incident with which I was to end *The Empire City*.]

:   Here is how my spirits rose at a bound. For their humble meal that I was buying, my Neapolitans took me to a dairy, clean, bright, and cheap. They bought rolls and milk. I got us three slices of cheese that looked good. I offered myself a cup of coffee that was not bad. And this was the first meal in a month that I had got from its prime elements by my own effort. My spirits rose at a bound. Evidently I can be happy in a place, in the world, only if I stake out a claim of my own and do for myself from scratch. Yet I complain that others don't come across for me!

:   In a foreign land, one ventures also to grope a cop. His uniform doesn't look authoritative.

:   Where you go to look you are also seen. The top of the tower that gives a long view is also visible from afar. They who maltreat a poet are also judged by him.

:   Others are as confused as I. The German boy takes me for an Italian because I am sunburnt and I speak German so badly.

:   What is the connection between sex and money? They become sexually excited, proceed with you up to the point where they are about to come, and at *this* point they stop and ask for money. (1) Somewhat comically, it has the effect of saving their capital for a wise investment. (2) It is a device to ward off guilt: "I'm doing it for money, not because I like it." (3) Or more positively, it is a device to regularize lust by integrating it with the demands of the ego and society: the money for a casual encounter is like a

wedding ring. (4) All these are true in both America and
Italy; yet in Italy today I am wrong. For the fact remains
that this soldier gets 17¢ a day to spend, and what shall he
do with his free evenings in Venice with 17¢? He hangs
around waiting for somebody to suggest something to do,
and perhaps pay for it. It is in this position of passive expo-
sure and dependency, where he can make no decision of
his own, that he fights desperately to regain some initiative
and manliness, to get spending money. (5) In the city full
of things and activities all of which cost money, to be
without spending money must be very equivalent to being
deprived of sexual freedom; and then sex without money is
like second-best or defeated sex. As a man does not want
the sexual act as such, but wants it with his "type," whom
he has sought and won.

For neurotic reasons of my own, I refuse to pay
money. I complain to myself that the mixture of love and
money makes "personal relations" impossible; as Wilhelm
Meister said to the Countess, the exchange of the money
closes the situation. When I refuse, the soldier has to back
out. I then "generously" give him money for food or cigarettes, so he can save face. My attitude is hopelessly ambiguous and unfair. I hope for a relation developing, but I
must prudently refuse to be the all-sharing friend, for in
fact I don't have much money; I must be parsimonious.

: Yet the *navy* is really no good, here as elsewhere.
And I am taking revenge. I wilfully excite them and then
say I have no money, disappointing them doubly. This is
truly perverse—I've never played such dangerous games in
my life, for fun and spite. But—the poor kids—their shoes
squeak—and I give them money for cigarettes.

: Hitler's concrete bunkers that dot the beach are popular retreats for quickie love, a good example of beating
swords into ploughshares.

: Rough trade spends the hot afternoons on top of the
bunker, conversing with a medical doctor and two doctors

of philosophy, all much traveled, courting him. Who of his friends has such cultural advantages? Lord knows how it addles his brain! The doctors, conversely, learn another thing or two from one another.

: He keeps from bumping into him inadvertently by following him all day at a distance.

: I cannot even weep for it, but throw wide my hands in despair. This beautiful adolescent, Renato, hard on with desire and determined to be satisfied—why should he favor me, except that I look at him with admiration and make his advances for him? But I am without lust and such satisfaction as I get is in his pleasure. Such an animal! a few short years ago I would have burned for him and trembled for joy. What has become of me? and what is to become of me?—Too beautiful: I can't even remember what he looked like, but now nothing else pleases.

: A further exploit of, alas, San Paolo di New York. It's pouring and we huddle in the bunker, all in bathing suits and chilly. A cute, probably queer, sailor from Rome who avoids everybody; a good-looking spoilt German who dislikes me because I cruised him; a German set-designer from Hamburg, intelligent, urbane, and self-tattooed from head to foot; an Italian intellectual who keeps setting me right—except he is wrong—on the mores of the Italians. And we are all waiting around avoiding one another and nobody having any fun. I finally become annoyed and go into the deeper recess of the bunker to change my clothes and brave the rain. There stands an ugly old man who becomes excited by the sight of my momentary nakedness and gropes me. "Go to it, old man," I say, "if that makes you happy." He gives me a hard on and bares his ass, saying pathetically, "Bello culo, non? Bello culo?" I fuck him, a good job, he is wriggling with delight. (I hope I don't catch anything.) With the noblesse oblige of an American, I also give him 500 lire. Clothed, I return to the others and am full of self-righteousness—I explain the

symbol of it to the intelligent German who can understand, and I stride out into the rain.

: An Italian garden is roundabout scraggly and sometimes shockingly invaded by the *Schlumperei* in the background. They seize on an adequate large plot and put intense care into the small details; or they make a rock garden in the wild place itself. In principle, this should be just
my dish of tea, to settle in a finite locale, "no more than
you can cover with your own two feet," and decorate it.
But they miss the energy that comes only from the Whole.
There is no village form. If one does not empty the background and provide a frame, the isolated big fragment is
hard to maintain. There is no beauty in mere details. Disorder invades.

: I had many thoughts pell-mell in Venice, but yesterday not another thought. So today I have left.

v. monuments

: How to live with the monuments? for after all, people have to live here and now.

A. In Venice, the people live in the Monument,
carefully preserving it as a fixed capital from antiquity. But
it does not function as part of their going business—the
Palace has no Council, the Cathedral is not prayerful; nor
do the Venetians produce economic goods. The income is
from the tourists, who come to see and share in the same
Monument. It has 3 forms: (1) hotels, etc. at tourist
prices, a continual tax or toll, legitimate like any tax for
luxury accommodations. Unfortunately, such an income
does nothing for the people's own need to produce. Many
are left unemployed. And the values of the present, what
people aim at, are necessarily the values of the visitors, the
"rich Americans," who wield real power and must be

pleased. Even more unfortunate, the visitors, like all people on vacation, are at their worst and often deserve contempt. (2) So a second form of income is to get the visitors' money for nothing, to get it by mirrors or conning, and so share at once in American power. Conning raises the people to equality with or superiority to the tourists, who can be held in contempt as dupes. And there is continual begging and personal badgering. All this is humanly disastrous, for it makes human contact impossible and finally it makes the Venetians self-contemptuous. (3) Better is outright robbery, which takes the visitors as tribal strangers or invaders, which they are. But then, of course, the visitors cannot stay. A refinement of simple robbery is legally creating an artificial barrier and charging a toll to cross it.

B. In great cities like Athens, Rome, or Cairo the situation is simpler. The inherited capital from antiquity is not the place where people live, it is more like a natural resource, a gold mine that pays off in tourists, and that it pays to preserve and improve. Small places like Delphi or Olympia are nothing but museums and the people are like curators, especially since the Greeks make a thing of their history and the antiquities are always busy with bus-loads of schoolchildren and adolescent soldiers. The fabrication of Greek souvenir copies is a considerable industry and not very phony, since many of them are excellent and stylish; just as the fabrication of folk-ware is a considerable industry and also not very phony; and authentic commercial products, like nuts and oranges and shipping, that sell on the international market, do not exist badly with the others cheek by jowl.

C. In Paris, on the contrary, up to the last decades there has been a most excellent handling of the monuments. Not to preserve them, but prudently to *conserve* them, using them by accommodating them to the going productive concern. This is like a son inheriting a fortune and using it for new enterprises. Then the visitor comes, looks up to, looks around at, and shares in, if he has business in Paris. But one senses that recently the continuity has snapped; the Parisians will no longer transform this inheritance—the old style is no longer gradually transformed, and the modern building is unbelievably shoddy. But unlike the Venetians, the Parisians do not accept our living in their monuments; rather, they are hard and angry with visitors. The Venetian robs you and wants to be liked; the Parisian robs you and couldn't care less, or perhaps even means to humiliate. They cling to a conceit of themselves as Parisians when it is no longer their Paris, and therefore they make it nobody's Paris.

D. Florence is something else again, different from the integrated transformation of Paris and yet much closer to the monuments than Athens or Rome. The Florentine monuments are not very adaptable to community need; they are tough and grand and there is an hiatus between today and their antiquity. Nevertheless, the Florentines have gone on among them and do not live as if in a musuem. There the things are, you—and your car—rub shoulders with them. This is the place in the world where it might be seriously worthwhile to question the man in the street and ask, "What is your favorite statue here? How far back does your memory of it go? Did you play tag on it? Do you have anything to say in connection with that?" What has been the effect of living with their past the way they do? I cannot at all predict the answers.

E. And there is still another way of living with the Monuments. I quote the mechanic at a gasoline station in Pisa: "You liked Florence? Pisa is just a little town." He raises an oblique forefinger. "That Leaning Tower. Last year it moved three millimeters. They keep pouring in tons of concrete." "When will it fall?" I ask. "Ah, when it falls! when it falls!"—he has entertained this idea with relish—"What will happen then? *Unico nel mundo!*" Stuck with a freak.

vi. Florence

: A stranger, and strange, and more and more estranged, I am hardened in it. I am surely projecting my own mood, but Florence is a good screen to project on, rocky, rude and tough, though humanly kindly enough. These old buildings do not express what is sweet to me, common sociable spirit, but the hard imposed conception of a man, and yes, the man not even pleasing himself but austerely fulfilling his conception. For instance, the wilful arch connecting the nave to the Duomo: it is terrible, but tolerable just because it is so powerful. They seem, here, to be terribly fond of heroes who have decapitated something for the public good and are holding up the head for all to see. Are we then supposed to be serenely joyous with our civic triumph and not perhaps a little uneasy in the collar-bone?

: Everywhere there are *named* individuals. It seems to be that unlike most Italians the Florentines have managed to draw strength from the Whole and to maintain the Whole, and they do it by the unifying insight and decision of single men with individual styles. This is what Burk-hardt said. Nor does one get the impression that these individuals form any band of friends. Yet if we put it this way, it is sociologically impossible. There would not then be any city at all. The feeling here is tough, but it is deeply feeling and there was (and is) a city. These are not individual pirates and free-booters. In Santa Croce one guesses at the answer: Praise! just and unstinted praise! (To be sure it's not *hard* to praise justly and unstintingly Michelangelo next to Dante next to Machiavelli, and on the opposite side of the aisle Galileo. But that's just it.) Here, the city did not give you support, not to say love, neither beforehand nor as you went along. You had to fight even for the opportunity. It is not a world in which to be happy; and the outcome of the struggle is scarred by

a desperate, hardened individuality. But then, forming a
social cement—a bitter nourishment, an incentive for the
next combatant—Praise, and in it nothing grudging. As I
see this, and hear the silent praise resound, I think, "I
too!" Instead of feeling as usual that my time is slipped
away, I feel I have plenty of time to carry out something
worthy of praise, as indeed I have the soul and knowledge.
It is simply necessary to put away my yearning that betrays
me, to be supported, loved, and happy. Isn't it what I always urge on my young, to do something great to make me
proud? "I too! You too!" These are my thoughts as, desperate for a little freedom and pleasure, I risk my fool neck
on a motor-scooter in the mountains, when I have not yet
learned to drive, and consorting with criminals. Good! It is
this contradiction that I am going to prove is the right
way.

:   The Head of John the Baptist is on the salver with
the halo still a-shining. In these pictures of the deathbeds
of saints, there ought to be a moment when the halo can
be switched off like an electric light.

:   David is a little light on his long legs; one is reminded of the vulnerable pins of Babe Ruth. In the *Pietà*
in the Accademia, how woefully the pitiful legs have given
way.

:   In the harsh and noble Bargello one comes on the
delicate and sly figures of Donatello.

:   *Perseus:* instead of the withdrawn pelvis and campy
posture, Cellini should have given him half a hard on and
the hero conscious of that as he holds up the snaky head.
Since he undertakes to be in this business, the hero should
enjoy it.

:   The pomposity of these notes—regular Thomas
Mann! It comes from being frustrated and nevertheless
having to feel something or other beside rage. Perhaps I'll

become boring in a new way for me, another advantage of travel.

:   The disheartening academism of Beethoven and Michelangelo—poor kids, they were so unhappy and protect themselves with stuff and guff. (1) They start with a powerful sexuality. (2) But an equally powerful super-ego and/or ego ideal, making it impossible to get run-of-the-mill satisfactions. (3) Narcissistically, they impose their individual conception on the world, and this makes it hard to reach them with help, for the help always has to come on their terms. (4) They get back at the world with bitter griping and reduce other people to shame. (5) In order to be irreproachable and, alas, in order to have some world to share, they take over all the world's conventions and values. This is the stuff and guff. (6) Bearing all this burden, nevertheless they have another ounce of strength. . . . They long to be loved, they succeed in making themselves feared, which is also what they want. Well, I do not fear them but love them. *O hypocrite artiste, mon semblable mon frère.*

:   Florence, harden my soul, harsh one lavish of praise. Admittedly thou art second best, for best is to hope on for paradise—but a field of action, if one has another ounce of strength.

:   I am playing the same fun and games as in Venice. Yesterday Nando, a pretty unsavory hustler, tried to inveigle and rob me. I got rid of him, but then gave him 45¢ for a meal, out of misplaced pity and my usual guilt of having, if only passively, encouraged him. Then I am annoyed with myself for having given him 45¢. Well, today he spots me in the P. Signoria but doesn't know I have spotted him. At once he sics a colleague on me, a ridiculous "masculine" type who struts around me and tries to strike up an acquaintance. I maintain a stony non-recognition, as if he were an article of furniture, and watch him go off to consult with his hidden chum. Sure enough,

Nando at once speeds off on his bicycle and comes back
with a "donna"—I must want *something*. I am satisfied
that he has at least hustled for his 45¢.

:   I am back to the relation of Love and Money here,
that is so odd. Two Sicilian soldiers obviously like me; I
give them something to do, I express my affection with
cigarettes and beer, I like them, they are truly sweet. I sol-
emnly explain to them that I will not make love and pay
money; I much prefer to give them spending money and
just be friends. I am sure this is adequately communicated
with my six weeks Italian. No, they will not have it. "For
nothing! for nothing!" they insist. They want to make love
because they are hot and we are already friends. I let myself be drawn a long walk to the park. Giuseppe, who is
not very attractive but a very sweet and pathetic boy, keeps
playing me tunes on his harmonica, including an outland-
ish memory of *Oh Susanna*, to make me want him too,
since I expressly prefer Guido. By the time we get into the
thicket, it is I who pick a dark spot to sit down. We start
desultorily to make love, they more eagerly, pricks bare, I
with little lust or heart for it. Generously, Giuseppe urges
on his preferred countryman to enjoy himself. Guido heats
up, begins to hug me and press against me—but he will
not kiss me and he maintains always a fixed smile. Then he
is about to come—and at once he stops: "Give us some
money—just a little!" It is *entirely* symbolic. Nevertheless
I am disappointed and at once I stop and get up: "Let's
go. You said you wouldn't ask for money." I leave them
brusquely and go back toward the avenue. They do not
attempt to restrain me, certainly not to rob me, though
they know I have several thousand lire on me and they are
two. On the avenue I wait for them—a little afraid because it is still dark and deserted and I have doubly disappointed them; but I feel they are too nice boys to quit
without having said good-bye to them. They are a long
time in appearing. I presume (hope) that they have jerked
off. At last they appear. I say a friendly good-night and give
them half a dollar each and they are grateful and pleased.

"I like you," I say, "but you must not make love for money!!" For heaven's sake, who in such an incident is proving what to whom? I go off thinking my own thoughts and I will leave Florence tomorrow.

: If I stay with my Lambretta, I will learn the poetry and superstition of travel. Here is the only case of favoring wind that I have ever experienced: packing to depart, I want to readjust the back seat to tie on my valise. In the tool-box, however, there is no wrench, but only an old spark-plug. I tie the valise on the seat as it is. Finally I get free of the maze and traffic and I cut out gladly on the highway to Pisa. At once the motor dies. What a miserable start! But I see that the connection has slipped from the spark-plug because the nut is lost; and now I happen to know there is a nut on the old plug in the tool-box. I fix it and off we go. *Fortuna!*

vii. Riviera

: Real tough guys sit on the rear seat of the motorcycle and drive sprawled forward, masturbating on the vibrations of the machine. More fortunate folk go in pairs one close behind the other, like pairs of fucking insects in flight.

: Ferenczi is right, it's in our blood. There is a long gruelling ride on rough roads, but the goal is the Sea. Signs of the littoral appear, sandy soil, salt smell, the salt-plain, and my heart leaps up more than can be accounted for rationally. *Thalassa! thalassa!*

: "I want to go and look at the stars," I say, "they're brilliant because it's so dark here." "He comes to Italy to look at the stars!" says the unemployed 23-year-old, "the Italian stars are no good either." (Marina di Pisa).

: Below in the garden, the boy is playing with his dog. He whistles softly, *"veni qui,"* but the dog won't come. I whistle softly, but the boy won't come.

: But the dogs and I speak a language older than the Tower of Babel. When I go down the street, they come to *me*, because I smell good and wag my tail.

: To prove that he is hep, the adolescent gets into what he "doesn't want to do." But it turns out that he's not hep, and he hopes that what is "against his instincts" is really only his virginity that wants to be violated.

: I choose a pleasant and secluded place to meet people. This logic gives me leisure for long agitated thoughts.

: I expect that some one who is shiftless in all respects will keep an arrangement he has made with me. Naturally I am relieved when he doesn't show. If only I could fail to show!

: What a study it would be to compare the situation as it is with how I imagine it is! Yet my friends would be proud of me (and weep) to see how I do my best, indefatigably. It is simply that the task is too hard and I get confused.

: The voice of many young Italian men is delivered buoyantly but above a little choke that squelches the chest tones, like a smiling horse with a bit in his teeth. They often have a little bob of the head, taking part in an interior conversation, like young alcoholics.

: You ask an Italian for a direction and he responds with enthusiasm, he comes verbally to your destination with a ring of wondering joy. "Marina? La prima a destra, poi tutto diritto, tutto diritto—*Marina!*" the ring of wonder in the joy of (verbal) arrival is as if he too were surprised that he ever got there.

:   "This must be Santa Maria della Spina, the sailor's church, isn't it pretty? But it hangs so oddly sheer on the shore—surely there was once a bridge here." So I mused in my loneliness. "It's even evident from certain signs that there was a bridge here, across to the Via Santa Maria and then direct to the Cathedral. There must have been a plaza for the Chapel at the head of the bridge." And it is at this thought, that there was once a bridge here but there is no bridge now, that I suddenly burst into tears. No bridge. No sailors. No way from the sailors chapel, 700 years old, to the Cathedral. . . . Holy spirit, if I took pains, as I did, to get the key from the porter across the street, to enter the little Chapel with its sweet rhythm of 2's against 3's, do Thou prosper me this voyage.

:   As you go one kilometer, you go ten. As you go ten kilometers, so you will go two hundred, from Pisa to Genoa.

:   Either by my own efforts or by chance, it's made clear that my hopes have been illusory, so that I now leave each place without the sense of unfinished business, indeed with a strong sense of finished business. Thereby I sleep well o' nights, but it means I ought to go home. I leave each place a day too late—that is, as soon as possible, the last day bearable. I am reminded of the married couples among my patients who battle and tear each other to pieces for the excitement, and to whom I fatuously try to prove that they could be happy together, for they have money, children, each other. And here am I with freedom, my motor scooter in running order, a little money, and the wide world.

:   After the hard climb, at the pass all are giddy and euphoric. There is an inn with flags, souvenirs.

:   Geologically the Riviera is too new, picturesque and therefore hardly habitable. Every habitable spot is infested by a horde of people. They sometimes make of themselves an enduring monument. Everywhere in northern Italy there is stone for building, and through this intermediary they fit into the color of the place. But the place is too wild, tossed by the earthquake, the strata of petrified mud wildly upheaved and broken off, and no river valleys. In Canton Uri, people directly confront their too wild place and *this* is the meaning, that it is lonely and dangerous. But the Italians make everything into landscape, a stage-set, with panoramas and vistas. (We would not speak of a Swiss "landscape" or "vista.") The Italians invest in human rhetoric, are intensely cultivated, but it is as if on a stage and they are doomed to poverty by the inhumanity of the sett ng. It is odd to watch them at one of our Wild West movies: to us these are childish backdrops, but to them they are legitimate ballad-epics, for they have not yet reached the period when horsemen can freely course over mountain and plain. The country is too new geologically, too new industrially, and in between there is an intense cultivation of human rhetoric. (But in Greece, given similar conditions, people make a more manly and animal adjustment, as if they were free Swiss from antiquity.)

: In order to get my old Lambretta registered in Florence, I had to become a member of the Italian Touring Club. £2500. "And what is the advantage of being a member of the Italian Touring Club?" "It saves you from certain inconveniences—" for instance, not being able to get a registration. But it's not funny but disastrous, for this medieval brigandage, creating a barrier in order to charge a toll, is general in the system and it clogs the movement of real goods and services. There is a peculiar formalism about the Italian way of managing. Every transaction is rationally analyzed and subdivided, but there is no process, so the parts do not make a whole. One man sells you a ticket, a second punches it, a third fails to collect it—soon your pocket is full of bits of paper. (The cartoon is probably accurate: there are ten mailboxes for different categories and destinations, but the collector dumps the contents of all into his one bag.) Obviously they are trying to create jobs, but the pay is subdivided, for nothing has been produced. Ten minutes late, the bus starts off in a great rush, and knocks down a passenger trying to get aboard. This is rhetoric. But the beautiful side of it, that Silone conveys, is the wondering joy if anything is actually, not symbolically, accomplished at all.

: The lanky-legged adolescents out camping with their fathers continually bite their nails to the quick.

: They take a towel when they go swimming, the same who when they masturbate won't let the sperm touch their flanks. In New York rowdy Irish, here otherwise sweet Italians, but the same cause the same effect.

: Let me try to contrast the homosexuality of America and Italy. In America there underlies more of the normal homosexuality of ages 6 to 12, the gang "overcoming the Oedipus complex," and exploring first among the like. At adolescence there is a strong and combative reaction to this, but it is superficial, and what underlies can be released for the "educational" homosexuality of antiquity, conformity to a model. On the other hand, because of the general anti-sexuality and the spiteful mothers there are serious problems about all sexuality as such. In Italy it is different. There seems to be less free growing up and almost no adolescence. Then there is little normal homosexuality, but rather a regressive feminine-identification on the part of some, and "active males" who enjoy any sexual outlet whatever (phallic types). So far as I can see, this development has no cultural value whatever. In general in Italy, any sexuality is acceptable, but the equal cooperation that transcends oneself seems to be rare. On the other hand, since Italian early childhood is better and warmer than ours, they have more capacity for enjoyment and more resiliency in difficulties, they are less "neurotic." Nevertheless, one rarely meets a man, one who has developed into manhood the hard way by alienation and overcoming alienation. The majority are mama's boys. Such

things must have been otherwise during the Renaissance,
or it is unthinkable.

:   I'll take a swim, then lunch; and so the afternoon too
will have passed away. And tomorrow I'll go to Genoa and
the day will pass away. And so after many days my bitter
life will have passed away.

:   "The wrackful siege of battering days": it's hard to
know whether this image was better in Shakespeare's time,
or, as is likely, even *more* corny.

viii.   Paris

:   "Cela ne vaut pas la peine—" to get up and make a
salad, to attempt the pick-up. But you must not say "It's
not worth the trouble" to eat the salad, or to fuck given
the occasion. No one has that right. You must say outright, "I don't want to."

:   Meeting a new person, we go through a compulsive
song-and-dance to establish in his eyes some picture of ourselves, to make sure that he takes *this* for granted. E. puts
on his frantic camp of being Mme. X. or the witch on the
broomstick. I vent my low-pitched gripe of what a splendid and failure of a writer I am. I must do it to counteract
some inner guilt or doubt; for an artist without fame, guilt
and doubt come to the same thing. Yet when I walk along
the quai and see the dozens and hundreds of books by
other writers, disgust rises in my gorge. It is not in this
company that I want to be a writer, and I do not want to
be a writer at all. And I am writing it down and making
literature.

:   "The French way of becoming a great artist is to hit

on a new method; artists of other countries must produce great works." I see how this comes about in Paris. There are not only tight little cliques, as in America, but busy and combative exchanges, a community of the cliques, as not in America. The main critical exercise is naming dozens of artists according to their cliques and methods. Pieces by Edouard in this vein used to strike me as peculiarly noisy, but I see it is a local mannerism. An advantage is that it gives an artist a fairly immediate "fame" and a fairly immediate audience. But it leads to a premium on quick formulation and works that are definable without having a compelling exemplarity, for exemplarity comes from touching some depth of common sensibility. So the disadvantage is that the "audience" is a gang of competing cliques and not an adequate sample of all the audience there is. The kind of "fame" establishes one socially, but does not establish one as the voice of something in every soul. Such fame does not console an artist's guilt; it merely shouts louder than his guilt. With us in America, there is less of such a knowing audience. It is much harder to survive and continue, perhaps too hard. But if one does, or could, the result is more monumental. Lonely individuality grown to humanity. It is at this point that there should sound the unstinted Florentine praise, to enable the champion to perform further exploits with confidence and a good conscience. But any such melting and effusion of praise would turn America upside down. Instead, when the Americans are moved they at once pay off in money and "celebrity," the same rewards as are given to everybody else. The true fame of an artist, however, is an irrational authority that he thenceforward possesses, for he is known to be simply a force. Prudently, but not wisely, the Americans will not surrender such authority to any one. By default they let artistic authority slip into the hands of real-estate promoters, park-commissioners, and TV-producers.

: To translate, one must have a style of his own, for otherwise the translation will have no rhythm or nuance, which come from the process of artistically thinking through and molding the sentences; they cannot be reconstituted by piecemeal imitation. The problem of translation is to retreat to a simpler tenor of one's own style and creatively adjust this to one's author.

: My antipathy to the Parisians is perhaps only the "narcissism of small differences." They too accept only such novelties as they can incorporate into their structure without changing it. The result for us both is economical, self-confident, and piddling, innocently and cunningly bourgeois. It is an impregnable defense. But from time to time I am delighted by the pure childlike smile they flash me (and that I flash) quite without sensuality.

: At last I hear from a Parisian what some of us have long dreaded: "America is the Rome of Europe's Athens." Just this we must, and can, prevent. They really do not know our best, e.g. Merce or Aaron Siskind or me; they know what is notorious and "successful," which is of course what their intellectuals seek out and interview. (I recall a gang of us shamelessly pulling Simone de Beauvoir's leg and underlining her preconceptions about American literature; but she was so didactic, and ignorant, that one could not do otherwise.) Nevertheless, they are probably right about Rome and Athens, and we "best" are really the new Christians in the mélange.

: Only the culture of man is novel and interesting. And when, as has happened with me, one gets out of step with that culture, everything ceases to charm. I come to see people huddling like roaches in busy ruins. I go looking for neolithic man. The unsympathetic among my friends do not fail to point out that my ideology of nature has the most cheerless arid style. But of course, for only our culture could cheer me.

: He would paint from the model, but he has to be alone when he paints.

: I am God's loyal boy whom He doesn't understand, and He lovingly treats me in a way that really isn't good for me, but I put up with it because of His good intentions. Or it isn't that He doesn't know, but that He can't. He is, like me, in pain. "Some One is worried about me," said Kafka. So I put on a brighter face—my mother's peaked smile—to make Him feel better.

: It is usual in little hotels of passage to find a piece of soiled underwear hidden in a bottom drawer. It is the offcast of fellows who put up such a front of masculinity and correctness that they cannot bear to expose to the laundry their weaknesses, whether of shit or sperm or vaseline; and of course they are too shiftless to do for themselves. Having little money, they let their filth accumulate for a few days, and then they conceal their shame anonymously and flee. We others get the piece laundered lily-white and add it to our store.

: The young man brings me his poems. He "wants to be a great poet" and he already thinks he's mighty good. Though I don't say so, nothing in particular sends me and I am bemused at his ambition. He obligingly goes on to inform me that I could have done something fine if I hadn't been soured by ill-success; indeed, he has written an epigram about me to that effect. In a tone of elegiac fortitude I agree with him. I might yet have a last period, of transcendent work, I say, but in my middle period, of public communication, I have certainly missed out. (All bullshit.) "Well," I say, "when you make the grade in a few years, don't forget to reach me a hand. Don't be like S. and B. who kicked me because they had looked up at me." All in all I spend five hours studying and commenting on the verses he keeps handing me, greedily asking me questions; but he is not at all interested in looking at a few verses of mine. "Why do you care so much about my judgment?" I ask. "You used to be my idol." "So? You never let me in on that secret." He cannot think of a word, thing, or action of his that he had ever bothered to give

me, but he is offended that I didn't know that he had
adored me. Now he is my enemy.

ix. Amsterdam

:   Like a seaman or a traveling salesman with a stoical
endurance of the Way that gives no comfort, I take quiet
pride in the fact that my health stands up, I have not lost
my passport or money, and only a little of my baggage.

:   I am sitting tired on a bench in the square, and he
sits down next to me. "You are made happy by Amsterdam?" "It is a beautiful city, but I am not happy because I
am lonely." "No! I shall be company for you—what is it
you wish?" I think he would do anything he could to preserve his idea of his city. "Are *you* happy in Amsterdam?"
"Yes, Amsterdam! I shall never—how do you say?—forget
my Amsterdam."

:   Amsterdamer humor: "He lives there in 35 rooms
with his one wife, for he hasn't any other wives." They
attempt it in every sentence, a joke with a dying fall at the
end, while the English rain keeps falling down. "The harbor is not so big as New York's, of course, but it is 42
meters deep while New York's is only 40 meters deep.'

:   I despaired of ever achieving those restrained yet ele-
gantly-flowing direction signals of the fellows on their
motos in the South; but now I see the same up North, it is
simply that they are balancing on the turn, and I too am
doing it.

:   The problems of scientific logic and philosophy—
what is the smallest adequate structure of a symbol to
serve as coin, how to communicate accurately so as to
share a real world, Occam's razor to go light on the bag-

gage—these are the problems of Phoenicians, sailors, merchants, and other travelers who must survive and do business in strange lands. They accustom themselves to pidgin signs for a speedy adjustment that does not need to last long; they do not need to worry about long range consequences in ethics, politics, and pedagogy. Artisans, contrariwise, are pragmatists and operationalists; they are concerned with available materials and how to get the work done. They pass on their skills to apprentices by forming correct habits of manipulation and rules of thumb. But peasants, physicians, poets, and priests are, alas, more passive to the cosmos and history in which they are stuck. So they continually multiply overdeterminations and cling to text and commentary. They are always in the presence of the disastrous long-range consequences of antiquity; and they are responsible for the unpredictable future behavior of the children. They engage in patchwork, and they dream up magic formulas. On the other hand, as natives and landowners they have endless time, the mistakes will iron out, though meantime the patients die like flies.

:   When you're a stranger, you don't eat according to your taste. You praise it if it is edible.

:   I ask a direction. (1) The manual worker screws up his brow, seeks to orient himself internally, finally comes to an inner clarity, and then makes several attempts to get me to see what he sees. Of course he doesn't speak English. He repeats his direction in faltering German, several times, for he assumes that I am as slow-forming as he. But during all this he comes closer to me, offers me a cigarette, talks about the weather and his coming holidays. (2) The bourgeois proprietor of a good tobacco shop at once knows what he knows; he guesses I am an American and speaks to me in English; he assumes that I grasp the direction at once, which in fact I don't quite. He acts as though he had other business to attend to, but he doesn't. (3) The intelligent youth dopes it out both internally and verbally as one process; he acts as though he were walking it out for

me as an experience—it is not as though he were reading a
map but going a going that *he* easily goes and he shows me
the way. He has a full appreciation of my difficulty as a
stranger, and he concludes with satisfaction for us both,
"There it *is*."

:   It is Schreiers-Tooren, the Weepers Tower, and I
suppose that, now I am here, I have come on a pilgrimage.
For it was from here—so says the plaque put here by the
Greenwich Village Society, whatever that is—that Henry
Hudson sailed in 1609. The Harbor Master lives here, and
his tides and times are posted at the door. The weather-
vane is a pretty gilt Half Moon. I sit on the dock and
write on the back of an envelope, and I write on a paper
napkin during a glass of beer in Dam, and when I finish
my poem in my lonely hotel room, at the words "Many
are the lovely northern rivers," I finally begin to cry.

:   On Joann Blaeu's Map of the World, 1648, there is a
lovely expression of ignorance, e.g. of the American north-
west or the Australian southeast, by breaking the outline
and indicating neither land nor sea; instead of rounding it
off of connecting it up, on the irrelevant principle of logic
that something must be there or nothing. To express ignorance so adequately one must be very precise about
what one knows.

:   The travel book of a great age of exploration, e.g.
Tasman's, is a rare case where literary values—vividness as
well as accuracy, and first rate drawings—are a life-or-death
part of a practical enterprise, just like the work of the ship-
wright and the astronomer. Most often literary values are
rhetorical for practice, or are para-practical altogether.

:   At 16, frantically repressing his disorder, he is forever
grooming his hair, both exhibiting himself and warding off
social disapproval. At 18, he runs his shiny motorcycle into
a car and is concerned neither about his own injury nor the
damage he has caused, nor about the cop's questioning

him; but he frantically and obsessionally goes back to inspect his machine, has it been dented?

: The boy and girl on the dance floor are whooping it up, in American rock and roll but with their own adolescent inventions. They take fire, the other dancers step back, and the onlookers scream "Go! go!" The boy stops in dead bewilderment. Has he done something wrong?

: I have been stopping dead twice a minute to gaze in admiration at another Dutch-blond cyclist making the turn and threading the traffic—dammit! there's so much traffic in Amsterdam, and especially the bicycles, that it takes 20 minutes to cross Leidseplein.

: Thousands of Amsterdam dogs are descended from the identical mutt in the old pictures, and they sit nicely at table.

: In the Rijksmuseum I see a little picture and my head swells and glows and I begin to sing to myself. I am enchanted and I am satisfied that I have come so far to see this little picture—it is Vermeer's *Street*—also puzzled as to just what its magic is: is it perhaps the wilful asymmetrical composition in the patient pervasive texture, or the blue foliage, or. . . . At this moment the lecturer comes by and explains to his flock that this little picture is the highest-priced in the gallery: the owner of Dutch Shell paid $200,000 for it thirty years ago to get it back from the Americans; and "How," he asks my question, "is this little bit of a picture worth that much money?" My immediate response is that I am just as pleased that I know an expensive thing when I see it. Then I am annoyed that they have taken away my own little picture, which I could fancy stealing. Then I engage in my usual high-level consolation that there is a common sensibility of mankind, with which thought I cease to have any pleasure from that picture—at least for now.

: In a painting by Vermeer, you can take any couple of inches, just enough to include any shape in the texture, and you have a smaller painting by Vermeer. The only other example that I can think of, that has this phenomenon in equal strength, is nature.

: The grand and masterly Rembrandts, and the way the little Vermeers amiably keep pace with them and linger in the soul. If only we had a grand and masterly writer in America, so that I could smilingly and modestly follow his pace and occasionally run rings around him!

: It's not hard to understand the lust for collecting, for "possessing," the pictures. It's hard to tear myself away from these paintings that Van Gogh made in 1890 which give me back my revealed world—if I could see this world long enough and at the right moment, then I could carry it away and see it everywhere, as no doubt I used to but I don't remember. But I get dizzy and leave the museum; and it's an illusion anyway. No doubt it's better that these things are on public display in Amsterdam (Venice, Florence, Paris, New York), whenever you choose to come and look, as the beauties you look for on the streets are a means of getting you out of the house. I ought to, I would be happier if I could, take this revealed world as my home. And I guess I really do. In these little trips to old museums I am content and I sing. I have earned the right to be at home here; I am a native son.

: Elsewhere I often choose Heineken's beer when I can afford it. But in Amsterdam it's just the local beer with the same old taste.

x. Paris

: I can't imagine what I'm doing here again, aimlessly walking past the cafés. "You're boulevardier-ing, like the others." No, but I'm not *doing* it, that's just the trouble. "Probably they're not doing it either." Ah, then I'm doing it.

:   I have a form of argument in which I reduce the issue to a formulation in my own previous work, and then it's proved to my satisfaction. The other hasn't heard of that formulation, and perhaps it's false anyway. But I have become my own classic text.

:   The problem is to be able to say something that is not my party line.

:   When he tries for what he wants and doesn't get it, he is angry. When he tries for what he doesn't want and doesn't get it, he is gloomy.

:   The cure is difficult, for the beauty of the beauties who are our Type has two roots: (1) Beauty is a natural sign for real powers, sexuality and health, and admirable traits of courage, gentleness, alertness. (2) It answers to our repressions and neuroses and unblocks such powers and satisfactions as we do have, e.g. avoiding Oedipal and other childhood inhibitions, or having prestige value because of social convention. If only the first cause were operating, we should not much speak of human beauty, or we would regard it as a minor amiable trait among many. But because of the second, the beauty of our Type compulsively dominates our existence.

:   If I wrote witty epigrams I'd have a grand success. But it is just wit and paradox that I try to neutralize, because I find the common substance more interesting than the contrary attributes. My genius is to make epigram dull.

:   He scowls. Does he know he is scowling and mean to communicate that, or is it the natural sign of a more drastic action, and watch out? So with smiling. When I smile I mean to communicate. But do children know they are

smiling? Do they mean the others to know they are
smiling?

:   Blocked from major artistic experience, A. mentions
always some related minor figure, partly to sabotage the
discussion, of which he is envious, partly to share in it in
his own way, amiably enough. But B., whose power and
ambition are greater, rather mentions some denigrating aspect of the great figure himself, though without revealing
anything significant. A. reaps the reward for his modest
claim by coming to love his small fry, whereas B. can only
learn to hate his big fish.

:   Modern letters likes to treat the scene of Embarrassment, the situation where there is a strong tension of feeling but an inability to find words. There are long pauses,
banalities, fumbling beginnings void of content, and so
forth. (1) Edouard points out that the characters are petit-
bourgeois, for neither the aristocrat nor the workingman is
animally embarrassed. (2) It is a sign, too, of the adolescent rather than the young mature hero. Neither a child
nor a man who has found himself is embarrassed. (3) It is
a sign of the alienation of society from the live interests of
its people. People can no longer find public means to express their feelings, and soon they cease to know their feelings.

:   Now that I have a date and a ship to leave Europe, I
am easier here and enjoy myself more.

:   Just because it achieves so much, Paris poses most
strongly the paradox of making a city beautiful. It has remarkably an overall unity of color, a congruity of style, a
humanly possible building height, and always a good sky.
With a strong structure of broad streets and continual and
various points of monumentality, it is indeed one vast city.
And the monumentality is not pretentious, because it is
modestly scaled to the background; and it is not frigid because, though rarely very good, it is always graceful and in

good taste. Also, as I have said previously, Paris has come to terms with its past monuments by progressively adapting them to present use and building in a changing style without a break (until recently). But the fatal defect of the city beautiful is that it does not study the relation of the exterior and the interior. There are back streets, where the close and domestic things of life occur, and the beautiful structure is imposed on this other city. And even in the formal buildings of the great structure there is no indication from the outsides of the great boxes what goes on within; or rather, one can guess only too well what the interior is like, for just the not very good but modest and urbane decoration of the exterior is chilling and heavy in the interior, where everything is in bad taste. The Parisians themselves behave as if a culture were imposed on them that they bear courageously, but their city is bigger than all the Parisians instead of being the same size as each man, woman, and child. There is no urban esthetic possible without first solving the problem of the expressive relation of interior and exterior; but once this is solved, there is no city beautiful possible.

: The Sainte Chapelle is the model of Paris. Every appropriate effort was made to beautify it. None of it is very good, but on the whole it is quite good and even interesting. But one gets an uncanny sense of the formative touch of St. Louis; everything that he touched turned to ice. The one stroke of life, the clashing green of the Rose against the prevailing purple of the other windows, is a replacement. No no! the best touch is the little diagonal peephole of Louis le Malin, through which he could "attend" the Mass without being seen. This *sournois* spitefulness (Pascal!) is the thrill of life in France.

: There is something blasphemous about portraying the Creator with a halo. Whence comes this halo?

: If you order butter for your bread in Paris, they will bring you a ton of it and charge you accordingly. I am disgusted to see such a quantity of butter. But if you ask for buttered bread, at the fixed price, the butter is spread very thin indeed, just according to my stingy taste.

: I spoke French better a month ago, before I began to write English verses again, and before I was set on returning home. To speak fluently, you must swim in the environment as the only world.

xi. ship

: A ship's barber is a mine of tourist opinions, and he will see to it that *your* opinions are confirmed.

: I go to sleep easily—it means that I have done my best, and failed. I have dreams acutely painful to me, but they do not wake me up. I dream that Susie is crippled, my wife is living with another man, etc. What is the wish? I am telling myself to resign myself and live on, to stop investing so much energy in obsessional denial to protect my darling self-image. For at present I exist like the Bourbons, saying that nothing has been changed, no real defeat has been suffered, even in things not only now irremediable but quite uninteresting, which I cling to only to save face for myself. I dream these dreams the way a child puts his hands over his eyes or hides under the blanket, to practice at mama going away.

: In the game, because of chivalry, fear of hurting, or fear of riling up, I inhibit my shots against a weak opponent. This spoils the game for me and I get out as quick as I can.

: I have been writing something good [yes, the exploit of St. Wayward, Book V, ch. 1 of *The Empire City*] and I have been getting on not badly with my new friend. These things have laid me open to strong feelings. For the first time in a couple of months I hear some fine music, *Carnavals*, and the effect is devastating, I am too deeply moved, defenseless, If *now* my friend would come to my aid! but he rejects me; the circumstances are as usual impossible, and my wish is in any case impossible. Nevertheless! I *finish* what I am writing to its terrible last sentence, and after that I am as if a dead man, flattened against the rock. Well, instead of remaining bitter and becoming mean, I choose to put a happy face on it, to be jovial. In the game I play topnotch, coming from behind and dragging my weak partner with me to victory. I make two small slams in the rubber of bridge. I am animated, so that my friend clings to me and squeezes my arm—always if I stay within the limitation of Moses our teacher on Pisgah.

: There is courage in realizing that the others are even more hurt, embarrassed, restricted in scope. The truth is that we walk around in a vast hospital of chronic diseases.

Winter 1957-1958

i. method and language

: It is time for the historian of culture again to collect our present sense of the Universe, with its galaxies and implosions and expansions, very post-impressionist and expressionist; as contrasted with the long-reigning neoclassical abyss of Bruno and Newton, studded with quiet stars and subject to circular laws.

: From three miles up, the houses, cars, roads, and lakes do not look like themselves smaller, but like toy houses, cars, and lakes in an architect's model landscape. That is, they are seen in a different context altogether, "not real." Changes of size do not form a simple gradation, for our unchanging field of vision always gives a frame, and what we see in it must be interpreted as we can. We must ask the Darwinian question concerning "absolute size": what is the survival function of just *this* scale of vision—just as we must ask concerning Euclidean geometry, what is the survival function of *seeing* the "axioms" of this kind of geometry. Such things are not simply relative; they are anthropomorphic, but they *are* anthropomorphic, and the human animal has a special sensory nature.

: Ground whatever you are talking about in something that you are not talking about, that is its ground, and be aware of this relation without exploring it. Any subject that is discussed is, *eo ipso*, somewhat self-contained; but its givenness, its "reality," is from what is not discussed. The clear example is always Darwin: he illustrates but does not explain Variation, and proceeds from there, using Variation as his material cause. Kant's criticism gives a Warrant by showing the limit of any self-contained subject, and drawing rules by which, being outside the subject, we can still treat the subject. The ground, or matter, must be "empty," and yet the figure must be "in" the ground. There is no "prime" or featureless matter, like dough for the cookie cutter; but matter is the unanalyzed potentiality for just *this* form or change. We do not talk about flutes in analyzing the song of the flute, but, as Aristotle said, only the flute has such a song.

:   A thinking or a flow of talk must have a climax and an end. We do not "go on from there" but just begin again, though we may use the products or achievements of the previous action as material for our new action. In Aristotle's treatises this always occurs beautifully at the words, "Let us now make a new beginning," when "the army is reformed after the retreat."

:   The kind of periodicity of climax and new beginning is not the same as the sine curve of Yang and Yin. It is related to the phasic notion of accumulating latent energy and breaking into existence.

:   "King David was the petty warrior-chief of a federation of tribes." No. Say rather, some petty chief is a King David. To be sure, some chieftains are unchronicled and others are drily chronicled. But the quality of the chronicle, the style in which such a thing is written, is a natural sign of the humane importance of the environment, the world in which one is, or is not, King David. However, there is also the historian from "outside," perhaps from another culture, who writes up a petty chieftain as if he were King David. But this is not a chronicle.

:   Meaning is concrete and *therefore* transcendent. It is how the thing sits in its ground. So Bosanquet says that a philosophical treatment is one that is concrete and central.

:   At a discussion led by the theologian Gogarten of Goettingen, after he had given a few halting answers in English, we suggested that he reply in German and the chairman would translate the gist of it. The Professor was, I think, a bit disappointed at not being allowed to carry on in English, but so we proceeded. But more than half the audience were themselves German professors who haltingly asked their difficult questions in English, till we suggested that they might as well talk German and make themselves clear to Gogarten directly. By this time, however, Gogarten was thinking in his pidgin English—I know just how he felt from my experiences with Italian—and he began to *answer* in English, much more confidently than before; he was impatient with their questions in German. Unfortunately, they, who spoke much better English than he, had by now relievedly dismissed their English and they couldn't understand a word he said in English. So now the chairman had to translate Gogarten's English back to their German!

: Gogarten insists that there is only one history, not a sacred and a secular history, and that the Christian reads this one history in faith of the "imminently coming" God. (He convincingly refutes the criticism that this is future-thinking or living in the future, by showing that in any interpersonal relation we do not presently "have" the other, but we always speak to him "as he comes.") But I think his position is needlessly abstract; he could show how *in* the history we meet and must meet our faith, for instance, if we *reason* very hard about what occurs: it will crumble into un-Nature. In general, the Lutherans make much too sharp a distinction between faith and reason. They quote Paul, "We walk in faith," but do they imagine that others, non-Christians, take a step without faith, e.g. that the ground will bear them up?

: Christian theologians have been drawing ammunition for the reality of their faith from Auerbach's style-study showing that the Greeks could not represent reality. (Homer and Sophocles vs. Genesis and the Gospel.) But I think Auerbach unwittingly proves the very contrary of what the theologians want to prove. He fails to ask, "In what conditions does a man *write* a book?" Had he asked it, he would have seen that the Greeks would never have thought of *representing* "reality," which is something that must be lived; as Kafka said, "Man kann nicht Erloesung schreiben, nur leben." For the Greeks, poetry had quite other aims, of dream, recreation, or community worship; and the totality of *that* function was the reality. In this respect, Homer reads just like a Border Ballad. The foreground he presents is sharp and clear because the background is quiet, without neurosis or problem of community function. One must rather ask: what is imperfect about Christians' faith (and what is the neurosis) that they must *represent* reality in a book and spread a Gospel as a story?

: "So *you* think; and what if just the contrary is the case?" Then I'm wrong and have been wrong, and I trust that the evidence of the contrary will work in me and make a salutary change.

ii. art

: If we narrate from within the feelings of the character, it is hard to convey how he is with the others and in the environment in ways that he does *not* think and cannot feel; thus we lose a main part of the *inner* truth. Here at the lunch bar there are several different perspectives: (1) Each is thinking his solitary thoughts. (2) All are like pigs at a trough, solitary but not alone. (3) And they are indeed eating. Also (4) I am writing this waiting for G. to get off work, and nothing else to do but think impatient thoughts.

: In the ballads I've been writing, I try to convey the Freudian ideas in popular jargon, for it is our present common wisdom. E.g. "she makes him guilty so he can't get it up." Paradoxically, just this ordinary community enterprise forestalls their being published! If you say "erection" it is psychoanalysis and you can't publish in the literary review; but if you say "hard on," it's a bar-room ballad and you also can't publish in the literary review. [1966: A couple of blessed decisions of the Supreme Court and now we *can* publish "hard on" in the literary review!]

: In *Tristan* the climax of the love music in the second act is interrupted by the discord of Mark's return. Then at the end of the third act, when we are supposed to hear the climax clear, we hear forever in our souls the discord. Whatever he intended, *this* is what Wagner conveys, and what he truly meant. In *Otello,* on the other hand, the music of the kiss climaxes softly at the end of the first act. It is mentioned but interrupted in the prelude of the scene of the murder; but we now long for its completion, and we hear it forever at the close. Wagner is a romantic: the ending of love *is* chaos and death. But Verdi is classical, and the terrible murder for jealousy is indeed an act of love.

: Without having known them, I hear on the radio the *Four Last Songs* of straus, and what a formally proportioned and unsurprising dying-piece it is! At the reminiscence—but not like a quotation—from *Death and Transfiguration,* I weep; so! after 60 years, this is what he meant to say, but now so simply and without struggle. There is a haunting flute-trill at the end, G above high G on my piano. I am haunted by this ending, I do not wish it to end. To cope with it, I begin a sonnet "And so—" but my agitation and surplus of excitement is such that I cannot write it well (as yet?). Next I think of sharing my feeling —I will mention it to Sally, I will speak of it at my brother's tonight. Just now I can 'phone Glenn, who is musical. But his line is busy, so I write this note.

: [1966] The irony and paradox of High Art because it tells the historical truth, not the conceptual truth nor the critic's truth. How Nietzsche would have hated Zarathustra's Dance, the *Biergemuetlichkeit* of a waltz scored precisely for solo violin *à la tzigane!* Yet that fiddle arpeggio is one of the divine moments of the 19th century. Just this jazz was Strauss's existential and chthonic (!) revelation, very close to the *gaya scienza*. And finally it is the Tin Pan Alley and academism of *The Rhapsody in Blue* that is our authentic American voice that brings grief, because it was *in fact* the pathos of the poor Jewish boy making out in our greatest city, such as it was.

: I go vainly looking for love, come back tired, and write a lively anacreontic. Expectedly, the content is gloomy, a means of domesticating my disappointment. But why the animated and even merry tone? It is the release of spirits and speaking out after the dangers and tongue-tied inhibition of the hunting. Already on the way home I began to sing.

: I complain that when they name the novelists, the critics, the poets, they never mention me. Now Fiedler does mention my name in a discussion of fiction, and I am not so much pissed off as discouraged by the stereotyping which is inevitable, it seems, in such omnibus chats. What he calls by my name has no relation to me. *I* am called a super-Jacobin bent on Bohemianism! What irritates, however, is his critique of the "attitude of dissent that has survived the grounds of dissent . . . a vestigial Trotskyism." It is news to him, perhaps, that we do not have a good society in America 1957. (Nor was I ever a Trotskyist.) And I now learn again that I "left" the *Partisan Review* because of my disagreement with its policies, rather than that they wouldn't print my pieces. I have never left *anybody* who has access to a printing press!

: Rivals, e.g. in Sheridan's play, is a ready comic subject, for nobody has yet lost anything. A common twist is that both rivals lose to a dark horse, and this can be very comic, for it proves that the prize was not essential. But the play of the Defending Champion is usually pathetic and cannot be comic. It is already pathetic that the hero must defend; and the encroacher is both criminal and desperate as a have-not. The only chance of comedy—but it is glorious, to be sure—is the Black Knight cracked open in defeat, and forth leaps the Green Knight of Spring.

:   I give a reading at a bar, flanked by a few feeble poets and amateurs. What strikes my friends is how unliterary my poems are by comparison with theirs. Perhaps this is because I *know* just what wry lilt in my line is from Catullus, what stance from Horace, what period from Milton, what gimmick from Donne, and so forth. No doubt there is also something of my own, but this is just what I cannot know.

:   In tales of young love, a certain amount of sexual detail is conventionally permitted, nay demanded. In accounts of promiscuity, any amount of sexual detail is permitted and expected, since the whole work is taken as primitive or marginal experience. In stories of adultery, very hot detail is expected, as part of the defiance. But in stories of marriage, the convention is that there must be no sexual detail at all, whether of felicity or misery. But to me it seems that the sexuality only of marriage is worth writing about. The story of young love is monotonous in principle. The interest begins with the marriage, where the usual book ends.

:   After writing the first page of the Laddy's Deed, I experienced again the sudden woe of finding my pleasant anecdote turning into an important story, as its implications began to emerge and to demand of me to probe my own situation and reveal myself. The heaviness of a hard task opening before me, and the need to compose a work worthy of the theme; and woe because meantime nobody gives me anything, no solace, no acceptance, no sex, hardly even praise. Writing the story, of course, I felt the contentment and excitement of being able to do something adequate; yet I wrote it in a state of profound depression, withdrawal from life. I have "finished" it, but I do not go back to it.

:   With piecemeal chapters, I can proceed with Book V of *The Empire City*. As I now have two chapters, I can have six. But I still won't have a book until I can bring into action Horatio, whom I left armed to the teeth. For what fight? I do not conceive the fight. If I were not a coward, I would recognize *my* fight, and then I could invent a great fight. It becomes increasingly clear to me that my art does not do the right job for me. In principle, a work of art should help to solve an inner conflict; but with me, it is to the extent that my inner conflict is solved that I find I have a work of art. Then the work defines and affirms for me whither I have arrived. (This sounds like the dynamics of Goethe.)

:   The last scene of *The Family of Abraham* realizes again what I am trying to do in the theater—the program mentioned in the preface to *Jonah:* to convey the wonder and drama in an everyday action, conversing, sitting down to a cup of coffee. It is ironical that it requires five long acts to convey this simple thing in its concrete, and therefore transcendent, meaning. . . . And why is it this particular esthetic program that I work at? Because I am hungry for earthly paradise, and this is it.

:   The effect *largamente* is what artists aim for. Rebekah's exclamation "My Lord—" in the last scene of *Abraham* I have marked *largamente*, I think correctly. But the passage came to me a little luckily, so it is necessary to *mark* it for the actress, unlike the climax of the Chromatic Fantasy, where the *largamente* is methodical (masterly) and cannot be played otherwise. *Largamente* follows what is difficult and ambiguous, and it means: broadly, all at once a total affirmation.

:   In the classical style, the subject is everything. Given a big and simple subject, everything else is given just by being appropriate at every moment, and not underwriting. But such a big simple subject is hard to find, I mean one in which the poet is really involved. To get big effects with other subjects, one must rely on attitude, on inwardness, on leaping upward—and these are non-classical. In the last act of *Abraham*, which is classical on the whole, Isaac's lament for Lezar is non-classical. It would be inappropriate for him to say nothing, but it is not accurate for him to say just this.

iii.   myself

:   As I come to consider myself a more mediocre person, my standard for the ones I chase, my ideal, is far more modest. At least this makes them more numerous, if not more available. I make less demand on the chimeric relationship and therefore my own approach is easier, more confident. Unfortunately, my lust has also diminished. Which is the cause and which is the effect?

:   I go an unfamiliar lonely way along the river, but when I finally enter a familiar stretch of rocks, I am not less fearful but more. It is that the new scene roused my curiosity and exploration, motives which in me are prior to fear altogether. As I showed in *A Visit to Chartres*, I am not timid to take the steps into risk, but I am exceptionally fearful when I have taken them.

:   My wife does not want me sexually; she wants others. I do not let her go freely because it pains me and I will not let myself increase my own pain. This makes ordinary sense. But in a deeper sense I am destroying myself, for I am not, in the teeth of pain, nevertheless affirming the right state of things, the general freedom, including hers. Having so betrayed myself, I do not get a hard on.

:   With the departure of my friend G.—whose presence here was not always joyful-making yet did give me
something to look forward to, to do—now New York is
like a city strange to me, like New Orleans, open for roam-
ing, lonely. I could commence on a new tack, in new
neighborhoods, if I could conceive a new tack. But as I
peer at my face in a plate-glass window, I see I am lined,
middle-aged, unattractive. I was lucky to have had him, so
chastely sexual. I am less ugly when I am lively and made
love to.

:   In my way of having a living (I do not "make a living") I seem stubbornly and cleverly to make real the situation that I want: I give service as I can and I am given
gifts. But I do not have enough "opportunity" to be active, for opportunity is something that must be aggres-
sively wrested from the environment, one must "make" it.

:   Lucky am I among men, to be able to be waiting for
Earthly Paradise in a bar on 33rd Street, in the shape of a
farmboy from Milton, Vermont! When I consider how
hard it is for others to be deeply pleased, and how easy for
me—if only my simple-minded herald angel would have
come, as I almost expected he would, instead of standing
me up.

:   I write "herald angel," and I am reminded of the
verse in "Driven Back on the Walk," "I think it is the
Messenger of Death." Indeed, fear contends with desire.
My lust is for an easy-going love, to which I pay attention
and give myself without much stinginess and little fear of
humiliation—I have been able to give myself with extraordinary perseverance to a foolish effort for paradise, without feeling I am wasting time or that I lack justification.
My fear is as if when I was small (but I do not remember
it) the big boy cruelly twisted my arm and threatened to
murder me if I told. Then lucky am I among men! to be
goaded all my life by the struggle between two such grand
and simple contenders as practical lust and physical fear.

Careless of reputation, insult, hurt feelings, appearances, social success. There seems to be no sado-masochism in my love-death; my contenders are real enemies—except that I exaggerate my risks when I have not been satisfied. I am likely to turn out badly, but let me point out that I am 47 years old, "already no mean feat!" say I proudly.

: These bitter and frustrated daily walks abroad—and the glass of beer in the bar I fruitlessly frequent—are the prayerful service I do to the lord of my life.

: They tell me that I don't have enough "self-concept," image of myself, dignity. I doubt it. The areas where I have notions about myself are those where I gripe: "Nobody in America can write like that, I don't get my due" or "I give and nobody takes care of me"—these are just the areas where I am frustrated. I boast where I fail. "Self-concept" seems to be simply a defensive maneuver against rage and grief, and better off without. If I had to write a description of myself, it would be pretty close to the consensus of my acquaintances. (Naturally I may be deluded in thinking so.)

: I repeat twice a week, with suffering, the situation that I am waiting for some one; I am not so much desirous as expecting to be desirous when the occasion arises; but he stands me up. Pathetically, I do not feel that I am "repeating" the situation, but that I am indeed waiting for just this one, telling over the positive and negative signs that apply in just this case of C. or B. or L. But it is clear that I am again waiting, period.

: For a day prior to waiting, there is a spell of ambivalent hopeful desire and fear. The hope *includes* the hope that he will not show and the wish that I myself may be "prevented" from showing. The fear is grounded in not knowing what risk I run, because of the unwary and precipitate nature of the first pick-up. A couple of hours before the appointment, however, I strongly fantasize our joys and want to masturbate. I don't, because I am waiting for the actuality which at that moment seems lively and realizable. After I am stood up, I am despondent and don't want to.

: My disadvantages are so many—I am not young, not attractive, I do not fit people's expectations, I am formidable in the wrong way, I am impatient and too direct, I am cowardly and not direct enough, and I am pressed for time because of other obligations. Thus, I have no claim to hope, I am bound to disappointment, and I would do well to resign myself and suffer less.

: I interrupt sucking on his cock to look at him with a smile and ask, "Do you like it?" "Yes, do you?" "I like *you*," I say. This sincere remark wins me, when we part, a kiss of gratitude and affection, "You're a nice guy." But also it produces afterwards a conflict of feelings in him which, I suspect, makes him avoid me henceforth. It is probable that since they disapprove of what they are doing, they are not supposed to like the partner in it. My friends have explained this to me, but it is just this that I do not dig.

: I seem to have more moral courage than the average. I don't have much, but by comparison. I stand up for my friend, for the unpopular cause, for the truth, etc. But I guess it's simply that I have stronger ideas. Ideas give the support of their own structure of consequences, and they also motivate, noblesse oblige. It also works the other way: the courage to speak out and so objectify and structure one's feelings, gives one stronger ideas. Similarly, if I were big and knew how to box I wouldn't be such a physical coward; but this also works the other way: if I weren't such a coward, I would know how to box.

: Long ago I sold my reputation for a song, never regretted it, and do not regret it now. And indeed, the song has kept coming to me, it has been a profitable contract (except in money and fame). Why has *this* transaction worked out, whereas everything else I do is a failure? Because here I made a real decision, accepting the consequences. [1966. It is interesting that I wrote "everything else is a failure," not thinking of my admirable children, who today are my first boast. Yet because of them Sally and I were putting up with a good deal of unhapiness with each other. We did not mention them; we took it for granted. At that time I apparently thought I had a "life of my own" to lead, which I managed badly. I still manage it badly, but it is not such a big deal.]

iv.   psychology

You mean, he holds you so tight you can't move?

"No, not too tight, but so close that there's no alternative. His belly on my belly, thighs on my thighs, and so close that my arms must close around him. I don't want to; my thoughts are elsewhere."

—Fantasies about somebody else?

"No, thinking about other things. I used to try to escape, but his knees become sharp as you curb a horse. I've learned there's no use, he's going to have his way. I press my knees together, but he thrusts a knee between them and they're apart. He gets his leg in there and forces my thighs wide. His hard on is heavy on my belly and he begins to move in rhythm."

—What are you doing?

"I turn my face away and think about the other things. But he kisses my neck and it tickles, and then he comes up on my cheeks, so I give up the other thoughts and freeze in this one dread. At this moment he lets up on his pressure and says, 'Why don't you relax?' I feel a little freer and I take a breath. And in spite of myself I reach up with my belly and have a fleeting wish that he would put his hard on inside of me. Then he has forced his way in.

I'm always a little forced. But it doesn't seem like he's pushing harder, but as if I were being opened up to let him enter, and I do open up to get his coming—" She falters in her narrative, as if she no longer has a coherent story to tell. She weeps a few tears. "He's too strong for me to fight off. He's a man."

—Do you have an orgasm? You could remember that.

"Sometimes. Not usually."

—I don't understand. Since you can't fight him off, why don't you give in and enjoy it?

"I can't. I'm forced. Maybe I won't. I don't want to from the beginning. If I did that I wouldn't be *anything*."

—Oh? You mean, you would hold yourself in contempt because he's no good?

"Not at all. My husband has all my respect. What do you think? that I would—I guess I love him."

—Then I don't understand. What is it to be 'nothing at all'?

"Don't you understand that that makes it all the harder for me, that I ought to? I am glad when *he* comes and *I* don't. Then he's like a child. I pet him—"

—When he's weak and harmless? You mean you love him then? As a man, *I* don't like that idea very much!

"I mean like a child."

: Under present urban conditions, it is hard to define Marriage of our American-European kind without finding neurotic components in the essence: ties of infantile dependency, fear of abandonment, jealousy, conceit, superego, Oedipus complex. It is hard to conceive of an aware and independent person as being "married," even though one might start by rationally choosing monogamous marriage as an economy of energies, the most efficient way of managing one's time and feelings. The chances of life soon confuse and dissolve such a merely prudent choice. There is always looming a more attractive and somewhat practical opportunity. It seems to be the play of non-rational clinging, resentment, guilt, dependency, need to imitate one's own parents, that preserves the marriage. The prudential advantages look like a "secondary gain of illness." But in a society where everybody is pretty impractical, a healthy man might paradoxically find himself frustrated and left out just on statistical grounds, because he does not get the secondary advantages of remaining married!

Marriages get a more rational meaning by being obliged to real necessities, primarily the children, that must be coped with unquestionably. These limit the working of the underlying fantasies that wreak havoc with the happiness of the partners. Objective necessity provides a workable and sharable tie. And in the course of time, too, those shared necessities become a fund of shared memories and experience, unsoured by hurt feelings and with demonstrable achievements. This is a rational bond of union, a friendship.

Let us distinguish two levels of irrationality in marriage. (1) More superficially, the way in which the partners are suckers for each others' manipulations. This is likely what gets them to marry in the first place, for it is only with this one partner that either can become involved and feel anything at all. When the going gets rough at this level, the irrationality can often be worked through and the persons be made aware of what they habitually do to each other. (2) This means working down toward the underlying non-rational level, of jealousy, fear of abandonment, the Oedipus complex. The person says, "I see that we are bad for each other, but I cannot leave him (her) anyway." At this level there are several cheerful possibilities: there may be a diminution of the energy of the neurosis by working out unfinished needs when the superficial barriers to contact have been eliminated; there may be a compromise in which the marriage survives as a home base for outside exploration—"I am reconciled to my parents since they let me have fun and friends"; there may be growth through simple aging and increasing *self*-justification—"I can do what I want since I have spent so many years doing what I must."

Confronted with persons who cannot abide their

marriage, try to find out if there is every *any* real satisfaction that they get from each other, occasionally a pleasant shared meal, agreement on the children, a moment of teasing, a moment of feeling protected, a good fuck once a month. If there is this much, say three good hours a week, it is probably best to try to keep the couple together. It means that there is no inexorable positive principle of separation—e.g. somebody else whom one of them might marry; and to have something, in a lonely and difficult world, is better than nothing at all. There is no doubt—it leaps to the eye as we look about—that in most cases married couples would for a time be healthier and happier if they separated; but they would be less real; and when the feeling of emptiness begins to irk, they would marry again even more foolishly.

We must then speak of the "normal neurosis" of marriage (as we speak of "normal jealousy," etc.). The normal neurosis has important secondary gains, which are enhanced by the fact that it is epidemic and that everybody concurs in its rationalizations: "A husband has no right to—you cannot blame her if—"

:   Perhaps the concept of "Normal Neurosis" is the defining mark of an "Institution." It is the non-rational system that seems to be, and is taken as, a law of nature, and so it generates its own persistence. If the permanence of an Institution is threatened, there is at once anxiety and a fear of emptiness. It is believed that except in the Institution, a particular social function could not be carried on, though indeed it might be carried on better. As if bridges could not exist without tolls, or children be born and reared without marriage licenses, or education occur without schools. Wherever there is an Institution, like Marriage or the School System or the State, look for the repression and transference.

:   That I have been getting little sexual pleasure from most sexual acts these days has caused me qualms about my health. But I guess the case is simpler. Because of my frustrations, I have adopted a quite negative standard of choice. I do not ask that such and such a face or motion or trait of character be beautiful and rouse my desire, but simply that there are not, or not too many, desexualizing features or traits. I go ahead not because I want her kisses, but because her breath does not smell bad. Giving myself such very plain bread, I have no appetite. I eat in order not to starve. . . . But this raises a problem, for people do not starve to death so readily. Why don't I bide my time? . . . And indeed, if I may judge by the analogy of the food, it is more the time that is unappetizing than the food. I rarely eat my family dinner with pleasure; and this is not because it is my family dinner, and usually the food is pretty good. Rather, just at that hour I am not usually hungry. So my sexual life with my wife is ruined because she does not make herself available at my spontaneous moments.

: After a long, slightly chilly walk, I have a bowl of hot soup, and I find myself singing.

: She uses him for her dildo and he her for his watermelon. Her love she reserves for an unavailable young man who rouses her jealousy, and he reserves his love for his business and the affairs of the city. It is a pity that they cannot get a simpler happiness, but we do not live in paradise. Rather than evaluating these things, let us merely try to make sure that no important functions of life are entirely unaccounted for.

: Having given up on lofty values and perception of essential reality, he proceeds well and actively with secondary values of learning and memory, taste, gentleness, earnest effort, competence. He says, "Great masters like Monet and Fuseli." He wills to believe that those who maintain very lofty standards are incompetent or insincere. Yet also, he does perceive lesser things more authentically than other people and he is a useful critic. Defending himself against some terrible threat of reality, he is the hero in every encounter: there is no Thou. Yet within the limits of his security as the only actor, he is continually turned toward others; he aims only to please, and succeeds.

: J. 'phones asking to be let off a date because they have something else, and could they have a rain-check? Another time, he 'phones to say that he can't come to a reading of mine because he is having dinner with E.B. Why does he 'phone and make the appointments? "Because," says Sally, "it is important for his 'other self' to be on terms with you." Oh, that's a great role for me! which I do not invite, but bring about (1) by coming across in their need, and (2) by muffling my own need.

: To see these fellows in the street with their foreheads habitually furrowed in perplexed inquiry, you would imagine that, inquiring so much, they must learn a lot, instead of nothing at all.

v. society

: The busy single-minded men, on the steppe and at Cape Canaveral, in their hundreds and thousands, taking their positions, springing into action. Bright-eyed and hot, fraught with the future of an immediate enterprise, but otherwise blind and in darkness. They frighten me. Also I love them and the thought of them gives me courage. They are ants, not vermin as in my other disgusted fantasy of human beings. I know their intelligent purpose. What frightens me is how their concentration on the enterprise, mutually supporting one another, allows them to cut loose from guilt and resentment, but also from love and compassion.

: Some items on Hard and Soft Money: We make a 10¢ phone-call to ascertain if 6¢ can be saved; this is especially likely if the expense for the phone is concealed in a future bill. We pay a 30¢ fare, plus time, to get a 10¢ bargain, but the fare is considered as incidental to "shopping," not to this particular purchase, and the self-justified use of time is an advantage, as "something to do." "Petty cash" is soft money, but the few cents saved in comparative shopping is spectacularly hard money, and the rich woman becomes indignant at a rise in the price of turnips.

In the defensive attitude in which I make a living, money is budgeted and is very hard. Sally has the medium attitude; she is always confident that she can make a living and expends what comes in. But soft is windfall money, unearned money; or sailor's money, money not needed for sustenance, since the ship provides room and board. The sailor's coin *rings* on the bar.

Christmas money is soft. This is related to the release of stinginess, anal retention. Similar is Mad Money or cases where emotion or emergency introduces an uneconomic perspective, like births, weddings, and funerals.

: I am usually ambivalent toward an existing Institution. Consider the U. S. Employment Service—what did people do before it existed? They asked around in the neighborhood; employers asked around among their relatives and connections; acquaintances made recommendations. These methods had obvious advantages in creating personal contacts, in involving people with one another, and perhaps in placing people in more appropriate slots. Thus, I habitually drift onto an ideal tangent, not ignoring the hardships of the old system, but speaking up for "what has been lost." If, however, I think of needs where we do not at present have an Agency—for example, to bring me into touch with people who would be glad to get and give what I would be delighted to give and get (our East Coast is seriously ravaged by an epidemic of lackanooky) I ask, what do we do? We hopelessly look around in the neighborhood, and it's lousy. I do not at all tend to go off on an ideal tangent.

: Some propositions of impractical people (1) A tooth

pulled painlessly and with little after-effect. Nevertheless,
"the experience of having a tooth pulled is *not* a joyous
one, perhaps because of its unconscious associations." (2)
"We have a date last night but he didn't show. He said he
meant to come but he got all fucked up and landed in
Chinatown. So we made a date for 9:30 tonight, but this
time *I* got involved with something else and didn't show,"
she said joyously. (3) G. feels humiliated and threatened
by the fact that the girl is so good-looking, so he launches
an intellectual onslaught to take her down a peg. She, attacked, puts on airs and makes asinine demands to defend
herself. "You see," says he, "my impression of her was correct."

: People have a disposition, in their spite, to judge the
hero by his bad end, rather than to praise him for his skill
and prudence in long staving off the bad end intrinsic in
his nature and its battle.

: The young sailor, good-looking and amiable but in-
considerate and probably not too bright, is trying with lies
and flattery and insistent caresses to get the woman to
leave the bar with him. She is thirty, homely, not without
spirit but obviously lonely and despondent, which is why
she's here. From time to time he comes away to tell me
and his buddies of his progress, e.g. that he had gotten his
hand under her blouse, unbuttoned one button of her skirt
under her coat—"but if I get the other one open her
skirt'll fall off"; "she won't touch my cock only with her
knee." Yet his lust is genuine; he can't stand still for his
hard on. With a buddy he audibly discusses in front of her
some other hunt that they are going in a few hours. There
is no doubt of his intentions, just to fuck her and scram.
Despite his lies and flattery, there is really no deception.
She, during these lapses of his attentiveness, is visibly
suffering. She is torn with doubt, to go with him or not to
go with him. She would get a spiteful satisfaction out of
rejecting him flat—you can see the resolve form on her
face. But then, what? Yet why won't she go with him just

as he is and as it is, since she wants to, for he is obviously safe and not a bad boy? Maybe she is afraid just because it does mean something to her and she will suffer afterwards and surely feel humiliated and degraded. My heart goes out to her, the poor dear. But what help can I be to her? She is The Suppliant, the powerful weak, the suffering woman, that the ancient tragedians and Rilke have celebrated so beautifully. On the other hand, I do not disapprove of the young fellow, whose need is also genuine, though he is a lout. The one unfair component in the situation is his impregnable solidarity with his uniformed buddies. Naturally this is what strikes me, for it excludes me too.

: In dismay I see my country going to its doom. My feeling of alienation has much diminished; but the venality and folly of the Americans thereby appear to me the more clearly, and now I have a premonition of defeat. I do not enjoy a private spiteful victory. What "we" have been saying all along has been true; yet I was not in a fight. At no moment, no not for one moment, did I put myself to helping the commonwealth—mainly because I was too lazy. I have sometimes, yes and perseveringly, spoken up and acted well, but it was for the truth and not for the commonwealth. Now I must bow my head. I do not get a hard on. I am in dismay.

: Hearing Sibelius' A-Minor Symphony—and I cannot sleep until I have said something for the Northern Hero, though he is far from what I myself feel or hope for. His passion is not sudden but habitual, and we learn here that passion means suffering. He is rarely comfortable in the weather. He is often solitary—there are no towns there. The snow and the summer-bright fens are no doubt beautiful, but they are not practically beautiful; he is vulnerable to the beasts and to his enemies, and he is always on guard. He is wounded and in brute pain and he will die. Surely the wild bard is a necessity for that man, like drink. That man exists in his long passion and I love him. I do not fear him. I would embrace him like a bear that might also hurt me. Somewhere in me it is my duty to tell his northern story, and I shall with dread seek in me the language and the memory. I have not yet broadly enough studied my Adam.

: We who require that the music be interesting, various and not too slow—oh that is an attitude of luxurious culture! To the simple man in us it is the great thing that the passion can be harmonized at all.

vi. God

: It is necessary to be just in order to act and grow spontaneously, without the hindrance of inner contradiction. It is necessary to be courageous in order to have a free space to grow into without obstacles. Courage is justice to oneself. Prudence and temperance are self-preservative; they guard against external and inner damage. Temperance is the prudence of oneself. Temperance and courage are pragmatic virtues; they may be practiced at, habituated to. In important ways, prudence and justice may be studied and learned.

Patience, however, is a theological virtue, a form of faith. Patience, confidence, hope, and charity are really the same. They cannot be practiced at but must arise from the existing situation, and it is not we who create the on-goingness of the situation. But they *are* given in the situation.

Holy spirit, the on-going creating of self-in-the-world, is not a virtue at all; it is not "*of* me." But the other virtues follow from its presence, if it happens to be present. It is named Truth, Beauty, Good; we know it by Wisdom, Love, Community.

For the most part, the lack of natural virtues cuts down the chances of exercise of theological virtues, for we do not have favorable situations. And the exercise of natural virtues makes probable the chances of theological virtues.

Is happiness a virtue? Yes and no. It enlivens and makes courageous. It diminishes illusions and makes simple and prudent. It tends to share out of its surplus and makes generous and just. It obviates greed (fear of starving) and tends to temperance. All this is what Spinoza meant when he said, "Happiness is not the effect of virtue, it is itself virtue." By this he meant to reverse the puritanic values and to say that, e.g., what gives pleasure is in so far good. But happiness depends also on luck and grace. In this sense, it is not a virtue but an effect of virtue. Happiness (or misery) is in the middle ground of what is "not of me" and what is "of me."

To say that happiness is a virtue, and can be worked at, is the same as saying that there is a Method to grace. It seemed evident to Spinoza that there was such a method. (As I write this, I have a flash of him and love that mild man.) It does not seem to me that there is a Method to grace; but I have no claim to an opinion, since I have not worked at the natural virtues which enhance the probability.

: "I do it because I want to."—Who are you to want? by what right? "I'll show you." This is the good answer. If he makes good his will because you can't stop him, he has established a sovereign political right. Or further, if he will try to do it anyway, to death, like the tigress defending her cubs beyond reason or fear, then his action is self-justifying, because he can only rationally be dealt with if the action is respected as his right. Self-justification is given by grounding his claim outside the realm of moral discourse, in some ineluctable behavior.

But what about compulsions? for the compulsive ineluctably acts what is countered by the ineluctable rational will of those who are socially stronger. The question must again be answered by the test of strength. If his action willed in the teeth of reason and custom in fact unsettles the social opposition, causing paralysis, shame, love, etc. in those who would stop him, then he avoids blame. But he is merely compulsive if he begins to have inner doubts. He is self-justified when he rouses their inner doubts.

: I find, as if empirically, that by the force of my intellect I am driven nearer to the truth, for after a test my intuition survives simpler and more evident. If only I could dwell securely in that! I know, I have experienced, that "the spirit bloweth whither it listeth," but I feel as if I did not believe it. Yet I behave as if I did believe it.

: My sexual behavior, void of both lust and satisfaction, may now be fairly and strictly equated to a false cultus-religion, an obsession. My seeking and waiting are its pieties and austerities; and the sexual act itself has just about the meaning of a ritual sacrifice, and is about as delicious as a communion wafer. This is a false religion, an idolatry. The question—and I must soon seek the answer or founder—is, What am I obsessionally warding off?

As I consider my behavior, for instance this catastrophic past week hanging around the bar full of young sailors on 18th Street, I get an insight into the religious history of mankind, which has never otherwise been clear to me. Religious observance is what I have been doing, and what the sailors alcoholically are doing. It all has a promise of Paradise in it. For me this has been the apparently innocent and sensible purpose of finding some one to love and be friendly with; but each one believes that his idol makes sense. But the idolatrous promise is an abstraction and a fraud, which I dare not, however, expose.

"Eyes they have but they see not. A mouth they have but they do not speak." Let down by my idols, I am now in the most disconsolate state that I can recall, for it is without pain, resentment, or melancholy. To come home and to be abroad are equally fruitless. On the contrary, let me entertain the thought—and practice feeling what it is like—of being for myself; since indeed I am isolated, and I am at least not in pain, nor resentful, nor afraid. This thought does not seem to be so terrible. It is no worse than the case I am in. Savior, save me in the case I am, or from the case I am in.

: Occasional signs point to my being right, and so I proceed as if I were right. If there were no such signs, would I go on anyway?

: Twice this week, I have "explained" to people—contrasting their balkiness to my disposition to come across— that I am nearer to the angels. Now what the devil do I mean by doing that?

vii. people, places, things

: Trespassing over the fence, you go through the forbidden gate and are again on legal ground.

: On the lonely piling sticking up out of the river, there rarely fails to be standing the seagull to complete the picture.

: I am doggy, dogged, and doglike. But I am not a dog, a dirty dog, or a gay dog.

: Backing into an empty space, the truck backs up at a good clip square towards another truck. "Hold it!" shouts a driver standing by, and rushes across to give directions. I, passing, make a mock face of dismay and cover my eyes with my hands, "Don't let me see it." "Yeah," says another driver from his cab, with imperturbable vindictiveness, "he's ascared to stick his head out the window and look where he's going."

: "So I suppose *you* could do a flying half-gainer?"
—What, do you think I *can't* do a flying half-gainer?

"No, I *don't* think you can do a flying half-gainer."

—Well, just you wait till we get in the pool and I'll show you who can do a flying half-gainer.

"Well, here we are in the pool and I thought you was going to do a flying half-gainer."

So he runs out on the board and does a neat flying half-gainer.

"Jeez, did you ever see such a jerk, he jumps in the water with his wrist-watch on?"

:   Poor M.! Now he picks up a trick who has syphilis and reports M. as one of his contacts; the City 'phones and M.'s wife answers. He is never spared any humiliating scene with his wife; he must taste the dregs. He is a true poet, not like me who structure everything. Last year he opted for his lover at the hot moment and went off, whereas I should have arranged things more reasonably and never have experienced an extreme of joy or guilt. He is not very bright; but he is bright enough for a poet.

:   Now a flock of birds is winging northward up the Hudson, low on the water. Faith they have in the advent of spring, as I have predictive knowledge of it. But the actual weather has been disappointing.

Ireland, Spring 1958

i. on the way

: To fashion in our lovely English tongue a somewhat livelier world, I am writing this book. (*The Empire City.*)

: When I listen to the rough and ready brass band, with a sprinkling of Salvation Army hats, at Paddington station; and the unabashed way in which the English still take part in "lower middle class" sings—I gain a respect for what Wesley and Whitehead did. With the bourgeois and industrial revolutions, the old sexy music was long done for, but there was this revival of the spirit in new conditions, culturally base but emotionally real, a folk music, equivalent to being "saved." Then I love Blake and Wordsworth the more; they started from *this*, and raised it up for me.

: An advantage of travel is that in foreign lands we find that people have epidemic character-pathologies quite different from ours, e.g. a Britisher's refusal to recognize that he is being groped, but he goes right on with polite conversation as he gets a hard on. The Americans must have their own epidemic diseases; we who do not share them are not *necessarily* crazy.

ii. Dublin

: The docks of the Liffey. There is nothing going into the ships but peat moss, Guinness's stout, and rusty scrap iron: the soil, the soul, and the ruins of Ireland.

: She's rubbing salt in his wound, hard to tell whether to sterilize it or to make corned beef.

: In my *Ballad of St. Patrick* I was certainly ignorant and unjust. (I don't know how to cope with this; I won't tamper with a fine poem just to be accurate, but I won't let anything pass that is unfair.) So far as I can see, the Irish don't drink much at all, not compared with the Americans. And as for brawling, never have I seen less. Even the kids just butt at one another like awkward rams. But then the question remains: what *do* they do with their repressed sexuality?—for the gist of the poem is not unfair. They put it into racing and gambling! I would never have guessed it. The men are mad for sports and the sports pages; if they closed up the Turf Accountants (bookies), they would have nothing. I should have taken the Racing in *The Play-Boy* more literally.

: The warm, though enslaving, family ties in Ireland make for a peaceful people. As soon as they emigrate to England or America they become rowdy.

: They themselves keep referring to their "stage Irishmen," but indeed, the Irish little see the Irishness of the Irish. While you watch the street-sweeper, his broom comes off the handle. In the office of the American Express, a counter collapses with a crash. Half of the chairs in the pretentious restaurant have broken backs; the defect is in both the design and the workmanship. At the best hotel, the cover comes off the salt-shaker onto your dish. The national flag of Ireland is the Irish pennant. Lively, they interrupt the orgasm before it even begins to rise; then they lose track.

: If only it were possible to get rid of imperial tyrannies without a postrevolutionary period of National Culture, including the revival of local languages, jealous boundaries, and a rash of puritanism. The young Pioneers have as their aim Total Abstinence, for "Ireland sober is Ireland free." It seemed for a itme as if the effort to revive Gaelic would dry up the loveliest flow of English that is spoken and written in the modern world. Certainly the Catholicism of Ireland would be less tiresome if it were not part of the revolutionary ideology. Without doubt, the baptism of fire, whether in Ireland or Israel, brings forth heroes in the community, and they wield a natural authority among the people. But alas, in the aftermath their authority expresses itself in the usual banalities of ruling and staying in power. Boringly, the old patriots hang on, with no special wisdom, but rousing guilt in those who would make a change. The Chief of State is old as the hills and blind as a bat.

: Irishmen I speak to insist strenuously that their late marrying is due to economic causes and not sexual timidity. They are unanimous on the subject, and "who else would know?" What you never hear, however, is any fretting about the sexual situation as it is. We see in this dramatic illustration how impossible it is to make a change by rational persuasion.

: But the Church *is* democratic, not like American liberalism. Consider a contrast. I recall trying to write for the mimeographed PTA newsletter at Matty's school in Chelsea; my idea was some kind of column that would bring up controversial psychological and pedagogical issues. I was at once rejected as not a competent writer; but if I had been a Nobel prize winner in literature, Madam Chairman would still have held against me, on the grounds that such matter was irrelevant to the Newsletter: "People interested in such things can read them up in the writing of experts" (namely, not me.) The Church is not snobbish in this way. The most important matters are for everybody, though people are allowed to hear only a censored discussion. With all their mumbo-jumbo and obsessional crossing of their hearts, people are treated as whole human beings. This is what liberals never allow.

: There are four bad young misses on the bus: the hard one with the ready sneer on her young face; the one with the Cupid lips and the calculating eye, who speaks out the corner of her mouth; the crazy one with disordered speech and a bad complexion; and the cry-baby with perpetually reproachful eyes.

: "Sit down *there*," says Mama, "don't make me tell you again." But the little boy wants to sit in the other seat in the bus, where he can look out the window. Papa, who is pretty drunk, backhands him. The boy cringes, doesn't sit, gets another crack. And a third that brings tears—it would have been harder, but we stony-faced passengers are watching the scene. He half sits. Stealthily he stands up again; and *then* he sits, having not completely lost the battle, for he was not *forced* to sit down. He has only lost his original wish, to sit at the window. We pass a church. All cross themselves with meticulous precision. Sally and I, seated behind, are uneasy, frustrated. Finally she offers the boy a piece of candy. He smiles happily and says No, with a furtive look at Mama and Papa. He wants the candy, therefore he refuses it. But the result of our attempt to ease the situation, to ease our own situation, is again to make Papa descend on him with a hiss, "Say No Thanks when somebody offers you something!" It's *always* all of a piece, this is one thing I have learned. It makes it tough.

: Rain-wear, these days, is more various and colorful than ordinary wear. Why? The technical problem has not really been solved and they are experimenting. Rain-wear is in a transitional period, so there spring up random sports. When the technical problem was considered solved, the rain wear was dull indeed, strictly "utilitarian." Now there is a more whimsical use of flimsier materials. Further, the unconventional circumstance—being out in the rain—permits more individual fantasy and carelessness. The shared emergency allows more direct expression; you may talk to anybody under an awning in the rain.

: The hustling photographer on the O'Connell Bridge badgers me to let him take my picture. I triumphantly show him my 11d., of which I need 4d. for the bus; I think this will get me off, but he says, "All right, give me 7d." (Presumably he is a voyeur; he wants to be paid—anything —just to clear his conscience!) He is pretty drunk. The print is not bad, except that the face is quite blotted out by a defect in the film. Seeing my disappointment, he insists on taking another snap; but this time he leaves a thumb-print all over it. "God damn it," he says, "it's 'cause I'm drunk." He insists on still a third. I am embarrassed, for my 7d.; but he is on his professional mettle, and this time he takes the greatest pains, readjusting the shutter and counting with the result that the film comes out badly overexposed. He is desperate—he *has* to get me a passable picture. The fourth is rotten according to a very low standard, but I exclaim with rapture, in which he grudgingly concurs (he's not that drunk). I carry off all four essays which, within half an hour, have turned black as night. . . . Another time I ask him, "Don't the cops ever bother you?" He charges up to five shillings for his fadeaways! "No, except that one there; he's always after a free drink, a newspaper, an apple." "Why don't you give him a free picture," I ask maliciously.

:   "He was a nice guy and I had a good time, so I won't go back and try to blackmail him." With this glowing testimonial he stands me up.

:   Trapped out.

:   There is such a thing as food and such a thing as poison. But the damage done by those who pass off poison as food is far less than that done by those who generation after generation convince people that food is poison.

> Force, fraud, speed of flight:
> know the exits, travel light.

:   A hand strong and warm and doesn't give itself. Not to me.

: In a dream I am having a hurried argument with, I think, Degas, and pointing out that drawing from the cast teaches us that the statue of the man is obviously more beautiful than the man, so that one gets over the impossible aim of presenting "beautiful nature." This saves us from sentimentality. One learns to give the natural truth brusquely: "That's just how it is." But he keeps saying that drawing from the cast is zany, and I keep hearing it as Zenny.

: The separate chapters in *The Empire City* climax too strongly for a dramatic work; there is not enough motion toward a single climax. The result is a picaresque epic. The same in my sexual career; it is episodic. And in the sexual act itself, I insist on reaching a climax, whether or not the conditions warrant. Yet there *is* a forward motion through the chapters—I am not writing short stories. It is, as in my life, a motion of increasing commitment, perhaps of simplification (?), rather than one mounting excitement to fulfillment. My character and destiny make more sense than my day to day and the life I lead. The meaning of *The Empire City* is not in its power of effect, but in its attitude, its way of being in the world. (Of course, it is just *my* way of being in the world that people reject.) To me at least, the endearing trait of the book is that it is always in there pitching, although in a confused game.

iii. around the country

: On the four corners of Abbeygate Street, in Galway, stand a cop, a priest, the Bank, and I.

: I smile and wink invitingly (I hope it looks so) at every passerby. In Dublin, the men were very friendly and responded with an elaborate shying of the head, right down left, like a horse shying. When circumstances allowed, this led to exchanging the time of day and other talk. In Galway, however, I seem to be met with no response, so I take them to be more like the Americans. I think I even notice a tight little head-shake that is positively rejecting. But now I recognize it for the same bully, horsey, doggy Irish greeting, only more directed, more meant. It is that more of the folk in Galway have jobs, so they are more practical.

:   Only among the Irish do I feel neither too roughly dressed nor too well dressed, but just right. Lord! how this must stem from my childhood on 151st Street and Amsterdam Avenue!—1917. And it brings me to a problem. These folk, with whom I feel at home—I could live happy in Galway, or even a smaller place, if only I wouldn't get into bad trouble, and maybe I wouldn't—these folk are quintessentially the Goyim. I cannot be one with these Goyim who are, spiritually and intellectually, simply in the wrong; yet I do feel most at home here. For a solution to the paradox I am driven to fantasy: it is to some other state, pastoral antiquity, everywhere apparent in Connemara, that I am turning. Or to the even earlier period, of the golden lunulae and sun-disks that warmed and dimly illumined my dark and cold soul in the Dublin National Museum. As it exists, the Christianity of these folk stinks and stifles. Perhaps in a more pagan form, full of sane superstititon, I could commune with it and say what I mean, whatever it is I mean. Such dogs as they have in Ireland! not only handsome, but still looking like working dogs and hunters.

:   In the Joyce country of Connemara it requires little imagination to understand how a 16th century clan chieftain and his lady might starve for elegance and jewels and Spanish stories to heighten to humanity a plain shepherd's and hunter's existence. For us these things are puerile and we need to stick closer to our "plain duty." When you see the kids in Connemara shepherded into a tiny school to learn to read, that's lovely; but for our kids in New York to

be chained in school rooms is ugly and wrong. They get
the saving Other thing; we get the deadening Same thing,
enforced against the young and defenseless.

:   There is a moment when the finery and romance of
the clan chieftain and other fanciful notables, playing at
being human beings rather than plain shepherds, can be
produced by the size and wealth of the community itself.
This is the great moment of simple high culture. Before
this moment, we merely have the high-born lady, protected from sunburn, in ballads and Spanish stories. After
this moment, to maintain authenticity, we must fall in
love with the City itself, as on the Ladder of the *Sympo-
sium*. When finally the social structure becomes too big
and complicated, we are forced into private High Art, as if
returning to individual folk-fantasy. A curious illustration
of this is the elegance of delinquent adolescents with their
hair-do's and sharp costumes: they are like tattooed bar-
barians whose Spain is the Stork Club. Their Law is the
feud code of Alfred.

:   Just as it was last year on the Continent, this little
city of Galway drives me to despair of America. It is so
pretty and variously unified, so much of a town; and then
you are quickly in the country. In all of America we have
nowhere what they have in many places.

:   "Hamlet": row houses on the Road. "Village": a
hamlet with some kind of community center, perhaps off
the Road. To this, may be added other rows of houses,
requiring lanes and secondary streets, (The rows and turning streets are stopped by the river.) "Town": where there
are squares and parks for the secondary streets.

:   "Parish": the neighborhood small enough for people
to attend early Mass. When there are several parishes,
with their squares, there is a "Town," which then has a
principal church.

: The Irishness of the Irish: the Tourist Guide to Galway has an ad for bedbug juice on the front page. (In fact, the Irish are very clean.) At Glendalough, their principal monument, there is planted square in the middle at the little bridge the sign: This Land Is Poisoned, presumably by some insecticide. You get to see the ruins of Bective Abbey by scaling a high wall and falling into the nettles.

: For the tourists, the Irish government has poisoned the pike and perch because these "coarse" fish devour the trout (*cyprinidae* and *salmonidae*). Now the trout are still more rapidly dying out because they are eating the snails, which pike and perch used to thrive on, but which are insalubrious for trout.

: He shakes the match-box. "Empty!" and he tosses it away. But luckily it breaks open—it is chock full—and he has to pick up the scattered matches on his hands and knees.

: The Irish do not lie, but they save face by the dishonorable technique of mental reservation. They cannot tolerate being in the wrong. A simple mistake on a job (and there are many!) is a cause of guilt for days, as if the child were caught masturbating. Naturally they then go on to more serious bloopers, out of spite.

: Various religions and rituals promise us salvation; one cannot possibly practice them all. Yet suppose one of them were the true one—perhaps a ritual last correctly performed 17,000 years ago by my neolithic ancestor. The pantheon and the blessed of that faith are patiently waiting in heaven for another human being to be saved, but alas, nobody among us knows how to dance correctly among the menhirs, nor are there menhirs.

: At a cattle sale in Tipperary: "£28. If I offered for 20 I'd have the whole town pushin around and fightin for him, and I wouldn't want to be responsible for a public disturbance." The trick is the violent dramatic inference from a non-existent premise, like betting on other people's horses.

: Into the flock is born a quite black sheep, in nature and disposition no different from the others. The other sheep, of course, pay her color no mind, but the shepherd prefers her as interesting, prizes her wool, and keeps her for breeding when the others are slaughtered.

: Sheep for the shearing is one thing; lambs to the slaughter is quite another.

: The hours, days, long months, and long long years that I have given to trying for love. Sometimes they do not seem to me to have been wasted. At other times, I try to imagine an alternative, and I am blinded by the dazzle.

: The Vale of Avoca, whose beauty was so highly praised to me, turns out to be a pleasant country valley, just as any ordinary country valley stream anywhere is as sweet as can be. It is a couple of poems by Tom Moore that have made it a famous place, and it happens that in one of the poems, "the mingling waters" must refer to just a particular spot, and the "shade" to even a particular big tree. We have, as rarely, the poem of the exact spot, and this is fraught with sacred interest. (It's not a bad little poem, though one wonders at the word "shade," since, as of 1958, there's very little sun in Ireland to warrant sitting in the shade.) They have thrown a fence around the tree and put a plaque on it; and I for one have come to visit it. And others come to visit it and have words to say on their lips. It is poetry; elsewhere there is nothing but scenery . . . Oh, the statue of Goldsmith! the Vale of Avoca! just for the immortality of it—poor pitiful mankind! I, who am a poet, am made solemn and sad for myself, and determined and proud, as I light my pipe where the bright waters meet.

:   The exact place where the poet sat and wrote the poem has the same virtue as a saint's relic. Go there.

:   Ruined monasteries are convenient for playing hide-and-seek, but ruined castles make good jungle-gyms. Even in their skeletal remains, the essential functions persist. If you happen by either, the lads of ten or eleven, who hang on the fringes of guided tours, will frantically and obsessionally tell you comic-book stories of ancient murders, and hold out their hands for a penny.

:   I walk five miles and climb a long mountain to view the Glen of Aherlow, in the Galtee Hills. There are shadows of liquid velvet. My breathing is better for the unaccustomed effort; I stretch out my arms with a lot of love for this place and its friendly people. Thus, in Ireland I go about "to see the country," the scenery; whereas last year in Italy—though the Apuan Alps are far more gorgeous—I sought out the cities, monuments, and rhetoric. Superficially, one might explain the difference by saying: You look at the scenery in Ireland because there's nothing else (indeed there isn't); the soul wills to be active and finds what interest it can. Yet this subjective judgment is also objective: for the same holds for the people themselves; they form their lives on, and become, that which is there *for* them. The Italians are formed by their past and history in the environment; the Irish more simply by their scenery and the fantasy and legend attaching to the scenery. In Ireland, sheep, cows, and dogs exist closer to the people, though other peoples also have sheep, cows, and dogs.

    In America I tend to tour in two ways: First, I always interpret the landscape economically, I notice the falls used for power, the waterways, the mines, the economic location of the towns. This aspect looms as the life-form and is very interesting. But then, perhaps because of the grotesque uniformity of that economic culture, as it has turned out, I now more and more seek out and boast of the Big Scenery, the Gorge of Niagara, the Smokies. I sternly think away the human references that spoil them. I close my eyes to the motels and hot-dog stands, do not see the grimy towns that I go through as I drive among the Finger Lakes. The country belongs to the ghosts of Indians, not to our ghosts.

:   Head in the clouds, or just in a fog.

:   *Mene Tekel* was written on the cliff, but in a script so foreign that we took it for the natural veining of the rock.

iv.   homeward

:   When I have a little boat, I creep along the shore and do not let myself get out of sight of land. Yet I complain that I do not experience anything different. If I were an experienced sailor, would I be more daring? As a writer: do I get out of sight of shore? The places I now visit regularly seem to me to be home waters; but some one else will have to judge that.

:   Deceived by his own wishes, in his private log Columbus systematically overestimated the day's run. But he kept a false log to deceive the crew, to make them think that they had not come so far from land, and this "false" estimate was in fact much nearer the truth. His truth-for-the-people was his real thought; for himself he whistled in the dark.

:   Having met enough discouragement, and driven, therefore, to commit himself to exorbitant claims and boasts, it was not difficult for Columbus to go on even to death. In such a case, it is not worthwhile to consider returning. The trick is to get other people to cooperate with your fantasies.

Summer 1958

i. art

: With its program of "professional standards" with small resources, Little Theater is inevitably pushed into the advance guard. It must exploit modest means to give high theater effects, and therefore it hits on an inventive style.

: Toward the end of *Hagar and Ismael in the Desert*, there is an Introduction and Sonnet. This suggests to me a play entirely of set formal pieces, like the numbers of an opera. And Greek drama, of course, was much like this. I have been too closely following the "story."

: In a dramatic speech, if the topic sentence occurs near the beginning, the effect is formal and rational. If the topic sentence is held off and the speech starts from the previous speech or something extraneous, the effect is "real conversation." If we avoid topic sentences, the effect is allusiveness and wandering, like real conversation.

: What is the meaning of the question, "Does it play?" Start from the fundamental relation of theater: A watches B doing something. It "plays" if the action of B is such that *watching* it adds to A's experience. Thus, the logic of an argument is not play material, for A could think it or read it without watching it. But a quarrel between B_1 and B_2 might "play," for the logic of the argument is partly determined by their gestures, tones, interruptions, etc. which must be watched to be known. Any spectacle or spectacular action, like acrobatics or dancing, plays by definition.

: Three kinds of theater: Artaud's action *on* the audience, objective poem of set pieces, identification *of* the audience.

: In *Whilomville Stories*, Stephen Crane makes no

mention of the sexual activity of the boys, nor of any contact between the boys and their parents. (There is a story of one girl and her parents, and she is portrayed as a demon of power.) Altogether failing to mention these things, he gives us rather well the boyish suffering, shame, competitiveness, and combativeness. As a writer, it would be impossible for me to omit these salient matters, and therefore I lose the tension of embarrassment that comes from *not* being aware of them, and that conveys its excitement to readers who share the same block. What I tend to give is the light-drenched classical picture that bores the popular audience or shocks it (it comes to the same thing). In dealing with Negroes, Crane follows the same pattern. There is one story directly about Negroes (it is pretty sickening); but most often the Negroes are, as in *Huckleberry Finn*, projection screens for what the author otherwise overlooks, so that they alone seem to have human friendship and contact.

: How to explain the extraordinary attention and esteem that are given to things that are not necessary and not, finally, very interesting, the Arts, War, Crime? First, there is the psychoanalytic explanation: In these the repressed or inhibited finds expression in a setting of necessity, explanation, policy, etc., that gives justification. In War and Crime we can do or watch what we otherwise forbid. But secondly, if we consider growth as the normal function of an organism, there will always be a pressure toward what seems useless and gratuitous, and even "not very interesting," since its meaning is still future. The growth proves itself as Culture. The gratuitous creativity of one man then gives a justified activity, learning, to the others, to catch up by informing themselves. Who listens to Bethoven does not incur the risk and guilt of being Beethoven, but everybody agrees that he has the duty to know Beethoven. A creative society is one that fosters, seeks out, and immediately responds to strange excellences. It gives a social justification where there is not a necessitous justification. This simple message, Foster Excellence, is what I must tell people. Even if it hurts. . . .

ii. society and myself

: A "minority" exists because of a psychic boundary, that makes a real or fancied distinction *relevant*, and the anxious clustering and self-identification of the "majority" to keep on the right side. The minority is always a repressed part of the majority. Prejudice is not merely a projection of the repressed *onto* the minority, but indeed, it creates the minority *qua* minority and maintains it in being. Thus, the minority is always right in its demands, for it is moral and psychological wisdom for the majority to accept the repressed part of itself. "Class," on the other hand, implies a more conscious alienation and banding together, when there are clashing interests and it is *profitable* for one class to keep another in existence. "Enemies," finally, are not very different from the non-human and could be annihilated.

Censorship is directed against the minority. Its aim is to keep the repressed in repression.

There are minorities of religion, color, morals, and manners. In the first centuries of the Roman Empire, color did not seem to constitute a minority. During the North African dominance, for instance, there must have been many colored people around. Were Tertullian and Augustine colored? Interestingly, I do not know. I do not recall any mention of color *prejudice*—the nearest is in Virgil's pastoral, "even though I am black." Nor was there much prejudice on this count in the middle ages, though during the Crusades the colored were Enemies. Throughout these periods, however *religious* minorities existed and were oppressed.

When and under what circumstances are particular

minorities called into existence? An obvious circumstance is that a group cannot adapt itself to a change of fortune and creates a scapegoat. Internal tension and anxiety are heightened, producing a feeling of worthlessness, which is then projected to lessen the pressure.

In New York City, God bless us, we have only "minorities"—except maybe the Jews. White Anglo-Saxon Protestants are not even a minority, but a rarity. Jackson changes his name to Goldberg so he won't be mistaken for a Negro.

:   The question to ask is: Who are your Jews, Queers, and Niggers?

:   Willy Poster explains to me why they won't publish my books, even though it is conceded that I am a good writer and people rather like me personally. He says he is surprised that I don't know the reason. It is that I have the wrong tone, just as you don't invite certain people to a party though you may like them well enough personally. A publisher may publish all kinds of things, but not, says Willy, "French post cards. Not that your books are *exactly* like that." I guess he's right. How to get used to being a pariah? "It will end," says Willy, "when they feel you are a poor beat animal whom they can put in that (poor beat animal) category." If only they knew it, they could start right now. Somebody, tip them off.

:   I wish that I did not feel *personally* wronged and slighted as a writer, in order that I could impartially vent my indignation at the publishers.

:   My denunciatory and spiteful behavior at a social gathering increases my difficulties in the world. It creates and maintains the very exclusion that causes my spleen. Afterwards I have twinges that I did "wrong," people won't like me. Yet I even more deeply feel that I have been too hurt, it's too late anyway, and so forth; and the excitement of venting my anger and spite is better than resting in the torpor and envy in which I would otherwise exist at these social gatherings. What else should they expect from a strong spirit in their midst, who is a failure and unhappy? At a gathering where there are several editors and publishers, how would they expect a disappointed author to behave? If this keeps up, the day will come when I can with perfect equanimity make an ass of myself.

September to December 1958

i. method and language

:   From the shore, it is a mighty bridge across the river. But from a plane or on the map, it is the bridge across a mighty river.

:   "In one acre of earth the amount of soil that passes through the bodies of earthworms exceeds fifteen tons annually." And this is a small fraction of the commerce carried on by the ants and slugs, beetles and nematodes, and little animals and moles. Also, consider that in a city like ours there are tens of millions of faucets and many millions of yards of pipes to supply them. And again, that electronic machines begin to approach in multitude of connections the many-millionfold nerves of a single eye, and that this order of tiny magnitude approaches the fineness of molecular and atomic structure. It is all one texture, like a painting of Klee in which the weave of the canvas is not irrelevant to the scratches and patches of the design. You may securely make a spontaneous gesture and it will move in, and move, the environment of things.

:   At a meeting of Gestalt Therapists, a committee proposes some basic courses. An opposition group says this is a stereotyped procedure "just like the others. If you want to teach or do research, work in the community." Similarly, at the Living Theater, with great labor they build in seats and a proscenium, though this embarrasses from the beginning the kind of flexible theater in which we believe, for instance in which we can perform an action in the manner of Artaud.

On the other hand, everything we do is located in a social environment in which things are expected to be done in a certain "professional" way. We may not like that way, nor the things that are done in that way, yet as soon as there occurs a chance of doing anything at all, we try to do it in the accustomed way, which—"objectively" speaking—is rarely the easiest way.

Dissent from it, and one is at once in a crisis and driven to accomplish something, anything at all, just as a proof. Oh, the works of mankind created in this kind of crisis, and necessarily abortively, that stand there like hulks of ships on the plain! never launched, and the shipyards have moved elsewhere.

: The dog's foot is the dog. If it's stepped on, the dog yips and tries, including her foot, to get out from under. It is by a figure of speech that we say the dog lifts her foot. Yet if her foot is amputated, she is not that much less a dog but immediately adjusts to the reality and compensates and is in the world running on three feet.

: Prediction is not the "confirmation" of an hypothesis, but its meaning, for truth is not the description of a state of things but the orientation of an ongoing activity. Truth is structured faith. By confirmation we mean encouragement that we're going the right way, we are well oriented. Thus, with a patient I do not have a "diagnosis" but a kind of vaguely articulated prediction of behaviors in the session which, as they come to be, make me press on with more confidence. For the principle of Operationalism I would substitute something like reasoned-history-plus-prediction. When I have any success, it does not occur to me that I know (or have known) anything about the case; but I boast that I am a "good technician," I can get on confident paths and bring something about.

: What is it to *say* it? Consider the cases: "He comes at a snap of the fingers" or "at a curt nod"; or even, "he maintains a stony silence on which the other projects, and obeys." In these cases, (1) the "speaker" has not committed himself verbally and there is a suggestion of humiliation or insult; or (2) pre-committal conversation can exist on an animal level, as one snaps or whistles to a dog, or makes love with one's hands without even "recognizing" doing it; or (3) exchanging a little nod or a silent accord may be *totally* committal, so that commitment to words is irrelevant. Except in outcries or poetry, where the self becomes the speech, speaking commits the self in a special but limited way, more than animally, but less than totally.

: Einstein says, "Considered from the point of view of sense experience, the development of the concept of space seems to conform to the following schema—solid body; spatial relations of solid bodies; interval; space. In my opinion this concept of the interval, detached as it is from the selection of any special body to occupy it, is the starting point of the whole concept of space." He then proceeds to the space of Descartes, in which we freely put coordinates; the absolute space of Newton; the fields of force of Faraday and Clerk Maxwell; and so to relativity.

I think the original psychology is erroneous. Space is given more simply and essentially as the organism's possibility of motion in its environment. If we say, "I am able to move my hand—I am extending my hand—" there is already implied in these sentences the sentence, "there is empty room." There is no need to speak of solid bodies. The room is given in the onset of the motion, and it is conceptualized in the spelled-out description of the completed motion.

Would not this more accurate phenomenology lead more directly to the characteristic propositions of relativity, that space is qualified by the momentum of force in it; that space, time, mass, energy, and space are integral? It seems to me unnecessary to take the long detour through Descartes and Newton. (What I am suggesting, if I remember, is the line taken by Leibniz.)

But is it possible, without the detour, to quantify and mathematize? Perhaps it is just by detaching from the *giving* of space and conceiving of completed "dead space" which is "out there" that we can cut it up into intervals and count them. I take it that this was Bergson's contention. Yet Leibniz meant to mathematize the *vis viva* and why not, therefore, the Living Room in which force realizes itself?

ii. art

: What the devil to do with the sentence "Who the devil does he think he's fooling?" You can't write "Whom the devil—"

: Poets, e.g. Valéry, speak of beginning with a "first line"; the trick is to find the rest. My own experience is that the first line is a spontaneous response to an *unnoticed* actual occurrence. Thus, on a hot day I pass into a shady place and, without noticing what has occurred, I feel how hot I have been. I then think of a first line saying this ("Like coming into the shade on a hot day / I didn't know I was crazy with the heat—"); and with the line may or may not come the realization that this had actually occurred. Such a line seems to the poet unusually "right" because it spontaneously expresses what is indeed the case. And this feeling of rightness inspires him to seek further. The first line, that is, is analogous to a stroke of wit, except that its content is not repressed malice or lubricity but an unnoticed awareness.

: At the 8th Street Bookshop I ask if they want any of my titles and to my pleased surprise they order five of everything I have. As I am leaving, the gentleman says, "I hope these books have some of those dirty poems I've heard about."

: In *Jeremy Owen,* as elsewhere, my technique is to dream up an incident or detail that is dramatically plausible and allows for some action, e.g. that Jeremy keeps a short-order restaurant, or that he finds it impossible to look directly at the Monet in the museum; then I find to my surprise that the incident has also a symbolic meaning. I am rather antipathetic to seeking out a symbolic action and dramatizing it. Important real episodes, however, like the launching of Sputnik in the same story, are both dramatic and symbolic on the face of them. Or better, incidents that are also symbolic on the face of them are naturally important.

:   I again feel my disgust of the naked faces of clothed bodies: so little flesh to convey the whole person. Like the face of the flatworm Planaria. Contrast the art of the Greeks. Generally the face is impassive; character and situation are given by the whole figure. Most modern portraiture is disgusting, though Rembrandt is not, because he portrays philosophical and moral states by the countenance and costumes—his portraits do not carry sensual meaning. For a change we ought to try the opposite convention: all modestly wearing masks over the face, but otherwise going naked.

:   Intense young men trying to write to "realize the thing," to catch its essence in words; they soon drift off and bog down. It is a poor program. Rather, write *from* what you have, what is already realized in your experience, not toward realization. Keeping the realized feeling as your supporting ground, simply describe or annotate or free-associate. Make no effort to catch the thing itself; it cannot help but convey itself in the confabulation. There is no use in copying off what you have "seen" or expressing what you "mean," for the work is only your words and their sequence. This is what Cézanne meant: the *reconstructed* reality.

:   I tell the editor of *Esquire* something I intend to say in an article that he has commissioned. "Oh, but you can't use that," he says, "because they'd have to think about that. You can't expect our readers to think." "Certainly," I agree, always cooperative. But now, writing, I do find it hard to get from one sentence to another without a sequence of thought. "Jazz it up," he says at another interview, "the apt illustration, the alarming statistic." The most alarming statistic that I can think of is the circulation of *Esquire*.

Meantime, my wife has been disturbed at my writing this piece—which, if accepted, will pay $500 more than the advance. She is afraid, I guess, that I might alter my tone or sentiments in order to have the piece accepted. But of course my piece, on mass leisure, has turned out (alas) just like the rest of my pastoral letters. Yet I am touched by her concern for my integrity. Reading the typescript, she is unusually enthusiastic. In her eyes I have avoided both the Scylla of bending to please them and the Charybdis of purposely offending them.

: The extravagant condemnation of the libretto of *The Magic Flute* by some, and the high and deserved praise of it by others, makes us suspect that the plot contains something non-rational. And indeed, it is the plot of the Queen of the Night. Naturally, the "difficulties" in this plot are explained, as with *Hamlet*, by sudden revisions and "strata" of the text (for which Alfred Einstein says he finds no evidence). The attempt to make the Queen simply a malevolent antagonist cannot account for the fact that it is she who gives the magic flute and the bells; and Pamina is her daughter. But if we take her as a kind of non-rational power of the id, as, namely, the queen of the Night—and therefore as the energy of dream and superstition, and an ally of violence—there is no difficulty. She is the necessary "soil from which our virtues proudly emerge," as Freud says: she looms in power in the midst of our trials. It is absurd to say that she tends to vanish from the plot, for she has the most sensational aria in the second act, a terrifying coloratura; but she *is* irrelevant to conscious striving and ordered achievement. That is, she may be banished, but not destroyed. And just so she appears in the libretto. Night disappears, with the first darting rays of dawn; a dream vanishes—you blot it out.

Turner's point that Papageno, like Leporello, is a foil who does not change, is not well taken. Both Pamina and Papageno are willing to die, by suicide, and this allows them to be saved. A petty flaw, however, is that Papageno is not completely metamorphosed into a peeping bird without human speech. Mozart begins the duet of Papageno and Papagena as if they *were* birds, but he does not go through with it.

: After all, in the Ninth Symphony the adagio *is* irrelevant—as the first critics pointed out. It is better to go right from the scherzo into the orchestral prelude to the cantata. If the scherzo went another round (as it endlessly could), the top would blow off; the noisy chord is what he wants to *begin* to say.

: Slow comic deflation, as in my chapter on The Moral Equivalent of War. The lovely esthetics of a Flat Tire.

iii. psychology

: I have just gone through *The Empire City* with the publisher's young editor. His suggestions were generally sensible, in a few cases very valuable, and usually modest. I thank him. He says that he is the one who ought to be, and is, thankful, to have worked on such a book, he has learned so much, and so forth. I ask if I can dedicate to him the short chapter written on his prescription (*Dead of Spring*, ii). He is tickled pink, but he fears that it might embarrass him with his boss. It is a typical interpersonal situation. We both make sincere statements of gratitude, but we do not enjoy the feeling of these; our tones are embarrassed and wooden. I am thinking, "He thinks if I agree to, and praise, a suggestion of his, it is that I am placating the publisher. But of course I know that he thinks no such thing, for it is evident that I am sure of what I want, though I am anxious about being accepted." He is thinking, "When I praise his book and say it has influenced me, he thinks I am a naïve country boy, and he patronizes me by agreeing to, and praising, my worthless suggestions. But in fact he is *not* patronizing, and my suggestions are not worthless."

: After a shaking bad experience with an unlucky pick-up who threatened me with a knife and robbed my house, while I, not even afraid, was immobile, I go through several days of painful fantasies. They vary in the following sequence. First day: I spring from my immobility with the most bloodthirsty expedients that come to hand. I crush his legs, stab him, clout him with bottles. Next day: I contrive to trick him and I flee successfully out the window where, if he pursues me up the fire-escape, I kick him in the face. Or I get away downstairs and he has to flee lest I call the police. Third day: His formidable father, a notorious labor-racketeer, or his desperate jailbird brother, comes to blackmail me, which failing, they beat me to a pulp. I cannot withstand their massive presence. Fourth day: One of *my* friends is in the other room; I summon him and we disarm the thief, then charitably let him off and toss him out.

At this point, I in fact call on Jerry, tell him of the incident, and ask how to get over the immobility, the inability to stand up for myself. He suggests I join the Y and punch a sand-bag. We go together and I pound away a bit. There then follows another fantasy: Mobile, I get the better of the thief, but he is accidentally killed in the fight, and now *I* am in dread of the police. (This is why I pull my punch.) I invent fictions to tell the police, e.g. I am a writer and wanted to hear the fellow blab, but he turned on me. I make everything as regular as can be—so long as the cause of it all has been annihilated.

: Is it his nearsightedness or his glasses that makes him sexually unattractive? If we see him as "near-sighted," he is pathetic and may rouse feeling. If we see him as "myopic," he is sick and freezes feeling. The value of the glasses depends on the interpretation.

Now the girl, who is stone-deaf, tells me with great disdain, and almost disgust, that she cannot be attracted to X. because he wears thick glasses. I am annoyed—I am wearing glasses—at her unfairness, she who has so much need to be accepted with her total infirmity and is a burden on others. I let her know, pretty brutally, that the man she is talking to is wearing glasses, and that she is stone-deaf. But then I consider that, deaf, she has not learned to moderate her harsh tone to conventional politeness. I ought to make allowances. Yet she reveals what others conceal, and why in hell must I always make allowances?

iv. persons, places, things

:   When George V died, Princess Alice burst in on the dowager Queen Mary early in the morning, crying, "The King is dead! long live the King." The Queen said, "You are never again to appear in my presence with your hair not made up." Confucius explained that this was her way of expressing her disapproval of Edward's way of life.

:   Two old acquaintances run into each other on 14th Street. Neither thinks that the other is much changed after so many years, but each has the same thought: "See, a few more years and he will be dead." This unspoken sentence colors their conversation somber and compassionate, and neither tries to One Up the other.

:   Seeing that artists tend to make good the year after they die, an artist gives out that he is dead and vanishes. Nothing happens. Twenty years later, in Mexico, he in fact dies, and the year following he makes good.

:   I used to cross the street safely by watching out for the cars. But now it's dangerous because I have to watch out also for the cop who will give me (and has given me) a $2 ticket for jaywalking.

:   Whore to Cop: "Why'n the fuck don't you restrict the scope of your business and mind it?"

: The painting by Albers leaves the wall, floats in the air, wafts its way into the soul like fresh spice.

: Alas, the motorcyclist with all that machinery between his legs and nothing better to do but go.

v. myself

: If I start with the awareness that I am not made for this world—it does not ask me for what I can give, and when I persist in offering it I get a poor response—then I am soon aware that I do belong in this world and am simply impotent. But this sentiment does not (yet) infect my writing. The English language responds to me if I address her, and I have recently written a few good poems. But I have no feeling that *I* wrote them.

: *Opus* 130, and out of the dance *alla tedesca* and "the little turn of the melody" in the Cavatina emerges the bygone age when I wrote A *Ceremonial*, inspired by a recital of Shan-Kar, the evidence of a happy social art, the cult promised to ceremonials. I will not write it now but sit with tears in my eyes. I am no longer in an open world. I am aware how it is, yet I do not feel my usual horrible restiveness, but in my woe as if depersonalized. Yet I am precisely not depersonalized, but all there, all one cosmos of woe. The sense of it is rich so that I no longer feel woe as woeful. Only I am at a loss what to do.

: I'm learning to be bored with these people who can't come across. I have not yet learned to cut it short.

: These days when I send out pieces to certain magazines, e.g. *Poetry*, I can expect them to take something. My satisfaction in this is negative: I am spared the annoyance of being rejected. With shame I realize how some of the younger fellows would be pleased and proud with this much acceptance; they would boast of it and show the published poem around. I never much did that, even when I (rarely) had the opportunity. Perhaps their pleasure is in a fantasy of easy next steps of fame. I by now have learned that there are no such easy steps for me. From the beginning I had too much self-esteem and was firmly entrenched in the fantasy that would *finally* satisfy me. It would, too. It will, too. So nothing along the way counts for much.

:   In Dublin I wrote a skimpy poem about the Australian runners; now I plan to write a splendid poem on Ballymoss, the Irish horse. How lovely are the Irish in their friendliness and lilting talk, and oh! in Ireland, the closeness between the folk and their dogs, and the sheep of Donegal and Connemara. Their horses too are famous victors in the world, for they are rightly trained with love. Americans and Russians are mighty nations for satellites, but for horses give me Ballymoss, who now—and so on, manner of Pindar. . . . And yesterday at Laurel the goddamned horse made his move too late and came in third and robbed me of my Occasion.

vi.   society

:   On a Panel at the Techneion Society, I was interested in what Percy had to say and in what Paul Wiener had to say, and they were interested in my remarks. Afterwards we were eager to go for a drink and carry on the colloquy. Last winter I had the same experience at a conference at Yale; it was the first conversation in a long time from which I had learned anything—the terms "hard" and "soft" money. I don't know if it is the common fate, but I usually have no conversation with my peers. When we meet at a party, they are distracted by whatever distracts them—perhaps talking to somebody more useful than my-self—whereas I am looking for an attractive boy or am gloomy because there isn't one.

Under the formal conditions of a Panel, however, (a) there's nothing to do but pay attention; (b) we've worked up some common thoughts to get started with; (c) there's an audience as stimulus and responsibility—and my peers and I do not play to the grandstand; (d) I have something to say and can say it rapidly and, to my peers, clearly; thus I gain their respect. Then, having established my right to exist in the world of discourse, I relax and get something out of it for myself.

: I am amused how in my essay "New Theater and the Unions," I describe the noble and protective role of the theater crafts. It is a homosexual fantasy of Big Brother in Brown Overalls with his arm around my shoulders; and I, meantime, have been saying, "You're a lummox, but I love you." Naturally this fantasy makes my whole argument unrealistic, yet sweet as sugar, and I'm pleased to have written it. And maybe it's not so unrealistic after all, for there is no doubt that the harshness of the Unions in the cases I am discussing is grounded in a positive hatred for the queer artists and their weird ideas; in the long run the best approach might be seduction.

: There is a spectacular advertisement in the subway-trains showing an auburn-haired woman embracing her auburn-haired boy of about 8. It is a lovely picture, the colors, the beautiful creatures, the warm unabashed sexual-ity of the embrace. (It is an advertisement for a hair-dye: "Does she or doesn't she?") Now it seems that this partic-ular picture is unusually subject to scurrilous defacement, including expressions of frank rage like "Scum like this should be wiped from the face of the earth." The couple is sweet—intolerable.

: A good deal of talk last night at Meyer's about writers succumbing to, corrupted by, the crude and subtle lures of commercial magazines and Hollywood. My guess is that the causation is the other way: first they are artistically defeated, then they are susceptible, and the rest follows. Integrity, once achieved by artistic victory, is incorruptible. It is no different than sexual potency which manages in adverse situations if once one has really enjoyed oneself. It constructs its own supports. But people give up—and conform—in places where the anxiety of art has been too strong for them, and they have resigned.

Willy Poster kept shouting that an institution is stronger than a man. No; any man is likely to be stronger than any institution—a GI can gold-brick the Pentagon. It is true, however, that the "world," society in its manifoldness, saps and destroys us. Thus, a man stands out against the world; he is defeated; defeated, he is corrupted by an institution; rewarded, he identifies with the world that he dissented from. I feel myself especially liable, for my need for a proud patriotism is so strong that, if Washington gave me any encouragement, I could become simply idiotic.

:   In his farewell Circular to the States, George Washington felicitates us on "the lot that Providence has assigned us, whether we view it in a natural, a political or moral point of light." Reading it, I am struck with hopeless dismay for my country as she is, and I am agitated by the need to do something for my country. What is this patriotism of mine? I can distinguish in it three different passions. (1) My remembered childhood love for the rocks and rills and the Hudson, starred with tears of Paradise— and none of this is being conserved. (2) And in a social group, I cannot tolerate for anybody to be disregarded or allowed not to have his say; everybody must belong and have something to which to belong. So I am thunderstruck at how people carry on without thinking of our country. (3) And I have a prideful will that my own situation should be grand and worthy of a man—I express this both in competitive praise of America when I am abroad (which is irritating) and, more usually, in rebellious dissatisfaction with what I see at home that is not grand and worthy (this is also irritating). I cannot say "Right or wrong my country,"—I need her to be right, and if she is wrong I must try to make her right. I am continually dissident, willing to cooperate but in fact neither allowed nor willing to participate. Yet I cannot simply shed my patriotism and embrace an internationalism that would be more "rational," though as an anarchist, of course, I want to get rid of national *boundaries*. I am an anarchist patriot—a curious kind of thing.

vii. God

:   Emerson to Thoreau: "The few cases are deceptive. Though Homer should starve in the highway, Homer will know and proclaim that bounteous Nature has food for all her boys." Yes. But it's not because Homer knows that it's true, but because, being Homer, he wills that Nature be Mother Nature, that Nature be as grand as Homer. He'd say it whether or not it was true.

:   Thoreau to an editor: "Time and Co. are, after all, the only quite honest and trustworthy publishers that we know." Time, Death, and Co.?—if we put it this way, it rings differently. Thoreau's pervasive "equanimity" about such things is grounded in a theory of literature as self-subsistent museum-pieces. He then calls this man-speaking-to-man-across-the-ages-and-the-seas. But I want a personal and contemporary response to me, because I need it to inspirit me to produce something great. I really don't care too much about fame; I'd like awfully to belong and be greatly used. Thoreau says, "The blacksmiths met together looking grim and voted to have a thunderbolt, if they could only get some one to launch it; but all the while there was not one man among them who could make anything better than a horse-shoe nail." (His spite rouses him to lovely writing: notes from the underground.) This has *not* been my experience. When they give me an Occasion, I can turn out a fine occasional poem.

: Nothing can be done except simply, for a small company; the attempt to reach many and exert a big effect exhausts energy in the means, perverts style. Yet there is only one world and only that great world can inspirit me. The subjects I treat, and the literary tradition of classic masters that I write in, these are as-if I were writing for a great society; and I am starving to death with the emptiness of this as-if. Good! It is in this impossible dilemma that I work and must not quit. Rally! Full speed ahead in opposite directions! So I now rally and feel less a quitter, and I compare our situation to the Whore of Babylon that confronted the Reformers. God give me strength.

: Some of the young people expect me to be more sage, or even a Sage. A bleak and lonely state. But all they see in it is the activity and success that stream from the Sage. I, however, am stuck in the situation of clinging to my threadbare personality and yet allowing something to stream through me. But I can't grab at that streaming and say Mine! I know better. Unfortunately, neither can I abandon myself to the stream and say only Thou.

: What I write, e.g. *The Empire City*, in retrospect chills me and dissatisfies me. I am not in touch with material humanity, people in their plight. It comes home to me again as I read of the awful hospitals of the American Revolutionary war, or the suffering on the prison ships. But it is so in other ways: my slight diffidence in the gymnasium, my immobility with the young thief with the knife. I look about the room now, and if I could only more unguardedly touch with my eyes the wood of the furniture! I shut off experience, I am thirsty for it, it is simple to get—but I am a coward.

: Angus Fletcher says, "Readers admire Satan without regard to his evil nature, and they disbelieve in the final withering away of his God-like form." He is wrong. When we admire Satan, he is given to us in a mythical and highly abstract setting, in which he is a figure for our pride, our fictional conceit of ourselves. But then Milton, with enormous art, introduces more and more scenes of interpersonal feeling, till we suddenly realize, with dismay, how miserable mankind is, how miserable we are, how miserable I am. Finally I am filled with disgust for myself and how I cause some at least of my own unhappiness; and before this blast, Satan's God-like form does indeed wither away, in loathing, disgust, dismay.

1959

i. people, places, things

: My bulb don't light with microgrants. Needs Mega-bucks to make it shine.

: Easter 1959: "A host of golden daffodils—$750 worth saw I at a glance."

: "What's the matter with the girl!"—she is behaving in a peculiar way that doesn't add up at all; till I realize she is an actress of the Stanislavski method preparing for an audition.

: "Are you thinkin o' what I'm thinkin of?" "No," she says coldly.

: It's May Day and I ceremonially sing, as is my cus-tom, *A May Morning*, each year more dismayed by the weak melody and the dreadful words. But I cope with the melody by varying it and with the words by forgetting them. I go down to look at the river. The weather is lovely.

: He's interested in architecture and uses incidents like sailing in a boat or fucking his mother as ways of describ-ing space relations.

: "No, lad, I don't have enough energy to take your throwaway, just enough to drag my heavy body home with the laundry."

: He's lying face down on the sand, involved in a masturbation-fantasy, as is obvious by his small motions. But his mother and father keep interrupting him, urging him to go in the water and have his picture taken with his more tractable brother. He balks. He is ashamed to get up with his hard on. His name is Charlie, his manner bland and far away, his speech a little thick and moronic. Mama is a sharp and lively one and airs her prejudices against the

Negroes who depreciate the value of real estate in South Chicago.

: I am ambling along in Miami and two policemen stop and cross-examine me. Since I carry no identification, they drive me home to check my driver's license. I, since I happen to be temporarily innocent (just lonely), warmly enjoy their company, their concern, and their direct questions. It's a pleasure to let them lead the conversation. I am sorry when they let me go.

: When we exchange names, he won't shake hands, says, "Ts ridiculous, all this holdin hands the city folks do." He comes from "20 miles outside o' Hamlet, N. C."; he went to school 11 years and got to the 7th grade, but can't read. After we have some friendly sex together, we hungrily clasp hands, clinging to comfort in our loneliness. I want to give him a gift. Money would not be acceptable, so I try to give him my corn-cob pipe. He blushes, but he won't take it: "Make him sick to smoke a pipe." Just as well, since it is my only smoke on a long voyage.

: Across our broad harbor the great ships trend slowly and sluggishly, while the little tug-boats busily dart about or push and tug the giants that are too crushingly powerful to risk maneuvering on their own in confined waters.

: Newly rich, much garbage.

: I easily slay the mosquito when it is biting me, for it is fatally vulnerable at the moment it is enjoying itself. The sun comes out. In the foam yellow at the surf-edge, like thick with sperm and roe, flash the brilliant rainbows of Aphrodite.

: Little Mozart putting a drop of oil on that cricket.

: "Yeah, I felt sorry for Maloney. He use to think he

was havin a ball when all the time he just made trouble, stickin the people with harpoons an all."

:   "I'm working so hard," says the bar-maid on 34th Street, "to see my father through college. Everybody's father should go to college."

:   My teeth that ache are usually those I have lost, a handsome majority. A secondary satisfaction is that I am not responsible to do anything about them, they won't get any worse.

:   A quick one! catches his own forward-passes.

:   Our plane to Cleveland is passing over the place on the mountainside where the other plane was wrecked yesterday in the snowstorm, killing forty. There is the wrecked plane, down there. Here we are up in the brilliant blue. Like scattered ends of ribbon shine the meanders of the rivers reflecting the sun.

ii.   method

:   Darwin says, "This experience taught me never to trust, in science, to the principle of exclusion." Because an unthought-of reason, of a different kind from the exclusive alternatives, might prove to be the case. This is a good weak-definition of science: it is logic without the principle of exclusion. As Aristotle puts it positively, Science demonstrates only from real, rather than dialectical, premises.

More usefully, we can say: Logic is science plus the principle of exclusion. This formulation gives the essence of "analytic propositions" with more materiality than postulate-sets, and without their arbitrariness. Logic is the structure of any bracketed-off "finished" system of inquiry.

It is only from a highly developed science, implicitly using much logical machinery, that we can understand what logic is. To conceive of "logic" as such, is a delusion. But sciences we have from the beginning, they are the human animal itself. Naïvely, we do not in fact look for a "criterion" of truth, but for what amount of articulation, structure, and comprehensiveness suits a present need to know.

:   What is the Model of exchanging one Model for another? E.g., the earth is a Sphere—this is a good Model for explaining many phenomena, including direct observations from satellites in orbit; and in this Model the people in Australia are walking upside down. But of course they *are* not so, neither if you go there nor if, remaining here, you speak about their history and culture. To explain these things we use a flat Model. What does it mean to pass from one of these models to another, as interest changes. What is the Model of the two Models? Perhaps the clue is to look for it as Background in a Figure/Background where Sphere or Flat are temporarily Foreground.

:   The proposition that science progresses but art does not progress seems plausible till one realizes that important parts of science do not progress because they have arrived; e.g. you boil water by heating it; you know where the babies come from. So there are achieved things in art, like Homer or Haydn, invaluable to know but quite pointless to repeat. The average standard novel may be quite fine and a contribution to solace and entertainment, but esthetically it is about as interesting as a new careful demonstration that you can boil water with fire. And as "communication," every new standard work is a *dis*-service, on Norbert Wiener's principle that every repetition of a clear message increases the noise.

:   Ideals of politics and esthetics—Freedom, Tragedy, Witnessing Conscience—emerge in the historical conditions of particular societies that require them. Nevertheless, contrary to what Wright Mills seems to think, they are not limited in application to those conditions, for humanity has also made itself different because of them. In quite different historical conditions, we miss them if they are missing. We are dissatisfied with our present conditions just because we have no Tragedy; we think we *ought* to Witness; we will die for this "irrelevant" Freedom. Conversely, even in our present conditions, we are moved by the Greek plays, we admire the Reformers, and so forth. We must conclude that such Ideals are *not* merely patterns of Culture, but are discoveries-and-inventions in human nature. They are what constitute tradition, what man *henceforth* takes with him, and is.

Again it is no different from the steadily accumulating body of knowledge-and-invention in the natural sciences.

: When Santayana says *Skepticism and Animal Faith*, he means simply "Faith." But he has to say "Animal" in order to counteract the unfortunate common usage of his time and make clear that he does not mean Ecclesiastical. He does mean "religious."

: "None *are*": the vulgar tendency to use the plural verb is correct. "None" is the contrary correlative of "some" or "any." If the question is, "Are any people there yet?" the answer is, "No, none are there yet." "Some" *implies* by immediate inference "at least one," but it *is* an inference. If you mean "no one," do not say "none."

: The "unity" of a Village, that Thomas Sharp labors to define, is like the unity of a short-story, also hard to define. It is different from "unity of function," e.g. of an industry or of a narrative. It is the smallest possible integration of every possible (relevant) function, so that we cannot stop with any function, but pass from one to another into a whole life of all the members or parts. An industry is noticed as it takes part in the Village. In a short-story, we do not "develop" a character as memorable, but just enough for the action, the atmosphere, the attitude. There are no episodes. Nevertheless, it is precisely not simplicity that makes the village-plan or the short-story; rather, individuality.

: My tendency is not to allow the isolated concessive clause that occurs in present-day writing: "Granting that so and so, yet we must say that—" I try, rather, to make the concession refine and limit the thing I am talking about, to make it a *further* cause or proof of the proposition, and not a concession from it. The limitation must be shown to be a positive factor essential to the case.

Usually, I am pretty *bona fide* in this. If the matter does not seem to me really as I say it, without exception that I can think of, I prefer not to say it. If I can think of an exception, I prefer to talk about a more refined conception. That is, I tend to *affirm* the concession rather than to concede it. An analogy is the use of shadow in painting: a shadow is an independent *color* and must add to the color composition.

I am often accused of making sweeping generalizations when I am not generalizing at all, but stating the essence as I see it. Of course I sometimes generalize outrageously for rhetorical effect; I assume the reader is not a moron and does not think that I am.

: It rarely adds anything to say, "In my opinion"—not even modesty. Naturally a sentence is only your opinion; and you are not the Pope.

: I both respect and am ashamed of my way of doing research. I read a few books and reports, titles that seem promising, including always two or three standard textbooks, to see what they think is solid enough and comprehensive enough to teach academically. Most of this does not prove to be informative; but it serves to satisfy me that I know as much about the subject as some of the authors —naturally enough, since I would not be engaged with it if

I were not dissatisfied with the usual opinions. With luck I come on a few propositions that are novel or unexpected to me, and I theorize them into my general view. If my own theory thereby becomes tighter and simpler, my inventive faculty is aroused. (This is Aristotle's method of collection—experience—intuition.)

Once my invention is aroused, I start writing as if I really knew the subject, for it is now *my* subject. And in some important sense, I do now know it. For I am honest and have a good memory, and I am sensitive to my *actual* experiences and hunches over many years. This past of uncontrolled observation over many years now crowds to my help, with apt illustrations and turns of the topic that surprise me, and that lead always to a still simpler view than I had had. And while this is occurring, I pretty continuously come on new information that confirms for me what I seemed to have spun out of my head: I notice it in the papers, on the streets; I am led to a study or report that has been generally overlooked, or not considered relevant to this subject. I might even do a little active experimentation, asking a pre-thought key question in various environments, and see what the response is; but I am chary of this, because it tends to make the environments not real, or my interaction with the environments not real.

Rather disgracefully, I sometimes use a quoted "authority" to start a discussion as if I were reasoning from the authority, when it is only a stylistic device for saying what I intend to say anyway: this must mean I am insecure in the realm of discourse, and need to prove that what I am talking about is the same as the "authorities" are talking about. Other times, however, when I have myself intuited something and shaped the discussion, I like to quote confirming authorities, and this is permissible; for it means that by my dreamy method of recollection I have emerged *into* the common realm of discourse. Indeed, I am most pleased when I conclude to some thumping important platitude that is plain as the nose on your face, and that all the best men have pointed out, and that everybody is now disregarding or even denying.

:   I rely heavily on the following method of argument: I make a list of unaccomplished or lost causes and accumulate them as a program for action. E.g. in the essay on academic freedom, I accumulate the lost traits of academic man and so paint a picture of the Ideal Faculty. In *Growing Up*, the Missing Community of social stability is found by summing the modern revolutionary aims that were in their time compromised and unfulfilled.

Socially and psychologically, this has the effect of making my radical rejection of the *status quo* seem spectacularly conservative. (In fact, I am conservative.) I rely on the natural strength of the unfinished situation seeking closure; the "present" is broadened to include more past.

Historically and metaphysically, however, am I not, by my selection, relying on a *built-in* tendency to failure, the accumulation of impossibility? I choose among the events of history those impossibilities with which I can accuse those who are today successful. But if I do this, I am simply defining myself as an artist: an artist is one who reacts against irremediable loss by denying it. The successful revolutionary is one who can make such a denial stick.

:   Lying half-asleep, I move my glasses or pipe out of harm's way. Later, though I recall my action, I am less willing to affirm it as real, and of course I remember it less well. This seems to indicate that by "reality" we mean the object of *alert* sensation and motor behavior. (Not that the real is "made of" sensations; rather, we affirm, believe in, alert sensations of the real.)

But the act by which I notice my sleepy behavior, and am later aware of its perhaps-fantasy quality, gives me also another aspect of reality that is real and concrete but has a certain bareness and vagueness. And I think that a part of what we call "generalization" or "abstraction" is this concrete but bare and schematic perception: the grasping of the object when we are as if half-asleep. In language it is expressed in the syntax, the kinds of construction allowable, rather than in the terms. In behavior it is expressed in the method and habit rather than the acts.

Such a concrete but bare schema is different from the logical abstraction of a name, e.g. "apple" as standing for apples, which is a definite rule for dealing with particular apples. My hunch is that Plato's ideas were, for him, concrete but bare reals of this kind, occurring in mystical experience that made them seem very vivid to him. I myself find it hard to think in logical abstractions, but I think readily and habitually in schemata. I am a Kantian.

: To maintain my opinions opposed to the vast majority, I remind myself that in many ways—their war, their arts, their schools, and so forth—they are evidently absurd; so it is likely they are wrong-headed here too. But I must apply the same method of reasoning with respect to myself. Since in so many ways I am evidently unhappy—in civic effectiveness, in sex, in my quest for fame—it is likely that I am wrong-headed in much that I stand for.

iii. language

: When I hear a loud inarticulate noise—the grinding brakes, the foghorn, the barking dog—I spontaneously imitate it, making a comedy of it. So a two-year-old cries at the noise of the vacuum-cleaner until I imitate it, making it human. This seems to be the infantile way of coping with a loud sound, by domesticating it. Origin of poetry in thunder?

: It is correct to say, "There is a sociological reason why they do not copulate" and it is correct to say, "You have to fuck in order to have children."

: I distinguish "subtile" and "subtle," idiosyncratically using the first to mean fine and the second to mean cunning. In general, I try to keep both the British and American forms in usage, shading them with different meanings. These are new doublets given by history, as after the Norman invasion we learned to distinguish warden from guardian, lawful from loyal, etc.

:   "The pathos of public housing—" "the pathos of suburban allotment—" "the pathos of living in palaces—" "the pathos of nursery schools—" "the pathos of life with mama (without nursery schools)—" These all make good sense. But "the fun of public-housing—"? "the fun of living in palaces—"?

:   Fix—fox—fux: "Now he's fux it, but good."

:   There is a beautiful modulation to the present tense in Wordsworth's "There Was a Boy." In the silence after the hallooing, " a gentle shock of mild surprise/ *has* carried far into his heart the voice—" He means to say by this that the boy is *still* alive, is himself as he has become by identification with the boy, on the Wordsworthian theory of perception. But in order to keep the narrative texture, he at once cunningly reverts to the weak past "would enter." And then comes the crushing blow of the ending: gone! My feeling is that Wordsworth is our greatest master of fundamental syntax, after perhaps Milton. Just his program of the apparent texture of simple speech brings into emphasis the more basic syntax of tenses, persons, moods, and voices, to carry the nuances of how it is re-experienced (told). I have compared Rilke and Wordsworth as masters of phenomenology—how the thing is had—but I give the palm to Wordsworth because he gets even closer to his actual experience as poet—how it is *told*, rather than experienced, dreamed, or invented.

:   In writing fourteeners, ballad rhythm, I have to seek for the rime of the 2nd and 4th line. But remarkably, the inner rime of the 3rd line, which I don't demand, occurs spontaneously and frequently, as if this were a most natural speech.

: The lovely paragraphs of common Irish speech, e.g. in Becket's *All That Fall*, occur when the speaker withdraws from his speech as interpersonal action, because of diffidence or doubt. Then he makes remarks apologizing for himself or ridiculing himself for speaking; remarks about the attendant circumstances but avoiding the act; remarks to embroider the thought and stall, and yet fill the void and save face. It is in this void that poetry blooms, the language "for its own sake." Every paragraph becomes a dramatic soliloquy, self-contained. Speech-for-itself is literature. The lovely paragraphs of Irish speech, and the depopulation of Ireland. They do everything with their blarney except fuck the girl.

: At Random House, Jason praises the "snake-like suppleness" of my style. How do I manage this continuity in motion? Primarily by avoiding asyndeton. In almost every sentence I use connective particles (but, nor, for), or connective references (this, such, the contrary), or connectives of attitude (of course, naturally, nevertheless!). Almost as frequently as in Greek. I get denseness, too, by very carefully placing my "onlys" and "preciselys." But also I get both continuity and speed by often using an unexpected word-choice that produces a further connection, e.g. a pejorative adjective when I seemed to have been approving, or vice versa; or an unexpected emphasis by position; or even a rhythm, compression, expansion, sudden summation serving as a *premise of enthymeme*. The enthymeme is given in the texture of the words, without my having to state it in propositions. That is, I combine overfull motion of thought with a continuous run-on of connectives.

: The ringing tenor of the Irish 12-year-old calling out "Bob Sil-ver" in almost true musical tones rouses in me my boyhood terror and unease, and makes me wonder whether this nearly musical speaking and out-calling from open throats is not our native speech, instead of the noise-clusters that we assume to be speech. . . . An earlier thought of this same afternoon has been that masculinity is to Go-forth-explore-enter-and-spend-your-gold-as-at-a-bazaar.

I will use these ideas (d.v.) for the Laddy in Volume V of *The Empire City*. He is not "responsible" for his offspring; he lets nature take care of that.

iv.   art

:   To see Cartier-Bresson wandering in two opposite directions on the windy avenue where the next speeding automobile will clip him, is a snapshot by Cartier-Bresson. Squinting through the finder, he huddles himself up small, so that nobody—he thinks—can see him; he waits for the "decisive moment" when the scenes seem right to him: that is, when it is his own body image. Projecting himself through the finder, he snaps the warm confusion of everyday.

Henri imagines, I think, that he is himself invisible, that he has become nothing but peering through his finder. He is very shy. Photographing our therapy group—oddities of America, probably for *Paris-Match*—he is flustered by our easy self-revelation. We try to include him and he hastily packs up and leaves.

:   Horace's dictum, that art is great or it's nothing, is in general sound. For otherwise why bother? How can the second-rate compete with the richness of ordinary experience? But the art of children, primitives, and action-painters poses a critical problem. It is clean, spontaneous, unpretentious gesturing, strictly equivalent to a graceful gait on the street or a neat play in a ball-game. *Is* one to write critical notices of such things?

: I have a kind of love-affair. Its ups and downs become a subject for our friends, their commiseration, spite, jeering, and disapproval; and I take part in this jabbering. Meantime, however, I am secretly practicing my solitary vice of making a poem and song of it, happy with myself in private. Like a secret dope-addict.

For me, the best relation of "life" and "art" is not frustration and sublimation, but success and celebration. Love poem is best orgasm.

: The reviews of my novel make it likely that I shall have become a standard classic without ever having been accepted as one of the writers. Here too I miss out on the moment of excitement and possible pleasure, just as in my friendly and animal dealings. And for the same reason. I do not meet the immediate surface needs of people—as a writer, I don't even try to—but I *am* attending to real underlying needs. This is probably the common situation of good writers at present: people couldn't care less—but then these writers become the standard by which the next generation will live. Thus literature becomes a minor art, and yet it will always be a necessary and major art.

: From time to time I write a Wordsworthian poem, e.g. on the dunes at Wellfleet, or watching the colorful planes go up. I think I can spell out the conditions that give the Wordsworthian effect. It is a scene where I have no business but to look, as if passing by. It is a scene of a few simple shapes, plain colors, or simple folk, that calms attention; but therefore any *sudden* noticing stimulates a mistake in association or apperception which, however, since I am a disinterested observer, rouses feelings only of surprise, wonder, interest: "What can it be? It seemed to be merely this, but it is strange." Lonely, unoccupied, I have only this object to love and from it I ask nothing; it vanishes and leaves me pensive.

Because the scene is simple and I am personally disengaged, I can describe it with childlike directness. Because of my loneliness, I am potentially engaged and open to surprise. The incident comes neither to fulfillment, for there is no desire, nor to disappointment, for the object remains itself, not *for* me. But the incident produces awareness.

We must look in the non-attachment for the affect. Latent in the non-attachment is a repression; why otherwise is one idle, lonely? *It is the repression latent in the non-attachment that occasions the error of perception; it is the release of the repressing that provides the energy for the poem.* Wordsworth is standing idle on Westminster Bridge; and with a pang he is aware that "All that mighty heart is lying still."

: Fine pianists today play as if they no longer believed in the instrument, though they marvelously interpret its literature. And to our taste it is a raucous and non-musical instrument; we are as eager for pure sound as the painters are for real colors. Yet when a player of the old style—Horowitz—has belief in the piano, the esthetic effect is strange and wonderful; his fortissimo, never ugly, makes us feel the box cracking—it is fearful; and the following mezzo piano is remarkably relieving and resigned. . . . He was playing *Pictures at an Exhibition.* Surely the Promenade, beginning forthrightly, modestly, self-consciously visiting the dead friend, is at its finale the truth: my soul free of those works and memories of my dead friend—and now full of myself, troubled—transcendent because of the tears of affection that have boiled in my eyes, for those interesting works of my dead friend—as I march sturdily *out of that place!* My head is bursting loud with the thoughts and feelings for myself and for my dead friend.

: Says Evan Thomas of *Harper's* Magazine: "Probably the ideal length of a novel would be 288-320 pages."

v.   myself

:   I lean over backwards—till I fall flat on my face.

:   When I describe Horatio surprised at the backward
flow of the ice on the river, I "explain" that it is an optical
illusion. But it is not an optical illusion, but due to a vor-
tex along the shore that I happened not to understand. I
have a lovely tendency to know what ain't so. Because I *do*
love the causes of things.

:   Getting the proofs of reviews of *The Empire City*
during the couple of weeks before publication is like waiting for the election-returns; to be elected means that the
book will not lose money. Apparently by now, a week before publication, my hostile publisher concedes that I am
elected; the reviews are many and enough inches long. I
join in with these feelings and find myself eagerly depend-
ing on the space and place accorded me by the N. Y. *Times*
and even *Time*, and I am crushed because I won't be noticed in *The New Yorker*. Meantime, no review betrays
any literary or genuine response at all, of having been
moved or instructed by anything in my book. I should be
deeply wounded—these reviews should prove I have failed
—yet I am fawningly hungry for their crumbs of praise.

How to explain my attitude? (1) I myself judge that
the work is sprawling and unplanned. (2) I have not
aimed to make my characters "well rounded and human"
and have defied the expectations of the very readers I now
woo, so I anxiously yearn for them not to notice. (3) And
I am afraid because of the risk I have taken in going toward reality, so now I need reassurance that I am a good
boy.

My hankering for success for this book is not a generous hunger for fame the food of art, nor even for a comfortable sum of money, a lovely thing; it is pathetically
that, if I am known and esteemed, then opportunities for

friendship and belonging will fall my way, in my life which is now at such a dead low of loneliness that I do not even try for sex. I pray, if opportunity does offer, I shall recover my spirits and become aggressive for the general welfare, making use of my small success to have some weight to throw around for good sense, justice, beauty.

[1965: In fact, a few weeks after the above was written, the publisher called back copies of the book and that was that.]

:   This summer I have lost my bearings. I think in a haze. The breeze of success that forwarded me for a while in the winter has left me in the shoals—the losing of my publisher, my play, the book of Ballads—I no longer know myself. I cannot succeed in my own way; neither am I in opposition. Then I tell myself: withdraw your demands of, your hopes in, these people; stony, make a *Florentine* work. Why make it? The obvious and sufficient answer seems to be: Since you do not like this world, make your own. I will try to write an *Adam*.

:   Lothair is, in a way, Adam. But *he* would consider himself an Adam-seeker. Yet to me he seems to be Adam himself. Is this something Adam does, seek Adam? I shouldn't have thought so. It is a mistake for me to seek and woo him as I do; Adam will come to his lover, if he is there and if the circumstances are practical.

:   It is impossible, "statistically impossible," that other people give me as little out-going affection as I feel they do. Yet when an affectionate gesture does get through to me, it does solve my problem. I feel weak, delicious, pan-icky, happy.

Unfortunately, the case is that—since I am pretty formidable—just those who could love me and want to touch me, hang back in embarrassment. I fail to notice them, although *they are the most attractive*, for luckily I do love the kind of people who could love me. Those who find me "interesting" or "useful," however, approach me boldly enough; I become sanguine, try like the devil to make out with them, and fail.

: I am remorseful. Because of a mere wish or fantasy I insincerely prayed that B. and I would be friends for a long time, "for 10 years." I did not feel right even as I muttered the words. He was just trying out, and I was being sanguine. Naturally my prayer has been spectacularly not granted in 3 days. I can pray efficaciously only when I am expressing what is the *case*.

: Lord! my recent solemn tone is a pain in the ass. As a writer, I'm never really with it and honest but when I'm having lively fun—and then I'm also mournful. I just want some luck, that I won't fuck up, and then I'll come across. Happy face bringeth luck. Luck bringeth happy face.

: Being a couple of days on Fire Island, I again visit the Sunken Forest, to see the holly, the cherry, the sassafrass. The holly that has smooth bark twined with the oak that has rugged. On the big hollies are carved many weathered initials—"as grows the tree, so our love grows"—but I have never cut my name into a tree. This tall pine grows aslant, not to lift its top out of the shelter of the depression. I delay leaving, keep exploring various unlikely traces of paths. Because I visit this lovely place as though it were the last time in my life that I can ever come here. I am sad. I don't want to die.

: Sometimes I draw a breath that is not painful. If then, aware, I draw other painless breaths, I become blank of any interest in the world, my plans, etc. On rare occasions, aware of how tired I am, I can lie deliciously, as if I had a satisfactory love, wanting for nothing.

: My mind is sick. I am fertile with good thoughts. I have a noble intellectual scope in the old style. I might get a fine simple pleasure from exercise of the spirit. Nothing prevents my writing. I can teach. Yet I am continually tormented by not being published, nagged by not getting credit, envious of those who get credit. There would be some reason in my attitude if we were very poor, but we aren't any more. How much better I would feel if I didn't have this disease! and people would like me more, for I would not be bitter, accusing. The happy state moves just beyond me, across a barrier, and as if I could drop the barrier.

: Spirit is too damned quick. Writing *Growing Up*, I rapidly sketched out an enemy, the Organization. I saw some weak points in him. I launched a few tiny shafts, well aimed and fearless enough to make me believe that in a rough fight in this war I should continue to be fearless. I made a few small hits. And now it is as if that enemy lay stretched out mortally wounded, and nothing left to the war but mopping up! He is no longer an interesting enemy and I find myself excited (again) by an underlying problem, how to educate the young now that I have doughtily *rescued* them from the dragon of the Organization!

vi. society

: "Though we have gold to give," says Thoreau, "they demand but silver." They *expect* nickel, or counterfeit, or that you'll pick their pocket.

: In the last chapter of Book II of *The Empire City*, "Our spokesman cried out „Peace!‟ In the original version of *The State of Nature*, however, what he cried out was „Freedom!‟ A decade of history elapsed between.

: John Adams said: "I must study politics and war that my sons have liberty to study mathematics and philosophy, geography, natural history and naval architecture, navigation, commerce, and agriculture, in order to give their children a right to study painting, poetry, music, architecture, statuary, tapestry, and porcelain." Nu? and where are we? Something was wrong with this program.

: "He belonged to that type of statesmanship which Washington had shown to be so powerful, revolutionary doctrine in a conservative temper" (Lord Acton). Yes. The doctrine encourages free instincts with the potential future, justified and right, something to work toward; the conservatism avoids the guiltiness of rebellious acts unless they are "absolutely necessary," and it allows nature to take its course without pre-imposing too many doctrinaire ideas.

: "D'Argenson saw so little that was worthy to be preserved, that he did not shrink from sweeping judgments and abstract propositions" (Lord Acton). One must fill the void with something. With us, the Absurd has become so huge that I feel justified in the Arbitrary.

: In Lord Acton's 25 lectures on the French Revolution he does not once mention the concept of Fraternity! though his analysis deals entirely with the difficult dialectic of Liberty and Equality. How is this oversight possible? (He speaks, for instance, warmly, though disapprovingly, of Michelet.)

Lord Acton's book is full of his kind of wisdom when he is dealing with constitutional questions, but he goes on the shoals when once the lot has been cast to the populist direct action of the General Will. No doubt such populism is, almost by definition, the finish of constitutional politics, but it does not follow that it is the absence of any politics whatever. To find relevant answers, one must then explore new social-psychological depths. So let us consider the Terror.

No matter what the Terror was as a purposeful policy—and such a policy must be stupid—its emotional consequences must be explored as something unique. It makes a difference when bloodshed is allied with one's own superego. The analogy must be to the crowds watching the hangings at Tyburn—Lord Acton does not think of this; yet even he cannot describe 1792-3 without heavily emphasizing the personalities rather than their parties or classes. But since we cannot avoid the psychological, the historian must then look for the categories relevant to social-psychology and the analysis of personalities.

Certainly, Fraternity does not imply Terror. Nevertheless, it must have been the case, with so sudden and spectacular a release from the structural inhibitions of age-old laws, enforced poverty and inequality, and the church, that there would be a resurgence of confused libido that energized Terror. To make love to you, sometimes they dance with you in the street, and sometimes they cut your throat in the square.

And for an historian, a salient thing to explain is the sudden emergence of the People's Army that for twenty years swept everything before it. How can this be explained without enthusiasm and the realities of Fraternity? Alas! 19th century nationalism is Fraternity back in chains and put to economic use.

The French Revolution is an example of a Revolution in which the counter-revolution failed—and the invaders were repelled—unlike the Spanish War of 1936. The Terror was an incident, maybe necessary, of defeating the counter-revolution. But this political reason quite fails to explain why, in the popular mind and in all histories of the French Revolution, the Terror looms so large. My intuition is that the Terror is essentially related to a *more than political* hope, to Fraternity. It is a distortion of Fraternity, *faute de mieux*. And it is our self-punishing warning.

:   A Forest Preserve is one thing, a State Park is another. The aim of the former is to prevent the wild situation from being swallowed up by civilization—thus, I can freely camp in the Forest overnight, because so it was in the beginning, although conveniences for camping may be provided if they do not "spoil" the reservation. But a Park is an amenity provided *by* civilization according to its own standard, and I may not freely camp there, I must get a permit. In the Forest, I camp as in the state of nature in a museum. If I try to camp without a permit in the Park, I am a squatter and disrupt the plan.

: "If I won't rub your cock," says the young reporter who comes to interview me, "at least I burnish up your ego, the next best thing." No. The use of prestige, as Freud said, is to win love. The young man gives me his fantasy of himself instead of his penis. But his sentence holds in the negative: one must not add insult to injury; if you won't rub my cock, at least give me a good write-up.

: The city is teeming with cops because of a wave of juvenile crime, and this gives me a kind of inner calm since the cops' ubiquitous presence makes it out of the question for me to risk my usual dangerous behavior. I am resigned to be good. Nevertheless, I should be just as pleased to get in hell out of here.

: I am walking briskly down 23rd Street after having finished *Growing Up Absurd*—I am carrying the last chapter to the publisher, "The Missing Community"—and suddenly I find myself whistling *The Star-Spangled Banner!* confidently fighting for my country against the system that is destroying her. A chief argument in the book is that the patriotic community is the *real* environment of boys and adolescents, and I am now living out my missed adolescence.

This book, and most of the rest of what I have bravely done this year—my out-spokenness with the Recreation Association in Chicago, the fight I picked with Webb and Knapp among the town-planners at West Point—have sprung directly from reading Washington's Circular Letter. That did fire me and gave me something to do. So books do have a use, and why not my books? So I live in my adolescent day-dream and walk briskly along 23rd Street whistling *The Star-Spangled Banner*.

:   At the publisher's, however, I learn with consterna-
tion that he will not publish my book. (Later, I find out
via the grapevine that some critics have assured him that
he would make a laughing-stock of himself by printing
such a book.) Indeed, he asks me to return the $500 ad-
vance, since I have failed to give him a publishable manu-
script! Rather amused, though not jolly, I tell him to see
my lawyer, though I have no lawyer. And what now shall I
do with my beautiful book? I am deeply hurt. I wanted
this book to appear before the 1960 campaign.

:   Writing the chapter on Vocation in *Growing Up*,
reading Max Weber's essay, etc., I understand Milton's
Sonnet on His Blindness more simply, as an argument
about Justification and Calling. I failed to make anything
of this aspect when I first analyzed the Sonnet in *The
Structure of Literature*. Now I should read "stand and
wait" as a period, with ending voice, a plain assertion,
rather than rising and expectantly, as a need for identification and self-affirmation.

:   The hives of the multiple-dwellings reawaken my
maggot-disgust: the people are so passively housed. There
is too much flesh and not enough spirit, not enough structure of each soul in the world. It is pulpy. It is bad enough
that we fasten onto spots of the earth in clusters like
roaches in the corner of a closet; but in this housing we
become maggots.

:   The Probabilism that Pascal attacks is exquisitely like
the ideas of our own Organized System. In this view, it is
not the truth of a proposition that is important, but that it
is the kind of thing that is discussed by "the" authors, it is
"newsworthy." This puts to flight any primary speech, ancient authors, or frank hard look at the facts. Needless to
say, the condition under which such a view flourishes is
that the dominant system of society no longer has a moral
belief or functional defense for itself; it stands for nothing
except to stay *in* by pork-barreling and log-rolling. Any one

who plays a Role in it, is a right guy. And as Pascal points out, this is crude antinomianism.

There are two kinds of antinomianism. The kind we have been discussing is the degradation of necessary casuistry—it is adjustment, socialization, the probabilism of the Jesuits, the cynicism and public relations of Madison Avenue. This antinomianism is really a spiteful defiance of spirit; it is strongly energized by repressed envy. Inevitably, it necessitates a rebel antinomianism, to defy society on behalf of spirit, like the Assassins or the line of· Cain and Ishmael; to bear witness by torment, in order to found a new, but undefinable, order of the world. "My Lord is so great I dare not be fastidious of idols; what difference does it make?"

: Here is a lovely example of our Organized System at work: My boy breaks his nose at school and the school handles the situation miserably, does not notify us at once, sends him walking three-quarters of a mile to a hospital (and St. Vincent's, to boot!). Next day, I write the principal about the poor management and ask them to proceed more responsibly in the future. At this I receive a blistering phone-call from the physical-training teacher immediately involved, who is in charge of first-aid: I have a nerve, he says, writing to the principal; he himself, he tells me, didn't *have* to do anything about the accident, for it occurred during his lunch hour; and anyway, he *did* act handsomely, he let Matty sit down in his office and he gave him a piece of gauze before he sent him walking. The principal, however, follows with a letter assuring me, etc., etc.—as soon as it is clear that I am not suing anybody, things calm down.

A few weeks after the above incident, I learn from Matty that a rag of advertisements is used in the classroom as a reader! and there are also many brochures of Consolidated Edison, Ford, Shell, etc. I write to the Board of Education and the Superintendent of Schools—copy to the principal. At once he pulls my boy, age 13, out of class and tells him that his father has a nerve to go over his head to the Board of Education. In a panic, he orders the offending material out of the school. Matty explains to him that I wrote to the Board because I want the things out of the school system. "If that's your attitude," says the principal to Matty, "there's no use in talking to *you*."!!

What is dismaying is the anxiety of the subordinate whose name has been mentioned; there is then no possibility of taking any objective issue on its merits. This balks me. I don't know any way to demonstrate except by evidence.

: It is clear from Khrushchev's directive on "education for life" (= useful production) that in our schools we put the cart before the horse and therefore cannot find the formula for either education or life. Certainly we should say "life for education," as Aristotle did: the polis exists for education and noble action. In religious societies the principle is obvious: they "live" in order to grow toward salvation.

Let every six constitute themselves as a committee to see that a growing child is given opportunity to grow up.

vii. God

: Do not practice what you preach, preach what you practice. By doing the first, you sacrifice your time of life to empty standards, and will act hypocritically anyway. By the second, you structure some meaning into the life of waste and might gradually improve. Speech is creative.

: What he has taught me—just by needing it and by making it clear in his speechless way that he wants it—is to take him seriously, to take some one seriously. An immeasurable lesson. How far will it lead me?

: Touched with love, not rejected but not happy, I pour forth kindness; I have always more energy to serve, and a confidence that makes it impossible for me not to do as I see best. When this happens, they love me immoderately, too much. The fellow who was sexually potent with me and could use me, as I wish, if he were simply my equal and trusting friend, is now overwhelmed and oppressed; so I do not have the equal friend I want. Yet if I inhibit my outpouring kindness, I am no longer myself.

They give me occasion to serve, therefore I love them the more, and thereby I am more sure not to be happy. This sounds like protecting myself by drowning them with benevolence.

: Our position is ambiguous. On the one hand we are the savage, obscene, and uncouth anarchists, rebelling against the solid Establishment. On the other hand, we are the handful of high-born, well educated, God-fearing and polite aristocracy protesting against the vulgar powers-that-be. To ourselves, finally, we are simple and all of a piece— there is nothing to do but stick to our principles, brazen them out, and try to diminish both our irrational guilt in society and our inhumane contempt for it. Yet the others suffer more from us than we do from them; they are made anxious by our animality, humiliated by our snobbery.

: Miami in July. As the air-cooler whirrs and the refrigerator hums, the house certainly is a machine-for-living, for environment-control. In a similar hot climate, a primitive would sit immobile in the shade of a tree, and a cow would stand in the water. The primitive and the animal are aware of the climate and of controlling the climate; we in this house are not aware of the climate and the house is equipped with thermostats that do the thinking. Machine-for-living is machine-instead-of-living.

: If for a few moments under the sunny pines on the shore of the sweet pond, I can dismiss—not forget, but bracket it off—that I am lonely, then a surprising love and joy for the beauty of the world sweeps over me. Ordinarily I am easily moved by anything beautiful, but it tires at once because I am impatiently set on my monomaniac desire and am not distracted from it. Works of art in a museum make me happy for a longer hour, since they keep presenting to me concentrated spirit to woo me. But in the beautiful world, if I calm my frenzy, I realize that the sweet and easy disposition of green and water and sun and breeze and gentle warmth and scent of pine are quite various enough for lasting happiness. An automobile horn sounds, my heart contracts, my misery returns.

: I take a last walk before leaving the country (Wellfleet). I am murky, choked, because the bay is beautiful. I haven't been happy here—I won't be where I am bound; but it is beautiful here, and it won't be where I am bound. I am resigned to not knowing what I want, nor how to go about getting it; but I am not resigned to misery, but choked, sighing, finding a difficult music in the sighs, short of breath to sing much of it. "Murky, confused," says Lao-tse, and so I am. I salute my little motor scooter poised for flight.

: A gentle curse (aimed at Julian Beck): "I hope you fail to realize the error of your ways and go on for many years in this successful career you have begun."

: The tenacity of the Jews to persist in America, though the "religion" continues to decline, is indeed significant. But the attempt to make of this persistence a social-cultural idea, like Ahad-HaAm and his "reconstructionist" followers, seems to me to be strangely anti-Jewish. It seems to me that the essence of the persistence is not, mainly, to be other than the Gentiles, except as a response to anti-Semitism, but just simply that the Goyim and their *goyim nachus* are not worthy of emulating and being assimilated. It is not that the Jews have the answers, but that we, by our historical good fortune, such as it is! are able to, be skeptical and a little disengaged from some of the gentile foolishness. We are befuddled, but not that befuddled, in our thirst for paradise.

It is not a "Jewish" idea that animates Jewry—such a notion confuses everything; it is the society of justice and the culture of paradise, which belong to all mankind, but for historical reasons the Jews have often been less confused about them. And so far as, among the existentialists, there has been a small "religious" revival, this *has* been its content.

: Already in the 18th century, the Protestants had become Catholic, and the emancipated Jews took over as Protestants. Now in America Jews have become Establishment and people the Rand Corporation. But we were taught *not* to put our faith in princes, and to dwell as if in tents.

[1966: And now there is a revival of spirit among the existentailist Protestants and the *aggiornamento* Catholics; but the suburbanite Jews have sunk into spiritual degradation.]

: A fortuitious collection of events: Yesterday I picked up a book of Kierkegaard's (*Concluding Unscientific Postscript*) and found it thin gruel, but was enchanted by the portrait of Lessing. Today, hearing Lukas Foss's *Symphony of Chorales* and finding it somewhat interesting, I wrote the little prayer "God, I have misbehaved—" and this led me to the other prayer, "At last I know (for friends have said)—" because the editor read to me over the phone Harold's review of *The Empire City*: how it is my public acting-out that has led to my dismal hardships. Harold is right. It is only this! And now that I see it is so, I am proud; I am not guilty but a witness. At this moment, having finished the second prayer and breathing the Reformation, suddenly I hear Mendelssohn's Symphony, so spirited and boyishly onrushing, and I am even *happy* with myself for half an hour! The sacrament of the public gesture! Since Harold has named it for me, I take comfort in it. Lessing. Where I felt dirty because unfulfilled, I feel clean because naïve.

: I don't feel any boundary within my body. If I touch somebody, it may always turn into sexual touching. If sexual touching is made impossible, I can't touch at all, and the other soon becomes repugnant to me, if not downright repulsive. I can't live intimately in the same house with those I *must* inhibit myself from having sex with. Their manners, their conversation become repulsive.

: My son, at the age of 12, has a beautiful attitude toward the animals. Conservative and loving, he will not harm an insect. He spends hours observing the fish and fiddler-crabs, and reads and learns about them. He cries out with admiration of the slimy slug. At the same time, without squeamishness, he will pull the wings off a fly with equanimity to feed his lizards. Fishing, he will live-bait the hook and be proud of and eager to eat his catch. But if it is not for eating, he will protectively, and with great pains, rescue it and throw it back. He likes to bring an animal home and cage it as a pet; but if he thinks it is suffering and may not thrive, he lets it go.

: It's a crazy world the dog lives in. She plays a game getting the rope away from you, and then at once brings it back and lays it at your feet. She likes you to throw a ball for her to leap at and catch, but then she won't give it back. Using her teeth—and not biting. In the conditions in which we live, we stay in touch with the others with games, but we don't, can't, mayn't get it for keeps, finish, eat it, kill them.

: Beneath my torpor emerges finally, as always, meaningless grief of unknown origin. It has been liberated this time by words of Pascal, "A thought has escaped me. I wanted to write it down. I write instead that it has escaped me." This touches me deeper than his thoughts of Jesus, but in being touched by his despair, I am touched a little by his love of Jesus. "All these miseries," he says, "prove man's greatness. They are the miseries of a great man, of a deposed king."

:   So I write these sentences true of my misery; but I do not get to write other sentences true of my joy and which would perhaps be contradictory to these sentences. It is not that the sentences I write are doubtful to me; if I did not believe them, I would not write them. But that they are what I *have*, to write, is both their truth and their error.

1960

i. people, places, things

: On the diner of a Pennsylvania train, what can one say to the waiter's "Is everything all right, suh?"—"Certainly, sir! within the limits of the genre of lousy food served on this railroad, tip! top!"

: Imagine a folk whose culture is dominated by the deity concentrated in some crashing physical wonder like the Grand Canyon, or Niagara Falls, or the mountain of Manhattan viewed from the bay. (No difference whether the wonder is natural or artificial, so long as the vast magnitude of the image imposes itself indelibly in the soul.) They will have an epical literature unlike the more lyrical forest or the sea that forms temperament.

In the 3 images I think of, the Canyon, the Falls, and Manhattan, there is a magical variation of light and color, as if the Thing were alive and breathing. And of course there is sublimity, a magnitude that surpasses the ability of the senses to take in. Here, one cannot see to the bottom of the Canyon, though I guess that crevice must be the Colorado, where is lurking a Big Fish.

: There are beauties uniquely of our epoch—the electric lights in their rows and clusters, the leaping throughways, the views from the aeroplane. But I have not much used them in my writing. I tend to recur, rather, to the July-soft tarry streets of my childhood, the old New York basements, and the waterfront of the Hudson. Now in San Francisco I have inevitably come down to the rocks along the water of the Bay where it is dingy and deserted except for a couple of fishermen. But part of the scene is also the curving jet of the plane across the blue. And beyond the Golden Gate is the China trade.

The fantastic lights at night are certainly like the Arabian Nights. And it is easy to feel that the aeroplane from Cleveland is a Roc, a most mechanical bird anyway, from which we look down on the lands and rivers till he settles to earth and lets us off.

:   At a 10th Avenue garage: "If! if! If de fuckin car had wings it'd be an aeroplane!"

:   Scowling at the *Sun!*—in my depression. So—so—O neolithic man!

:   "Kiss it good-bye" or "give it a good-bye kiss": which is worse?

:   A winning toothless smile—won't bite your head off.

:   The king debased the coinage so that during the centuries it eroded away and never an archeologist has dug up his stamped effigy.

:   If you bend down to suck him off, he will clobber you on the head with a hammer. If you drop your pants for him to fuck you, he will stab you when your pants have entrapped your ankles. Got to stay behind a chap like that.

:   His hands, burglar's tools, are violations of the Weapons Law.

:   On the embankment, the ladder that serves for those who fall in the water by accident is used by the boys who are forbidden to swim there.

:   Of the naked boys swimming from the dock: The tallest leans against the tall piling on the right; the strongest boy is sitting on the tin roof jerking off; the smallest, seated on the dock, is looking up at him with wide eyes and open mouth; and on the left, the thin boy is crossing himself before diving. Nevertheless, their chattering rings continuous and unanimous, the matrix of agreement in which they can dare to be different. From time to time, knees akimbo, they spring into the water like frogs, includ-

ing the boy with the hard on. All are in the grip of the
need to jump in the water.

: With a rush the dog goes after the stick and brings it
back, and crouches with it expectantly, for the play to be
repeated. Again. Again. But the fourth time, she expertly
leaps and misses, and returns empty-jawed. Nevertheless
she again crouches expectantly. She does not see the stick
lying in plain sight.

: I could believe that our little Lucy, killed by a car at
Eagle's Bridge, lives on in dog heaven, for it is hard to
believe that her happy indefatigable spirit is no more. If
she is there, she is waiting for us there, to shepherd us
together again, because her heart was nothing else but
love. Her spirit is in the room as I write this, and it is the
spirit not of a dog but of love, whether of a man or a
dog.

: Some fool up in a loft building gets in a tizzy and
throws a bolt of cloth out the window. From 22 floors up,
and it crashes down on the guy in front of me on the side-
walk and kills him. Who in hell would expect to be in
mortal danger from a bolt of cloth on 8th Avenue near
30th Street?

ii. art

: Breughel's *Icarus* is always read in one direction, e.g.
by Auden: Icarus falls down and people go about their
business and couldn't care less. But it could be read the
other way: Here is this crowded world, and in it there is
also Icarus falling down. This certainly sounds more like
Breughel.

: If I ever have a connection with a theater company, I

shall put on Corneille's *Horace*, adding the few touches
that are absent in this greatest of pacifist plays. (1) A brief
mad scene for Sabine, *after* she has apparently regained
her composure. (2) Her breakdown at the end of the last
act, after the king's smug judgment. (3) The gathering of
the confused muttering crowd again "about to mutiny,"
this time on-stage.

:   The light of an object varies in times and weathers.
Monet in his series gives us this in the one constant light
of the exhibition hall. How disgraceful that his work is
then exhibited in poor light, with no space to back away,
and calamitous frames!

:   "Sunt'n" for "something." This is much more lazy,
conceited, and spiteful than "sump'n," which is childlike.

:   Siegfried's funeral music succeeds, curiously, in being
grandly barbaric. How does Wagner manage this? By saying, "*My* hero. It's *my* hero who's dead." He dares, against
the entire spirit of modern times, to have a personal alle-
giance to his hero, and this restores him to feudal barba-
rism.

:   Thinking, in Switzerland, about naïve vs. sophisticated art, I wished for the orange-red benches of the Ti-
cino to be "neutralized," "made bodiless" by a French
gray. Now it suddenly occurs to me that that gray is the
color of a Norman town and like the Norman climate. So
perhaps what I mean by sophistication is the imposition of
an invading conquering culture upon the natives.

:   In Quintero's production of Genet's *Le Balcon*, the
6th Scene, the revolutionists, is omitted, and so the whole
last part of the play becomes meaningless. One has not
been presented with the "reality" and the reality becoming
illusion, against which the illusion is measured and becomes real. The omission is disastrous, for with a master

like Genet the meaning, the pace, and the weight of every speech depend on what has preceded.

D.B. tells me that Quintero cut the scene because it was acted so badly. In the miserable tradition they have been trained in, the actors acted like actors, expressing their actor-like souls, whereas the director, rightly, wanted them in *that* scene to be natural, not acting. Since they failed to convey the meaning anyway, he thought it would be less damaging to omit the scene altogether. But he should have canceled the production.

: In this play, Genet achieves the Pirandellian effect, the doubt of what is real and what is as you desire it, better than Pirandello. It is sometimes doubtful whether the Madame of the brothel is "real" as a character or whether she is a character playing Madame. But he gets his success at a cost; he makes the art-work be only his own poet-reality message to the audience. Pirandello risks the harder, and in our theatrical conditions perhaps impossible, task of involving the real audience in the art-work. Genet is self-deceived; he uses the art-work as a conceit to deny his impotence, an impotence no doubt spitefully willed by himself. And since he too knows this, he writes the accepted castration into the plot. But it does not help —there is no dramatic or cathartic effect to the ending. It is alibi-ing for the public.

Pirandello, rather, is the jealous husband who in his torment doesn't know whether Desdemona is *really* unfaithful or whether it is his fantasy. Nevertheless he must rant and torture her. He calls upon the audience to tell him the truth. To rescue her, to rescue him from himself. But Genet protects his own conceit by spitefully taking away the audience's reality too.

Yet *Le Balcon* is a grand work. It is true to our present nature, as we have become. It is at least a masturbation-fantasy, rather than a phony like other contemporary plays.

: "Time and change will surely show how firm our friendship's, Ohio!" "On the field of life's endeavor, bound by ties that naught can sever!" And so forth. There is obviously an ambiguity behind this impossible sentimentality. On the one hand the bright homosexual attachment must be frustrated and the endogamy avoided. On the other hand, youth *is* passing and troublesome responsibilities loom ahead. The undying loyalty is both a wish for it not to die and a reaction-formation against the wish to kill it.

It is a pity that there is no real poetry for this poetic subject of the Youth House. But our young people are embarrassed. Friendship is perhaps the major personal experience of life, but we do not have a good conscience about it. They say it was different in antiquity.

: The Architect is both artist and either professional or gentleman, both artist and either technologist or businessman. Accepting the conventional and professional role, he is socially safe. But if the artist part is strong, he becomes a tyrant, forcing his vision on recalcitrant material and on society. When he gets old, however, he is not a tyrant but a force of nature, respected. As an old man, he does not wrest authority, it falls into his hands. Have his fangs been drawn by then?

: There is something humanly wrong about the use made of the performers in part music, except chamber music. In principle, in polyphony, there is a genuine community, mutually dependent and mutually supporting, "the ages and sexes of humanity" each acting to full capacity. In later harmony, however, a man often waits idle and then contributes a mite, not otherwise than in a too advanced division of labor. In some pieces, most of the players serve to support or embellish the star or the starry group. In others, all are servants of the "objective" work of the composer and conductor. The supporting kind is certainly ancient and primitive, e.g. the balladist and his chorus. But I doubt that the "objective" kind could exist, or be performed, among primitives. Primitive community music *is* objective, but not servile.

: In *Wachet Auf Ruft Uns die Stimme,* the difference between the two duets is remarkable. The first, "Wann kommst du mein Heil," is all yearning and expectation, in high operatic style. The second, "Mein Freund ist mein" is light opera, as befits success in the romantic line. Married love, however, is not a subject for a play, and the chorale text is here the usual, "Kein Aug hat je gespuert" —unutterable, not looked at.

iii.   method

: Here is a remarkable linguistic analysis in *Tetrachordon. Malachi ii,* 16 allows alternative readings: either "Let him who hateth put away, saith the Lord God," or alternately, "The Lord God saith he hateth putting away." Milton comments, ". . . reject the second reading because it introduces in a new manner the person of God speaking less majestic than He is ever wont. When God speaks by his prophet, He never speaks in the 1st person, thereby signifying his majesty and omnipresence. He would have said, 'I hate putting away,' saith the Lord, and not sent word by Malachi in a sudden fallen style—shrinking the glorious omnipresence of God speaking into a kind of circumscriptive absence. As if a herald in the achievement of a king should set his helmet sideways and close, not full-faced and open in the posture of direction and command."

: It is neurotic to have "thoughts" that you "express" in speech. One just talks and it makes sense because of good habits and present context and contact. "Thinking" —usually appearing as long blanks during which nothing is

said—might be fear of ridicule or shame of exposing oneself; more deeply, it is repressed hostility and contempt,
fearful of retaliation. (All this is more to the surface in the
case of stammerers, who do not "think" but cannot speak
either.)

Nevertheless, there must be a normal use of such
"thinking," since it is a human power. Plato calls thinking
an interior dialogue, the questioning self confronting the
part of the self identified with the thesis, and the two try
to come to terms. We must never forget that the neurotic
is a weak or isolating case of the natural. As Hughlings
Jackson puts it, "Do not explain a positive effect by a negative cause."

: The intermediate between just speaking and "thinking" may be observed in a usual technique of stalling. I ask
a question; he repeats the question and then answers it.
This puts the dialogue under his own control.

: A man fishing is not a fisherman, and a fisherman is
not a man fishing. The amateur, who has more various,
subtile, and strict aims, may know far more about fishing,
but his knowledge is not so real. In general, the Artist or
Sportsman with capital letters has the most expertness,
and is looked to as the model; next the professional who
works for a living; next the amateur for recreation.

Most experienced poets could turn out better journalism than the journalists. I know that I can, and do.

: Let me return to the idea of the power that is in a
thing making it exist. This is the power added to it to
make it break into existence; and that it then *exerts* just
because the thing exists and must be coped with. When
Wm. Reich distinguishes 3 layers, the "polite superficial,"
the "repressed character," and the "biological core," he
habitually under-rates the surface. We can see in our present organized society how just this polite presentness dominates and shapes everybody's behavior because there it is.

Reich rightly rates the middle layer, because indeed people act with a catastrophic response since they are cut off from a satisfactory present actuality. And whatever vitality is released by by-passing the surface behaves according to his model of the organism as pulsating bladder. But he then extrapolates this bladder behavior to be the "biological core." I doubt that it is a core and that it is biological.

The chief trends of my own thought—natural potentiality, background and figure, creator spirit, strength and value welling from the real task, open experiment, naturalist rather than scientist—all are about the "power that is in the existing." I sit secure in this position, it proves itself in many problems, yet I cannot define it. I cannot get it "out there" to point at, and of course it is not "out there" to point at. What do I want? Do I want to eat it? touch it? say it? measure it? What I want is, first, a crucial experiment.

: It is useful to note down the cases where one has been proved in error by the event, and to find in what kind of things one tends to go wrong. By experience we learn to correct our predictions, but it is more important to learn *when* and *how* one makes false predictions.

: A difference between the "modern scientist" and the natural philosopher is that to the scientist the Unity of Science is, by and large, established: there is one Method and there is an attempt to invent, or agree on, one Language of Unified Science. But to the natural philosopher, the Unity of Nature is a faith, an heuristic principle, so that the various sciences work in free federation, each using the language and method that works for itself and accommodating to the others.

From the Unity of Science, poetry is excluded by definition, since it does not use the Language of Science; but it is often included in the exploration of the Unity of Nature, for it is an autonomous means of knowledge and a particularly accurate means of saying.

: Journalism does not make a book, because a book develops and gains stature by its inner coherence in a deepening or expanding argument. I objected to Dwight MacDonald's collection of pieces because it did not have an inner principle, though it was fine journalism in that it coped with important passing events and first brought them into discourse, a splendid function for a writer. The kind of learning sufficient for journalism, however, is not sufficient for deepening an argument.

I objected to Wechsler's book because, electioneering, he keeps saying "Yes but," in order not to offend any possible voter. Thereby he keeps from developing his own principle.

The handling of "newsworthy" issues prevents arriving at the novel definitions that alone can solve problems. The essence is rarely newsworthy. Coping with passing events does not make a book. Winning a debate does not make a book. A new definition is bound to offend both parties to a dispute, and it seems irrelevant to what people think they are talking about.

iv. society

: An argument against Kennedy's campaign for the nomination is that it might put Pope John in the White House. Oh, what a pleasant change that fat old man would be, instead of *any* of the candidates coming forth.

: The advantage of the indecisive man, Stevenson, is that he might do less harm because he is sensitive to consequences that would rouse his own guilt and anxiety. Then if, for a change, some really innocent and excellent opportunity would offer, he might snatch at it with pent-up relief, no matter how quixotic it might be, just to be able to act guiltlessly.

: The entrance of Mrs. Roosevelt on the floor of the Los Angeles Convention of 1960 was, to my ear, a live moment in official public affairs. The tone of voice of the reporters was vibrant, and journalists began to speak of a possible "miracle," the nomination of Governor Stevenson, by which they meant simply the occurrence of something not machined, for a change. There was not in that electric moment—which revived several times for another day—any important factor of rebellion or anger; this was unfortunate, it was simply a revival of dormant life. With anti-climax the cold machine ran its course to the nomination of Kennedy, and spirit again went to sleep. It lies there (underground) waiting, O my sleeping beauty. I don't mean that Governor Stevenson is much of a champion of vitality.

It is a remarkable fact of life, how quickly and unspoiled by adversity life springs alive at the mere presence of possibility, like Rilke's Unicorn that feeds on the possibility of being. What seems to be required for a longer breath is a daring and destructive will, certainly not the forte of Governor Stevenson. No such daring occurred at the Convention. The specific lapse was that in his rather eloquent nominating speech for Stevenson, Eugene McCarthy did not *over-ride* the 10-minute rule, since he had the majority of the crowd with him. If he had done this, he might have injured the machine.

My own response to such events is interesting to me. Instead of being disappointed, I at once set up a reaction-formation of finding new expedients. The treacherous vote of our New York machine delegation particularly disgusted me; I reacted by writing an angry letter how Westchester County deprives our poor boys of the use of its swimming pools, and I made an advance to the editor of the *Post* (in vain). Next day I thought up a more important role for Governor Stevenson than being President. (He has rejected it.)

This is what Dave Riesman calls my "nerve of failure." To me, it seems to be the obvious course, inasmuch as we do not intend to lie down and die, not just today. But Sally says, "*You* can think of something; others can't."

: Don't keep a workman waiting for his pay. In Business Methods, however, the relation between work and pay has become indirect. For instance, if a check due me is "in the works" of the Accounting Department, neither heaven nor hell can expedite it, though somebody in the office will lend me ten bucks. And consider my daughter applying for a fellowship; she must go to Syracuse for an interview, and she bills the State for the expenses. But a poor youth does not have $40 to lay out. Further, each application costs $10, for processing; this is a small sum to invest for all the foundation gravy that will be spilled, but it might be just this sum that is discouraging to kids whose parents are not part of the Organized System.

: In a suit for damages, a woman sues a dentist for incompetent work she has had to have redone: she asks for the new expense and a very large sum for her pain, fear, and waste of time. (1) She is entitled to the new expense; certainly one mustn't add insult to injury. But I do not think that damages should be given for the pain suffered, any more than for breach of promise. Misery of the spirit and pain of the flesh are our common and to-be-expected lot. This flesh of ours, its pains and pleasures both, does not belong to pricing and exchange. (2) In general policy, of course, it is unwise to penalize the dentist for a mistake, that seems to have been unusual in his prosperous practice; it is impossible to practice any profession if one cannot simply do one's best and risk making a mistake. But since he does profit handsomely by his successes—he charges high fees—it seems equitable for him to write off his failures and pay the second dentist (who happens to charge even higher fees!) (3) Pain is our common lot, but money *is* a consolation prize, has been since Hammurabi's Code. It is a sweet that heals bad memory. But the balm should come from society, from the public insurance fund for tough luck. The theory that the defendant must pay harks back to an old tribal view that he is his brother's keeper, in which case he *can*, even though unwillingly, offer consolation. Under present conditions, we all must console her. If, at present, the defendant is forced to pay for the injury, he is penalized without the corresponding satisfaction of being thereby received back into brotherhood, for there is no such brotherhood.

In fact, in this case, the verdict was for the dentist, without damages, on the simple grounds that it is unwise to penalize honest malpractice.

: My fantasy of what I shall do when I have a lot of money is: to give it to those who need it, whom I like, but in such a way that they can feel justified because they are "doing something worthwhile." E.g. I fantasize paying a friend to do some interesting research that I need (there is no such research, of course, that I would not prefer to do myself); or I underwrite a theater-group that plays my plays among others.

The factors in my fantasy are (1) to relieve the insecurity of poverty. (I am not speaking here of immediate *need*, hunger or emergency.) I think of how a few years ago Paul Williams surprisingly gave me $1700, for nothing and unasked for, and since then I have had continuing security; it saved me from the margin of poverty. (2) Usually, but not necessarily, I like to be somehow included in the secure activity that then goes on. (3) And I persist in the Calvinistic feeling that the money has to be given for some specific performance, otherwise the recipient will be dependent or resentful, and the gift will certainly ruin friendship.

The real situation at present—when I don't have much money—is that the existence of poor friends, who work long hours at uninteresting jobs just to pay their food, is intolerable to me; and I wish I could set them free. On the other hand, if my friends don't support themselves, I don't like it either. Both alternatives seem to me to be servile and therefore irrational, and therefore threatening to me. The only solution is to try to get them better jobs.

: I am about to buy a house and its piece of land, in New Hampshire. It is far away; I bargained for it on the way home from Quebec and I have only a dim memory of it, there are a half a dozen big maples in front and that, across the next field, it is hard to cut through the bushes to the Connecticut River. But thus I too enter into the tradition of having a place that, according to our ancient laws, is "my own." By law, others are *excluded* from it. The irony, of course, is that though I could lawfully summon the constable to keep other people out, in fact I wouldn't. I inconsistently hope that *they* will take seriously the system of property that I don't believe in, and that they won't break in.

It is "my castle," and with certain exceptions I there can do what I please. Unfortunately, many of the important things that I please fall under the "certain exceptions," so I have no Castle after all.

I trust, at least, that the headaches of taking care of my new property will be balanced by real satisfactions. But this equation too is meaningless, for I know that whatever one takes on as his own becomes his concern, preoccupation, duty, trouble—whether it be a house, a car, a dog, a daughter. Busy with these, we go from the cradle to the grave. But I *can* say one thing: my new house, although expensive for me, is *not* more than I can afford. It will lead me, but not hurry me, on my way.

: Since I seem to favor the maximum use of scientific technology where it is efficient—for it is morally degrading to a workman to do what a machine could do easier—and yet since I see this technology everywhere as dehumanizing, I am driven to the compromise of wanting only useful machines, where "use" means the maximum mass-production of little more than subsistence. I seem to want the salt to be scientifically mined, machine packed and machine distributed; but I do not want tennis rackets and tennis balls to be machine made! I suddenly understand the relevance of the peculiar sumptuary statutes in Plato's *Laws*. Plato certainly comes home to me as I get older.

: As I get older, I begin to feel myself as law-giver. The more drastic the changes in society that seem to me to be simply reasonable, the more unrealistic my own role becomes.

: To illustrate the distinction between General Will and Will of All, Bosanquet mentions Themistocles' use of the silver for the fleet that then fought at Salamis, rather than dividing the money individually. It is a good illustration, but it would be even better if he remembered that this stolen silver was being used for Athenian imperial interests against the General Will of Greece, and the end was the Peloponnesian War.

Community is not the sum of individuals. As I point out in *Growing Up* with regard to Recreation, even if all were getting real satisfaction from a hundred million hobbies and sports, it sould be a dismaying picture. For recreation on such a scale, we need the culture of the community or city.

Community might be defined as finding resources in other people, just by their co-presence. It is bringing together the old folk and the orphan children, rather than shutting them in separate asylums, for they find life in one another.

Bosanquet's *Theory of the State*, however, is muddled by dwelling on Sovereignty, Will, and coercion as essential to Commonwealth. For the most part it can be shown that coercive will thwarts and devitalizes community and Commonwealth, just as it does every other function.

: I am an anarchist not because I am "individualistic" or have any abiding faith in "spontaneity," but because I am comunitarian and hope for the Commonwealth, whereas coercion and top-down direction make people fearful and stupid. I fantasy abolishing the jails (which breed crime), but cleaving to the Common Law. The police will quell disturbances of the peace, haul off the offenders to the Magistrate, who will lecture them on the Common Law in the presence of the community, and set them free—hopefully calmed down! Such a procedure would certainly not abolish crime, but I think it would result in fewer felonies than we have at present.

:   Rather than furthering it, Sovereignty hinders the natural tendency of the folk to cohesion. It leads to private symbolic identification with the Sovereign. Inhibited, people feel small, and they then need big symbols.

:   "Ready to change sides with justice, that fugitive from the winning camp!"—Simone Weil.

:   Today I offered my services to the National Committee on Employment of Youth. Sometimes with misty eyes and sometimes with indignation, I suggested things that could be done to "fashion into fact the useful thoughts I have for the Americans." I felt the power of my disinterestedness, since indeed I have no ax to grind and don't want anybody's money. Again I feel how my social role is changing. I am no longer one of the aristocrats of Art, who has each one an independent realm and banner. And I am no longer one of the serviceable free knights, who adventure *noblesse oblige*. Rather, I am entering into the paternal royalty. Yet somehow this does *not* jeopardize or diminish my religious faith in democracy. It is possible to be kingly just because all are equal. I am beginning to understand that to rule and to obey are the same (and I should rather like the fearful experiment of being obedient).

:   M.S. tells us that he was fired from the Communist Party in 1950. I am curious what the charges were, since they couldn't still, at that time, be calling people Trotskyites. And indeed, the charge was a good one: "Cannot prove he is not an FBI man."

v. myself

: Sally recalls how, a child, she did not like to get off the subway at 14th Street, which was a vulgar stop, but preferred to get off at the less convenient Christopher Street, for that was a refined and interesting station. At the same age, I was ashamed to be seen with the *Daily News,* but I also would not read it in private, for my snobbery was deeply ingrained.

I think my homosexual needs, involving rough company, catch-as-catch-can chances, and dirty practices, got me out of a lot of snobbery, though homosexuality does not seem to have this effect on the tribe of up-town queens whose reaction against their drives makes them more squeamish and snobbish still.

: I pick up a young fellow on the train, though I don't like him—he reminds me of J.M., with the same combination of self-righteous conceit plus some gifts and no contact with his own body. Naturally, he greedily eggs me on, frustrates me, is righteous, and gives me a moral sermon. I ride it out. Now that he is a little more earnest, he is more tolerable, and I am betrayed by my usual guilt of having imposed myself where I was not welcome. So I find myself saying, "You're a good kid, I like you," when I ought to say by instinct, "You're a stinker." Then naturally, since I am no longer threatening—and indeed it is now I who am the cock-teaser—he inundates me with confidences about a serious sexual-religious crisis that he is going through, and he develops a strong transference to me. Glad I am to escape from this leg of my journey.

: There have been few days back to my 11th year when I have not had an orgasm one way or another. Given this much "drive," whether neurotic or not, the unhappy course that I have run may have been the best, as sheer self-preservation. I could not possibly have been as adventurous and promiscuous heterosexually as I have been homosexually. With women I always commit the future to a considerable extent; there is, in my experience, more danger of venereal disease; there are complications like unwanted paternity; and most important, the settled hatred and violence of jealous rivals and husbands is far more dangerous than occasionally being knocked down, threats of blackmail, or possibility of arrest. From my 10th year, I have memories of the trouble one gets into by fooling around with girls. I have an inkling, but no memory, that I had a bad scrape about my 14th year.

: There was an aspect of my troubles at Z. school which I did not mention in *Parents' Day*, the hostility of some people because I had literary ability that they envied and that I took for granted. I find it impossible to take seriously the fact that people who have writer's block are suffering because of it. Offhand and embarrassed as usual, I showed my sonnet about M. to X.'s wife, and to my surprise, she bit my head off with rage at my offhandedness.

If one puts on the dignity and airs of an Author, then people can save face or perhaps identify. I don't do this; but then—what makes it all the more galling—I speak with authority when I make a critical judgment. Perhaps worst of all, I usually take it for granted that *everybody* is gifted, unblocked, loves the excellent, and so forth. This Nietzschean callousness appears sometimes to be humility, sometimes arrogance, sometimes a democratic spirit. It wins a few; it mortally offends most.

: Not a song in my heart but several in my suit-case, I'm off to Washington to read a tape for the Archives.

: I am uneasy about the reputation I am getting for *Growing Up* and my recent essays. I feel I am going under false pretenses, for these things do not represent "me" in the sense that my stories and plays do. My current bright idea to cope with the emergency is to make it perfectly clear to everybody that I suck cocks, e.g. by sending *C's Birthday* to a magazine and retaining my own name in the story, though altering the other names.

:   After the lecture, the students want me for coffee; but the professors want me for a drink at the elegant ranch-house, and I go with them. My young friend is disappointed, because I do not choose what I really prefer, and what would indeed be more useful as well as more lively. Instead, I choose the conventional behavior to play it safe, for the professors might be offended at my declining them, whereas the students take the rejection as inevitable. But my young friend is in error, for I *never* do what I "prefer," but always what, according to my lights, best conserves the whole. That I "do what I want" is a projection of his own inhibited need. And probably my chief *use* is that I carefully preserve the conventional structure for the young and prove that one *can* maintain some vitality and honor within it. This gives them the possibility of having a past, which they have come to doubt. I am an ambassador between the Beats and the Squares, but I'm damned if I know who sent me on what mission, except just to prove that there *is* an ambassador and One World.

The University is lousy, but it is all there is and it does go back to Paris. So I try to undermine it and proclaim *Vivat Academia*.

:   I am having a dialogue with Kenneth Clark at City College, at a student forum, and he points out that the students are held to their grades, their "futures," their schedule of conformity. I sense that they are ready to deny it and I say, "If our talk were lively and worthwhile enough, they would stay on past the hour and miss their classes." At this, many applaud vigorously, and I could easily lead them into a lively rebellious incident, beyond the hour. But I judge it is not a "worthwhile" occasion, and I allow it to break up at the bell. I feel I have let them down. I do not *think* so, however, since I did not have anything to offer. If I had been interested in what Clark had to say, I should have gone right ahead.

: At a private showing of a documentary (John Huston's film about the shell-shocked), there are about 30 people. I am the oldest; I will die before them. What role ought I to be playing in this place? Why am I still devoting myself to handball and making love to youth, instead of finding the philosophic exercise that will give my spent life a meaning? Yet afterwards, when they gather in a circle around me and respectfully ask for my opinion, I am uneasy with this role that they assign me. I modestly proffer my opinions as mere impressions. I prefer to have them talk and to lead them on, and I am self-conscious if I talk too much. Is it that I do not accept being old, or that I do not accept my right, being old, to enjoy their youth?

In impersonal matters, however,—"Kid, get me a cup of coffee," "Drive me to the airport"—I have no qualms about exploiting the young. Any one who has suffered the hardship and anxiety of bringing up a couple of children deserves this kind of pay-off from the young in general—though not, to be sure, from his own children.

: Since I have apparently made a better mousetrap, I am now summoned twice a week to assorted Y.'s, V.A.'s, Colleges, and Conferences. This ought to animate me; I like to be in the swim and to be made use of. But I am suffering from the "nervous breakdown" of middle age retirement from my long and honorable career of struggling for bare acceptance. The bother is that I do not know what to do with being "accepted." My old story, my malicious utopianism, is no doubt what people want to hear; but now I do not feel malicious, only utopian. What shall I say to them? What *is* important to me? who am I? If I frankly declare what is the case, that I am this aging and confused, indolent and self-distracting philosopher, I shall again be irrelevant and out of the swim, for this is too hard a lesson for them. So, not out of malice but despair, Creator Spirit come.

:   He rubs me gently the wrong way—to my delight.

:   Mailer lectured him on the question of making a critical decision and "staking all." But I dislike to think of it so melodramatically. In my own prudent course, I have made a decision a few times, most recently in my odd "patriotic" choice. Such a choice is "impossible" and yet it has thrown me into a lot of effortful activity. I make much less sense than when I abstained or always came in biting and scratching. One deadly risk I take is to become quite stupid. Not that I will become square; I have always been square, almost a cube.

:   I am ashamed when he hears about the other young men with whom I've fucked. What am I ashamed of? I don't know, but it's for the same reason that I rouse sexual excitement in myself with him even when I don't feel sexy, to avoid the anxiety of feeling close. The way I experience it is that I "don't know what to do with" the excitement; orgasm diminishes the energy and therefore the anxiety. So I merge with him, lose my self-possession, and of course lose him as a person. Afterwards I am fearful and ashamed because something happened but I wasn't there.

:   I see him daily. We behave as though we loved each other dearly. This is interesting, fairly peaceful, and so forth. Yet I don't get much satisfaction from it. But if I were making an important new poem, I should get—I would be *justified* to get—satisfaction also from this love affair. I would give myself less to the affair and get more satisfaction from it.

:   He misses the appointment. I am not resentful but simply frustrated in my lust, restive, dejected. I do not accept that *he* has frustrated me but retreat to the safe position that that is how it is.

:   My problem with him is hard. He acts in a manner I
dislike, and I dislike him, for his self-centeredness, tactless-
ness, and self-destructive violence. He is one whom I
would ordinarily simply avoid. Yet it is only he in the
world who forces his love on me and, however willfully
and rudely, does often pay attention to me and my needs,
and sometimes he is acutely perceptive. Responding to his
attention, I commit myself to him so as to be able to avoid
him. This leads to my giving him idiotic querulous lectures
which, I suppose, attach him to me further. He inhibits
his resentment.

The fact is that he is too good for me. I do not mean
by this that I am "not good enough" for him, since I do
him some good and no harm. (The relation of being too
good for some one is not co-relative.) His wishes are
naive and reasonable: pleasure, to learn, to achieve something by using me, to admire me, ultimately to beat me out
and prove something to himself by it. Thus he easily pours
out his love. But I for my part do not know what I want. I
cling to him as an essential tie to life, but he is not "important" to me. Therefore I do not get a spontaneous hard on
with him. What *is* important to me? I don't know.

:   When I am with him, he does not seem to be especially problematic, he seems to be improving. When I
have left him, I become anxious, guilty, afraid of catastrophe.

:   He may admire me but he cannot *say* it, for instance,
"I was proud of you last night." This would allow me to be
free-standing in my strength so that the warmth of life
could revive in me. I acted well and daringly with the TV
dragon last night in Cleveland—I would have enjoyed a
glow of triumph if he had praised me and made me feel
not alone. But he had to remain in control and share not
by praise but by small criticism. In his narcissism he is not
natural but awkward and strutting (and skinny), and
therefore I do not get sexual heat from him. He is sometimes glowingly beautiful, with the physicality and purity

of a child of three or four, a pre-genital sexuality, to be kissed and embraced, and then to draw back and look at, and then again to kiss and embrace, without ever coming off except by withdrawing into myself to have it over with. Alas! I guess this unattainability is what beauty is—at least Freud thought so. But then, of course, he is never there *for* me. I feel this as an aching void. Sometimes I distrust him, other times I simply dislike him. If I allow my dislike to show, however, he at once desperately turns to me like the small child desperately looking into teacher's face as if the answer were written *there*. This puts me on the spot, for the answer *is* partly there, if I am willing to speak it out. So I rally into action, and then good-bye to anything in it "for me."

vi. God

: "God's doing ever is to bring the due likeness and harmonies of his works together, except when out of two contraries met to their own destruction, he molds a third existence."—Milton, in *Doctrine and Discipline of Divorce*.

: "Every valley shall be exalted and every hill made low, the crooked straight and the rough places plain." Alas; with all that engineering there will be years of detours.

: There is a difference between making a sacrifice and giving something up because the situation has gotten too thick. I don't like sacrifices. The apparent sacrifices I make are (or I make them into) self-affirming acts of compassion, noblesse oblige, etc. But in lucky moments I do sometimes give something up because the situation has gotten too thick.

: About to start on a long drive—and the tire is flat

and I have to repair it. It is reassuring to pour a libation to Nemesis before starting out.

:   During the rehearsal of a play, or sitting in the lobby, I wear a continual grin of delight at the incongruity and the co-existence of the make-believe and the real. The outcry from the stage, the actor coming off and lighting a cigarette, while I chatter with the girl making up the accounts in the box-office. The sweeper of the stage and the dancer rehearsing her step, each totally absorbed yet courteously avoiding the other—these are warmly real and also make a better play than will ever appear when the house-lights are dark.

When I walk down the street, however, and see the same mixture of role-playing and reality, the clothes patently costumes, and so forth, I am not at all delighted by it. Indeed, finally I become indignant and write essays and books against organization men, public relations, and sociologists who describe society in terms of role.

The crisis comes when I turn on myself as I sit here, making like a writer, and in my bathrobe, making like a householder. Always not quite doing what I am doing. I can snap out of the dismay of it, but I cannot leave off.

:   It is true about every one of us, but the Dignitaries now assembled for the Assembly of the United Nations—just because they speak so big and emptily and stand under such a glare of lights—are most obviously odd, awkward animals, contriving death, bondage, suffering for other millions of animals, many of whom are not so odd and awkward. Luckily most of their speech and activity affects nothing. Some of it has a kind of relation to "values," of justice, reason, fraternity, and so forth; if one reacts to this part without keeping the creaturely part in mind, one is swept by approval, indignation, boredom, contempt. But this kind of response is not adequate to the animal fact that indeed confronts us. I do not know how to maintain a balanced view. If I think of them as Ambassadors to the United Nations, I am disgusted because they do not live up to my "high cultural" standards of beauty, justice, dis-interestedness; if I look at them as animals, I am swept by my vision of huddled vermin. I swing from one unsatisfactory extreme to the other.

Let me turn it on myself. The daily life I lead—fucking X., seducing Y., pushing for publicity and money for my books—is all innocent enough as I do it, and is such vitality as I have; and always it entails fear, illness, being laid low, bill collectors, maybe jail. It is one causal sequence of my animal desires and illusions. To keep this in mind it is salutary to read historics like that of Henry VIII, where the folk, acting out their lust or love, or struggle for power, or honest piety, come to a gushing beheading. In this scene, however, I do not see that it makes any difference whether *I* suffer and die shrieking with fear, or affirmed in integrity like Thomas More. These are merely nuances of life style and I find it empty to make esthetic judgments. Savior, teach me! Praying, I become more confused.

I obsessionally look to see how many pages in this notebook are still to be filled, in order that then I can be justified in typing it all up to add to the previous hoard of it. In this activity, I escape. I am balked, heavy; my chest is in pain, choked with sobs held back because I have already often given in to them without avail. Maybe by this heavy confusion and fearful ignorance we are successfully prepared not to dread death.

: Zen is dilettantish. If the aim is *satori*, it is certainly not the Way, for if it can be known it is not the Way. Especially not an extraordinary or special experience or enlightenment, for the Sage is murky, confused. There *are* peak experiences in life; they are precisely a *warding off* of excitement, a short-circuited orgasm, as in epilepsy. We must practice rather to blunt these peaks, not toward stoic apathy but toward a more diffused confusion, *not quite able* to cope, struggling for Wu Wei.

The Zen "acceptance of imperfection" is dilettantism. According to what standard is the thing imperfect?

When there is no good and evil there is no imperfection. But once you have judged, it is your nature to try to be perfect. "You do not need to finish the job; neither are you free to leave it off."

:   Art is not work. It is work when I sit down to work *at* something, in a structure given to me beforehand, as is not the case with art. Work may or may not be pleasant. If the structure is given and I can do it, there is always the pleasure of simple activity; if I cannot do it, the work becomes drudgery, forced labor.

In Art, once I have started, there is of course a sketched or indicated structure that I work at, but this always keeps creating itself different, and the activity is therefore not work. This does not mean there is no obligation: "since you undertake to have started, you must finish —until it stops creating itself different."

What I write in this notebook is not work. My need to fill this notebook is made work.

:   What am I so hungry for that I am disturbed at the prospect of not being, of being dead? If there is something, why am I not busy after it right now? But I am not. Instead, I am mildly interested in the things I do go after, and I can also envision not getting them with equanimity. Is it the unknown—precisely *not* having these mild interests to be busy with—that makes me anxious? If so, I ought now to practice omitting them, and face the void. I write this on a train to Bronxville to get, or not get, a job that I am mildly interested in.

:   There is power in Henri Frankfort's theory that the Egyptian animal-deities were sacred partly because of the unchangeable Otherness of the animal kinds. It explains the drastic effect that Darwin had. This was not, as Darwin's contemporaries and Freud saw it, because man is taken from his proud eminence by being identified with the animal species. (One never felt, for example, that a totemic Indian was debased by his animal identity.) But it was that Darwin's proof of the continuity of the species including man took away the non-human Creation in which man could aspire to a dignity different from what he knew. We are then left, if we are not to vegetate in our personalities and idiosyncracies, with Abysses, Bridges to Beyond, and Existential Moments. We cannot think about Foxes and Bears.

Nevertheless, my own superstition, of the Creator Spirit, rather thrives on Darwinism, because by his conception it is possible to relate nature and culture. Reliance on animal and social history gives us a good support for jumping into Abysses—if not over them.

: As the year draws to a close—I am writing this on Christmas—I have begun to follow the advice that G. gave me long ago, to stop trying to have something to love, to withdraw desire from those persons who are not worth it because they are shut in (from me) or impractical (for me). So I am cold to my wife, cooling to my young friend, and not seeking elsewhere. Naturally this makes me feel "solid." Is this nothing but the advent of age, impotence, and death? (But the impotence vanishes with X., who has no other meaning to me except that she warmly wants me.)

It is a reasonable experiment to try as I turn—busy and sought-for in the public world, and lively when I am there—toward my 50th year. I am not happy, yet as of today I would willingly live till 80. I have already lived longer than many another rebellious soul.

VINTAGE BIOGRAPHY AND AUTOBIOGRAPHY

A free catalogue of VINTAGE BOOKS *will be sent at your request. Write to* Vintage Books, 457 Madison Avenue, New York, New York 10022.

A free catalogue of VINTAGE BOOKS *will be sent at your request. Write to* Vintage Books, 457 Madison Avenue, New York, New York 10022.

VINTAGE POLITICAL SCIENCE
AND SOCIAL CRITICISM

A free catalogue of VINTAGE BOOKS *will be sent at your request. Write to* Vintage Books, 457 Madison Avenue, New York, New York 10022.

A free catalogue of VINTAGE BOOKS *will be sent at your request. Write to* Vintage Books, 457 Madison Avenue, New York, New York 10022.

A SELECT LIST OF
VINTAGE RUSSIAN LIBRARY

A free catalogue of VINTAGE BOOKS *will be sent at your request. Write to* Vintage Books, 457 Madison Avenue, New York, New York 10022.

VINTAGE HISTORY—AMERICAN

VINTAGE HISTORY—WORLD

45 R65G